Mixed Methods Research in the Movement Sciences

Mixed methods research techniques, combining both quantitative and qualitative elements, have become well established throughout the social, behavioural and natural sciences. This is the first book to focus on the application of mixed methods research in the movement sciences, specifically in sport, physical education and dance. Researchers and practitioners in each of these fields are concerned with the study of habitual behaviour in naturalistic contexts, and with the concurrent and sequential nature of events and states, precisely the kind of work that multimethod research designs can help illuminate.

The book is arranged into four sections. The first provides a thorough overview of mixed methods procedures and research designs, and summarizes their applicability to the movement sciences. The remaining sections then offer detailed case studies of mixed methods research in team and individual sports (analysing hidden patterns of play and optimizing technique), kinesics and dance (analysing motor skills behaviour in childhood, and the complexity of motor responses in dance), and physical education (detecting interaction patterns in group situations, and optimizing non-verbal communication by teachers and sports coaches).

Mixed Methods Research in the Movement Sciences offers an important new tool for researchers and helps to close the gap between the analysis of expert performance and our understanding of the general principles of movement science. It is important reading for any student, researcher or professional with an interest in motor control, sport and dance pedagogy, coaching, performance analysis or decision-making in sport.

Oleguer Camerino is Professor of Physical Education Pedagogy and Head of Research and Observational Methods at the Human Motor Behaviour and Sport Laboratory (http://lom.observesport.com/) at INEFC, University of Lleida, Catalonia, Spain.

Marta Castañer is Professor of Human Motor Behaviour and Head of Observational Methods at the Human Motor Behaviour and Sport Laboratory (http://lom. observesport.com/) at INEFC, University of Lleida, Catalonia, Spain.

M. Teresa Anguera is Professor of Methodology of the Behavioural Sciences (Faculty of Psychology) and Head of the Observational Designs Research Group (http://www.observesport.com/) at the University of Barcelona, Catalonia, Spain.

Routledge Research in Sport and Exercise Science

The *Routledge Research in Sport and Exercise Science* series is a showcase for cutting-edge research from across the sport and exercise sciences, including physiology, psychology, biomechanics, motor control, physical activity and health, and every core sub-discipline. Featuring the work of established and emerging scientists and practitioners from around the world, and covering the theoretical, investigative and applied dimensions of sport and exercise, this series is an important channel for new and groundbreaking research in the human movement sciences.

Also available in this series:

1   **Mental Toughness in Sport**
    Developments in theory and research
    Daniel Gucciardi and Sandy Gordon

2   **Paediatric Biomechanics and Motor Control**
    Theory and application
    Mark De Ste Croix and Thomas Korff

3   **Attachment in Sport, Exercise and Wellness**
    Sam Carr

4   **Psychoneuroendocrinology of Sport and Exercise**
    Foundations, markers, trends
    Felix Ehrlenspiel and Katharina Strahler

5   **Mixed Methods Research in the Movement Sciences**
    Case studies in sport, physical education and dance
    Oleguer Camerino, Marta Castañer and M. Teresa Anguera

Mixed Methods Research in the Movement Sciences

Case studies in sport, physical education and dance

**Edited by
Oleguer Camerino,
Marta Castañer and
M. Teresa Anguera**

Routledge
Taylor & Francis Group

LONDON AND NEW YORK

First published 2012
by Routledge
2 Park Square, Milton Park, Abingdon, Oxon OX14 4RN

Simultaneously published in the USA and Canada
by Routledge
711 Third Avenue, New York, NY 10017

Routledge is an imprint of the Taylor & Francis Group, an informa business

© 2012 Oleguer Camerino, Marta Castañer and M. Teresa Anguera

First issued in paperback 2014

Translated by Alan J. Nance

British Library Cataloguing in Publication Data
A catalogue record for this book is available from the British Library

Library of Congress Cataloging in Publication Data

Mixed methods research in the movement sciences :
case studies in sport, physical education and dance /
edited by Oleguer Camerino, Marta Castañer and Teresa M. Anguera.
p. cm.
1. Movement education. 2. Sports—Research—Methodology.
3. Physical education and training—Research—Methodology.
4. Dance—Research—Methodology. I. Camerino, Oleguer.
II. Castañer, Marta, 1962– III. Anguera, Teresa M.
GV452.M59 2012
372.86'8—dc23
2011049364

ISBN: 978–0–415–67301–3 (hbk)
ISBN: 978–0–415–53227–3 (pbk)

Typeset in Times New Roman
by Swales & Willis Ltd, Exeter, Devon

Contents

Figures

Tables

Contributors

Juan Andueza is a researcher at the Catalan Institute for Physical Education (INEFC), University of Lleida, Spain.

M. Teresa Anguera teaches and researches behavioural sciences methodology at the University of Barcelona, Spain.

Oleguer Camerino teaches and researches pedagogy and human motor behaviour at the Catalan Institute for Physical Education (INEFC), University of Lleida, Spain.

Jorge Campaniço teaches and researches individual sports at the Universidade de Trás-os-Montes e Alto Douro, Portugal.

Marta Castañer teaches and researches human motor behaviour and dance at the Catalan Institute for Physical Education (INEFC), University of Lleida, Spain.

Javier Chaverri is a researcher at the Catalan Institute for Physical Education (INEFC), University of Lleida, Spain.

Susana Franco teaches and researches fitness at the Escola Superior de Desporto de Rio Maior, Instituto Politécnico de Santarém, Portugal.

Alfonso Gutiérrez teaches and researches combat sports at the Facultad de Ciencias de la Educación y del Deporte at the University of Vigo, Spain.

Xavier Iglesias teaches and researches combat sports at the Catalan Institute for Physical Education (INEFC), University of Barcelona, Spain.

Toni Jofre is a researcher in biomechanics at the Technological Institute for Footwear and Related Industries (INESCOP), Spain.

Gudberg K. Jonsson conducts research into social interaction methods at the Human Behaviour Laboratory of the University of Iceland.

António Lopes teaches and researches team sports at the Universidade Lusófona de Humanidades e Tecnologias (ULHT), Portugal.

Catarina Miguel is a researcher at the Catalan Institute for Physical Education (INEFC), University of Lleida, Spain.

Gaspar Morey conducts research into biomechanics at the Technological Institute for Footwear and Related Industries (INESCOP), Spain.

Iván Prieto is a researcher at the Facultad de Ciencias de la Educación y del Deporte at the University of Vigo, Spain.

Jose Rodrigues teaches and researches pedagogy at the Escola Superior de Desporto de Rio Maior, Instituto Politécnico de Santarém, Portugal.

Pedro Sánchez-Algarra teaches and researches statistics in biology at the University of Barcelona, Spain.

Carlota Torrents teaches and researches expressiveness and dance at the Catalan Institute for Physical Education (INEFC), University of Lleida, Spain.

Preface

The broad field of sport, physical education and dance has provided extensive material for research based on a wide range of methodological approaches. However, there is now a need to move toward research designs that offer an optimal integration of both quantitative and qualitative techniques. These designs, which have enormous potential, are commonly referred to as multi-methods or *mixed methods*.

In the context of this book the methodological integration of quantitative and qualitative approaches opens up new possibilities in relation to two aspects: (1) optimizing the dynamics and strategies of play and the decision-making process in sport; and (2) analysing the efficacy and quality of motor skills, technical abilities and specialized gestures in the specific areas of team and individual sports, dance and motor behaviour.

We believe that this text will serve as an ideal complement to other notable works and research on motor behaviour, sport, and methodological tools and designs.

Structure and organization

Chapter 1, written by the editors M. Teresa Anguera, Oleguer Camerino and Marta Castañer, introduces the *mixed method* or *multi-method* approach to research, showing how it seeks an optimal integration of various analytic techniques by combining both quantitative and qualitative techniques. The chapter describes a range of mixed methods designs that are currently recognized by the scientific community and which may be used to study sport and physical activity. The other five chapters in the book are then structured around fourteen case studies that provide a practical illustration of how these designs can be applied to sport, motor behaviour, dance and gestural communication.

Six case studies of team and individual sports

Chapter 2 comprises three case studies about team sports. In Case Study 2.1, Gudberg K. Jonsson presents both physiological and observational data regarding attacking play in rugby, and illustrates how to analyse temporal patterns

(T-patterns) in the latter. This way of detecting T-patterns in observational data serves as a reference for the other case studies in the book that also analyse these patterns. In Case Study 2.2 Oleguer Camerino and Xavier Chaverri focus on how the use of space influences the dynamics of play in basketball. The findings provide a basis for further research into interaction contexts and laterality in professional basketball. Finally, in Case Study 2.3, António Lopes and Oleguer Camerino use specific observational data concerning defensive tactics to analyse the dynamics of play and defensive systems used by elite handball teams.

Chapter 3 presents three case studies of individual sports. In Case Study 3.1, Xavier Iglesias and M. Teresa Anguera analyse the influence of environmental factors in the context of elite fencing. Case Study 3.2, written by Iván Prieto, Alfonso Gutiérrez and Oleguer Camerino, illustrates how to detect temporal relationships between the technical errors made in judo, and considers their consequences for the learning process. In Case Study 3.3, Jorge Campaniço focuses on specific technical behaviours and physiological parameters used in freestyle swimming.

Five case studies concerning motor skills, laterality and dance

Chapter 4 comprises two case studies that aim to extend our knowledge regarding the specificity and diversity of motor skills and of laterality in motor responses. In Case Study 4.1 Marta Castañer and Juan Andueza compare the spontaneous motor responses produced during two forms of motor behaviour associated with natural and urban contexts, namely children's outdoor play and parkour, respectively. In Case Study 4.2 the same authors, together with Pedro Sánchez-Algarra and M. Teresa Anguera, develop specific and exhaustive instruments for analysing the laterality of motor behaviour.

Chapter 5 focuses on dance and choreography. In Case Study 5.1 Marta Castañer shows how to observe and analyse dance performances, taking as her example works by arguably two of the most important choreographers of the twentieth century: Pina Bausch and Maurice Béjar. In Case Study 5.2 Carlota Torrents and Marta Castañer adapt the observation instrument used in the previous case study in order to analyse contact dance improvisation, an interesting speciality within contemporary dance. Finally, in Case Study 5.3, Marta Castañer, Carlota Torrents, Gaspar Morey and Toni Jofre describe how a motion capture system can be used to identify the kinematic aspects of contemporary dance skills, before comparing and contrasting these data with the aesthetic appraisals of these skills given by observers.

Three case studies regarding the optimization of communication in relation to coaches, teachers and instructors

Chapter 6 focuses on the study of communication in relation to teachers and professionals in the field of motor behaviour, specifically, physical education teachers, coaches and fitness instructors.

In Case Study 6.1 Marta Castañer shows how to analyse the non-verbal communication of physical education teachers, the aim being to identify their verbal and nonverbal communicative skills. In Case Study 6.2 the same author, together with Catarina Miguel, adapts part of the observation system used in the previous case study to detect the styles of communication used by futsal coaches in competitive contexts. Finally, in Case Study 6.3, Susana Franco, Jose Rodriguez and Marta Castañer study the behaviour of fitness instructors and the preferences and satisfaction levels of users with respect to this behaviour.

Target audience

In a changing world with such a wide range of technological means for obtaining and analysing data it is increasingly necessary to develop powerful and versatile designs that are able to combine qualitative and quantitative data, rather than regarding them as distinct entities. The characteristics of these new designs take them beyond traditional methodological approaches, which were defined as either quantitative or qualitative, and pave the way for a more integrated and broader perspective on research. In the context of sport, physical education and dance an increasing number of professionals are now turning to mixed methods designs as the way forward. As such, the present book should be useful not only to researchers on the subjects addressed herein, but also to coaches, choreographers and educational specialists. It will also be of interest to a range of postgraduate students, especially those in the fields of physical education, sport and dance, and regardless of the country in which they work.

Part I

The mixed methods approach to research

1 Mixed methods procedures and designs for research on sport, physical education and dance

M. Teresa Anguera, Oleguer Camerino and Marta Castañer

- **Introduction**
- **Types of mixed methods designs**
- **Advantages and challenges resulting from the use of mixed methods**

INTRODUCTION

Integrating the qualitative and the quantitative through mixed methods

Research in the field of physical activity and sport science has traditionally been based on the quantitative procedures that have been developed in other areas of knowledge, such as the biomedical sciences, psychology and, more recently, sociology. Over the past decade, however, this tendency in favour of the quantitative approach to the study of physical activity has gradually given way to a more balanced view (Heinemann 2003), one in which neither quantitative nor qualitative methods are regarded as inherently better. Rather, each of these methodological perspectives is considered to offer a different way of understanding and approaching the study of physical activity and sport. Furthermore, this is seen as applying to each stage of the research process, since both approaches:

- Guide the study objectives.
- Use various techniques for gathering data: for example, observation (recording a soccer match), a field log (notes on a basketball training session), an in-depth interview (how an athlete felt after losing), a structured questionnaire (about the quality of municipal sports services), a standardized test (of anthropometry or biomechanics), temporal measures (duration of maximum effort during a 400 m run), or psycho-physiological assessment (battery of fitness tests).
- Select the sample through specific techniques.
- Use a variety of procedures to present the results.

In this book we aim to show that quantitative and qualitative methods can be integrated and complement one another through what is generally known as the *mixed methods* approach, sometimes referred to as *synthetic interpretative methodology* (Vann and Cole 2004) or *qualiquantology* (Stenner and Rogers 2004). Whatever the term used, the process involves the collection, analysis and combination of quantitative and qualitative data in the same study. Some authors have likened the emergence of this approach to a 'silent revolution' (Denzin and Lincoln 1994; Johnson *et al.* 2007; O'Cathain 2009). At all events, the notion of mixed methods refers not merely to the gathering of different kinds of data about the same behaviour or episode, but also implies combining the inductive approach to concept generation (Bergman 2010) with deductive logic. Furthermore, the mixing applies to the whole research process, i.e. problem definition, data collection, data analysis, interpretation of results, and the final report (Wolcott 2009).

We believe that such an approach can offer a more holistic understanding of human motor behaviour and is well suited to dealing with its complexity. Although it has only recently begun to be applied in research on physical activity and sport, the broad potential of mixed methods is illustrated by the increasing number of related publications in this field (Hernández-Mendo and Anguera 2002; Jonsson *et al.* 2006; Castañer *et al.* 2009; Fernández *et al.* 2009; Jonsson *et al.* 2010; Torrents *et al.* 2010).

TYPES OF MIXED METHODS DESIGNS

The research design serves to guide the methodological steps that are taken throughout the process of gathering, managing and analysing information in any study (Anguera *et al.* 2001). In the context of mixed methods, which are based on the complementarity and integration of the quantitative (QUAN) and the qualitative (QUAL), a number of different designs have been developed in recent years (Teddlie and Tashakkori 2003, 2006; Grinnell and Unrau 2005; Mertens 2005; Creswell and Plano Clark 2007; Tashakkori and Creswell 2007, 2008) and our aim here is to show how these can be adapted to the requirements of research on physical activity and sport.

Different combinations of mixed methods designs

In broad terms the different combinations can be summarized as follows:

Multi-method procedure: more than one method but from the same perspective, i.e. the combinations QUAN/QUAN or QUAL/QUAL. In multi-method studies the research problem is tackled by using two data collection techniques (for example, participant observation or oral histories) or two methods of investigation (for example, ethnography or case studies), each one of which belongs to the same modality (QUAN or QUAL).

Example 1

We would use a quantitative multi-method (QUAN/QUAN) at the start of a season when we want to assess the performance of a handball team by using a battery of fitness tests that determine parameters such as the players' peak oxygen uptake or resistance.

Example 2

We would use a qualitative multi-method (QUAL/QUAL) in a study of the quality of municipal sports services, beginning with a discussion group involving the monitors of these services and following this up with in-depth interviews of a sample of service users regarding their level of satisfaction.

This methodological combination and complementarity runs throughout the research process: problem formulation, theoretical development, sampling, data collection and analysis, and report writing.

Mixed methods procedure: more than one method and from different perspectives, i.e. the combination of QUAL and QUAN. In mixed methods research the combination of techniques must offer a better way of achieving the objectives. There are two different approaches here:

- Mixed method design (occurs in one stage or section of a study). Mixed method designs use qualitative and quantitative data and analytic techniques in a parallel or sequential way. An important advantage of this is that researchers can then address confirmatory and exploratory questions simultaneously, and, consequently, both verify and generate theory in the same study.
- Mixed model design (may occur in several stages or sections of a study). Mixed model designs imply the combination of techniques in several or all the stages of a study (Tashakkori and Teddlie 2003): problem description, the choice of methodology, the kind of data collection, the analytic techniques used, and the inference derived from the results.

Example 3

Exploration in a stratified and random sample of the use of physical activities by young people during their leisure time, this being based on a group discussion (QUAL) about the level of satisfaction with the activities performed and a questionnaire (QUAN) about their involvement in sport during weekends and holidays.

The process of mixed methods can also be considered in terms of five key characteristics (Greene and Caracelli 2003):

- *Triangulation*, or the search for convergence in the results.
- *Complementarity*, or overlap in the different facets of a phenomenon.
- *Initiation*, or the discovery of paradoxes or contradictions.
- *Development*, or the sequential use of methods, such that the results of the first method inform the use of the second one.
- *Expansion*, or the study's depth and scope, which is revealed as it unfolds.

Example 4

These characteristics can be seen in a study whose aim is to identify gender differences in the use of physical activities, and which does so by means of: (a) observations (QUAL) of the behaviour of men and women in different sport-related settings; (b) administering questionnaires (QUAN) to men and women about their chosen activities; and (c) in-depth interviews with specific subjects (QUAL) about their level of satisfaction.

- *Triangulation*: of results from three instruments (QUAL/QUAN/QUAL).
- *Complementarity*: comparing observations with interview data (QUAL/QUAN).
- *Initiation*: contrast between the questionnaire and the interview (QUAN/QUAL).
- *Development*: interview on the basis of the observational data (QUAL/QUAL).
- *Expansion*: offer new activities on the basis of the results.

The different possibilities described above can be formulated in terms of types of design (Tashakkori and Teddlie 1998, 2003), which in this book will be illustrated in the context of research on sport, physical education and dance. The four main types are:

- Triangulation designs
- Dominant embedded designs
- Exploratory sequential designs
- Explanatory sequential designs.

Triangulation designs

The mixed methods approach looks for compatibility between points of view. The term *triangulation* has its origins in the field of navigation, in which the known position of two points and their angles was used to determine the unknown distance away of a third point (Smith 1975). Triangulation designs, which were first used in the pioneering work of Campbell and Fiske (1959), and subsequently developed by Denzin (1978) and other authors (Patton 1990), are well-suited to the complexities of research on physical activity and sport. Four kinds of triangulation are relevant here: triangulation of data, of investigators, of theory, and methodological triangulation.

Types of triangulation designs

Triangulation of data

Here we start from different sources of data in the same study and distinguish between the methods used to obtain them. A sub-type would be when there are data that converge in the same study but which were gathered on different days or by different people. All this needs to be harmonized so as to avoid working with contradictory data.

Example 5

In tests of a team's fitness the temporal parameters of the data collection must coincide, since the results obtained for players' strength (QUAN), resistance (QUAN) and speed (QUAN) on different days or by different researchers may be contradictory.

Triangulation of investigators

In order to minimize bias due to human factors, different investigators participate in the same study so that any such influences on the study results can be systematically examined. Obviously, the mere fact that researchers carry out or are assigned different activities within a project does not constitute triangulation of investigators.

Example 6

Studying the functioning of after-school sport clubs by using observers with expertise in analysing sports organizations, the monitors of the different activities and the children's parents.

Triangulation of theory

The results of a study are interpreted from multiple perspectives, thereby increasing the likelihood of knowledge generation. This means 'approaching data with multiple perspectives and hypotheses in mind [and that] various theoretical points of view could be placed side by side to assess their utility and power' (Denzin 1989: 241).

Example 7

Studying the physical activities practised by women, differentiating them by age, country or geographical area and from different sociological, psychological and ethnographic perspectives and paradigms.

Methodological triangulation

Different methods are used for the same research problem, with a distinction being made between within-method and between-methods triangulation. In the former, data are gathered using multiple techniques within a single methodology (QUAL or QUAN), which implies checking the internal consistency or reliability of the results obtained with each technique.

Example 8

Studying the effectiveness of a coach's communication in competitive settings through systematic observations (using video recordings) of his/her verbal communication during matches (QUAN) and survey interviews conducted with the players (QUAL).

By contrast, between-methods triangulation checks the consistency of results by comparing the findings obtained with various methodologies (QUAL or QUAN) and aims to determine their external validity (Jick 1979).

Triangulation is the most well-known and widely used among mixed methods designs (Creswell *et al.* 2003; Creswell and Plano Clark 2007) and aims to obtain different, yet complementary, data about the same episode (Morse 1991; Riba 2007) so as to better understand the research problem. More specifically, it seeks to complement the strengths and weakness of quantitative methodology (large sample size, trends, generalization, etc.) with those of the qualitative approach (small samples, interest in details, greater depth, etc.).

It is mainly applied when the investigator wishes to directly compare and contrast quantitative statistical results with qualitative information (QUAN/QUAL), for example, assessing the effectiveness of an exercise programme for obese children in which both their calorie intake and level of satisfaction are measured (see Example 9).

Example 9

Studying the repercussions of physical activity among obese children taking part in an intensive programme designed to change their eating habits and engage them in exercise under the supervision of specialists. On the one hand we would measure calorie intake by weighing them daily and monitoring the number of calories consumed at each meal (QUAN), but then combine this with interviews (QUAL) to assess their degree of motivation and adherence to the exercise programme.

Triangulation may also be used to validate quantitative results with qualitative data (QUAN+QUAL), for example, verifying that weight loss improves with greater adherence to an exercise programme.

The most common form of triangulation is the concurrent design, in which the investigator applies quantitative and qualitative methods (QUAN+QUAL) simultaneously, giving them equal weight and importance (see Figure 1.1).

Despite this concurrence, however, the two types of data are usually gathered separately and then combined by the investigator, before interpreting them as a whole. The data may also be transformed so as to facilitate the integration of both types during the analysis.

Variants of the triangulation design

There are four variants of the triangulation design: the *convergence* model, the *data transformation* model, the *validating quantitative data* model, and the *multi-level* model. The first two differ in terms of how the investigator combines the two types of data (either during data management/analysis or during interpretation), the third is used to enhance the results obtained through questionnaires, and the fourth is used when working with different levels of analysis.

The convergence model can be regarded as the traditional approach to triangulation (Creswell 1999) and involves the separate collection and analysis of quantitative and qualitative data about the same phenomenon. These data are then converged (comparing and contrasting them) during the interpretation (see Figure 1.2). The purpose of convergent designs is to enable researchers to compare results

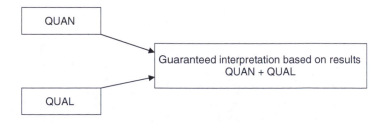

Figure 1.1 Triangulation design (adapted from Creswell and Plano Clark 2007: 63).

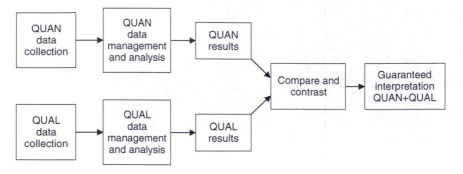

Figure 1.2 Convergent design (adapted from Creswell and Plano Clark 2007: 63).

or to validate, confirm or corroborate quantitative results (QUAN) by means of qualitative data (QUAL).

Example 10

Determining the relationship between the degree of cohesion among a team's members and the effectiveness of their strategies during team play by creating a sociogram (QUAN) at the start of the season in order to determine the levels of acceptance or rejection among the players, these findings being compared with data from in-depth interviews (QUAL) conducted with team leaders about the team's dynamics, as well as with the results of systematic observations (QUAN) of the team's offensive play.

The data transformation design (Creswell *et al.* 2004) also involves the separate collection and analysis of qualitative and quantitative data. After the initial analysis, however, the researcher then transforms one type of data into the other, i.e. qualifying the quantitative results or quantifying the qualitative findings (Tashakkori and Teddlie 2003) (see Figure 1.3). This transformation enables the data to

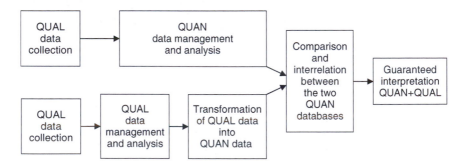

Figure 1.3 Data transformation design (adapted from Creswell and Plano Clark 2007: 63).

be combined (Fielding and Fielding 1986), thereby facilitating the comparison, interrelationship and subsequent analysis of both sets of data.

Example 11

In relation to Example 10, this would imply using the sociometric measures (QUAN) of acceptance or rejection in order to understand group cohesion. At the same time, qualitative data would be gathered by means of interviews (QUAL), transforming these data into observational categories (QUAN) referring to strategic play in real competitive situations. The two sources of data would then serve to compare and inter-relate the results and enable a combined interpretation (QUAN+QUAL) about team cohesion.

The validating quantitative data design enables researchers to validate and expand the quantitative results obtained from a questionnaire (QUAN) by including a number of open-ended questions that provide qualitative information (QUAL). The researcher therefore collects both kinds of data with a single instrument. However, because the qualitative items are an addition to the quantitative measure they do not strictly constitute a qualitative database. As regards how this design might be used, one possibility would be to include open-ended questions (qual) in a questionnaire about the level of satisfaction with a given physical activity (QUAN) in order to validate the quantitative data and thus offer a (QUAL+qual) interpretation (see Figure 1.4).

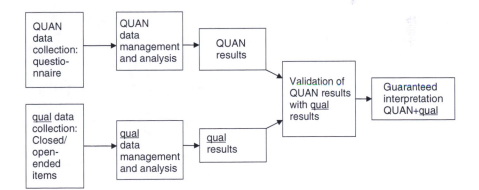

Figure 1.4 Validation of quantitative data design (adapted from Creswell and Plano Clark 2007: 63).

Note: Given the secondary nature of the qualitative data we have respected the notation in which they are underlined rather than written in capitals.

Example 12

A study of the quality and subsequent improvement of the activities offered by a large public sports centre. A survey was administered to users, based mainly on numerical ratings (QUAN) of the quality of the monitors, facilities and services, but information was also gathered (qual) about activities that users would like to see offered in the future.

In the final variant, known as multilevel triangulation designs, researchers may collect quantitative data on one occasion and qualitative data on another, either concurrently or sequentially. This is followed by the analysis of these data and the subsequent obtaining of results. The results from each of the levels are then considered together so as to enable a combined interpretation (Tashakkori and Teddlie 2003; Bryk and Raudenbush 1992) (see Figure 1.5).

Example 13

A multilevel study of effectiveness in learning a new sporting technique that considers the conditions of the setting, the task complexity, and organic, psychological and perceptual factors among players. On the first level we would make systematic observations (QUAN) of training sessions, while the second level would involve gathering the opinions of players (QUAL) using a field log in which they recorded their impressions, within which (level 3) we would embed the results of a satisfaction survey (QUAN) that asked them about the utility of and their adaptation to the new training procedures.

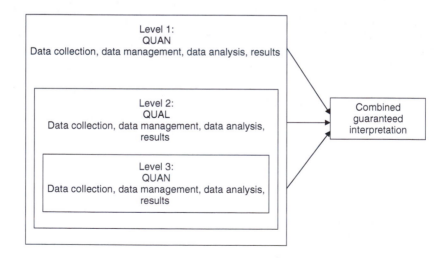

Figure 1.5 Multilevel triangulation design (adapted from Creswell and Plano Clark 2007: 64).

Advantages and challenges in using the triangulation design

Triangulation designs have a number of strengths or advantages:

- They make sense intuitively and this makes them attractive to researchers.
- They are efficient, since data of different types can be collected simultaneously.
- Each type of data can be obtained independently.

The challenges they pose are as follows:

- Researchers need a certain level of expertise in order to make the results obtained from qualitative data compatible with the quantitative results, identifying convergence between them.
- There may be discrepancies between different samples, with different initial objectives, different sizes and different selection criteria, etc.
- Integrating qualitative and quantitative data can be difficult.
- There is a need to develop procedures that enable the transformation of qualitative and quantitative data, whether quantifying qualitative findings or qualifying quantitative results.

Dominant embedded designs

In the dominant embedded design the researcher works with one dominant type of data (QUAN or QUAL) and then obtains data of another kind (quan or qual) as a secondary support. These secondary data therefore complement the primary or dominant data set (see Figure 1.6)

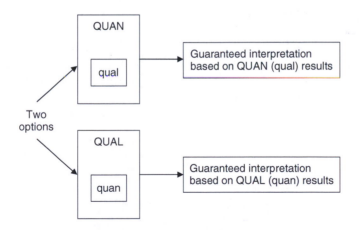

Figure 1.6 Dominant embedded design (adapted from Creswell and Plano Clark 2007: 68).

Example 14

In the chapter related to analysing motor skills and laterality we describe a study in which laterality was first explored using a recording instrument that provided quantitative data (QUAN). These data were then contrasted with qualitative data (Qual) obtained through interviews with experts in physical education. These opinions served to develop a more dynamic version of the original instrument, which was then used to obtain a new set of quantitative (QUAN) data.

One of the most important challenges when using this design concerns complementarity, since the dominant data alone are not enough to solve the research problem. However, these designs are useful for complex experimental studies, particularly those of a longitudinal or continuous nature, such as research on fitness levels in large samples of the population.

Variants of the dominant embedded design

There are two variants of the dominant embedded design: the *correlational model* and the *experimental model*. In the embedded correlational model, qualitative data are embedded within a quantitative design. The researchers work with quantitative data (QUAN) but also collect secondary qualitative data (qual) that are correlated with the former as a complement throughout the research process, thereby enabling an interpretation based on (QUAN qual) results (Figure 1.7).

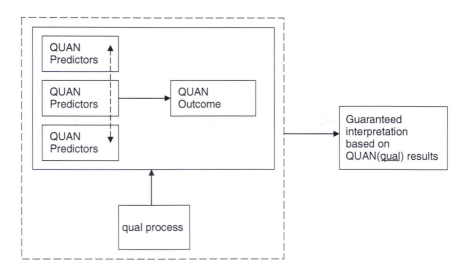

Figure 1.7 Embedded correlational design (adapted from Creswell and Plano Clark 2007: 68).

Example 15

In a study of communicative interaction in a group of elderly people attending an aqua aerobics class, observational data (QUAN) were obtained by videoing the pool-based sessions in order to identify how the participants interacted with the monitor, the material and each other, thus providing an overall view of their performance. This was then contrasted with the participants' own views regarding the communicative experience, these being obtained by means of in-depth interviews (qual) with some of the elderly people (Camerino 1995).

In the embedded experimental model, qualitative data are embedded within a dominant experimental study. The qualitative data may be introduced prior to the intervention, during its implementation, or subsequent to its completion (see Figure 1.8).

Example 16

In a longitudinal study of changes in self-esteem among people involved in an intensive fitness programme aimed at controlling body weight, the following steps were taken: prior to the intervention the daily habits of participants were identified through qualitative monitoring in the form of personal diaries (QUAL); during the programme their weight was measured daily (QUAN); and after the programme in-depth interviews were conducted to gather their opinions about the effectiveness of the intervention (cual). The study was completed with an interpretation based on the results obtained from the whole process (QUAN cual).

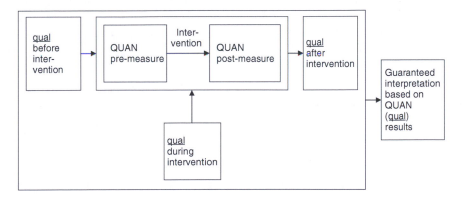

Figure 1.8 Embedded experimental design (adapted from Creswell and Plano Clark 2007: 68).

This strategy is useful in studies about the consequences of physical activity, since the researcher needs qualitative information prior to the intervention in order to tailor it accordingly, to develop appropriate measurement instruments and to select participants. After the intervention, qualitative information is useful in terms of complementing or comparing the results obtained.

Advantages and challenges in using the dominant embedded design

The principal advantages of dominant embedded designs are:

- They are relatively easy to apply since one of the data sets takes precedence and the complementary method require less data.
- It is easier to obtain the data since one of the two types is given less priority.
- The dominant data are quantitative, regardless of whether the study is correlational or experimental, and this is likely to make these designs more readily acceptable.

The challenges faced when using dominant embedded designs are:

- The researcher must specify the purpose of collecting each type of data, whether dominant or subservient.
- It can be difficult to integrate the results when the two methods are used in order to tackle different research problems.
- The researcher has to decide when to collect the qualitative data (before, during or after the intervention), this decision depending on their purpose (shaping the intervention, explaining the process followed by users, following up outcomes, etc.).
- The researcher must decide which qualitative results will be used in the quantitative phase. The latter cannot be planned prior to the collection of the qualitative data as this could introduce treatment bias that affects the final results obtained.

Exploratory sequential designs

In the exploratory sequential design an initial set of qualitative data is used to develop or guide a subsequent quantitative phase (Greene *et al.* 1989). The basic premise here is that prior exploration is necessary because no instruments or measures are available, because the variables are unknown, or because there is no existing theoretical framework. Thus, this design begins by collecting qualitative data to explore the phenomenon and then builds towards a quantitative phase (see Figure 1.9), the results of which are then linked to the initial qualitative findings.

Figure 1.9 Exploratory sequential design (adapted from Creswell and Plano Clark 2007: 76).

Example 17

A study of non-verbal behaviour in physical education classes according to the teacher's level of training. After a broad exploratory (qualitative) phase aimed at detecting types of interaction between different teachers according to the subject matter and their level of training, an observation system was developed based on a categorization of kinesic behaviour (Castañer 1999).

Despite the initial exploratory nature this is the most appropriate design for studying non-specific and intangible phenomena where the variables are still unknown (Creswell 1999; Creswell *et al.* 2003; Creswell and Plano Clark 2007).

Variants of the exploratory sequential design

There are two variants of the exploratory sequential design: the *instrument development* model (emphasis on QUAN) and the *taxonomy development* model (emphasis on QUAL). Both start with a qualitative phase and then move on to a quantitative one, the difference being in how the researcher links the two phases (Creswell and Plano Clark 2007).

Researchers use the instrument development design (emphasis on QUAN) when they wish to develop and implement a quantitative instrument on the basis of previously obtained qualitative data. In this variant the qualitative and quantitative methods are linked through the phases of data collection, data analysis and results (see Figure 1.10).

Example 18

A study of children's exploratory motor behaviour in school play areas, without any direct intervention from monitors. A questionnaire was developed (QUAN) after an exploratory qualitative phase (qual) in which types of interaction were detected.

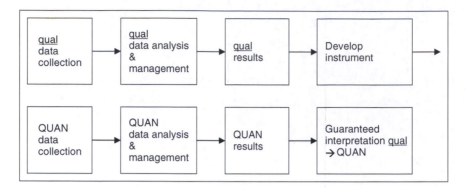

Figure 1.10 Variant of the exploratory sequential design: the instrument development model (emphasis on QUAN) (adapted from Creswell and Plano Clark 2007: 76).

The first step is thus a pilot phase to explore the research problem with a small number of participants, and the results obtained are then used to guide the construction of items and scales for a survey instrument. In the second phase of data collection the researcher implements and validates this instrument quantitatively.

This variant is used when the researcher wants to emphasize the quantitative aspect of the study. In our field this kind of design is recommended when the aim is to generalize findings about the effects of physical activity on different groups so as to contrast and explore in detail the effectiveness of a programme. In these cases, considerable importance is placed on the qualitative information obtained regarding the effects of physical activity, this being a step prior to the development of quantitative indicators.

The taxonomy development design (emphasis on QUAL) is used when the initial qualitative phase enables the researcher to identify relevant variables, build a taxonomy or classification system, or develop an emergent theory. The purpose of the second, quantitative phase is then to test or explore these results in greater detail (Morgan 1998; Tashakkori and Teddlie 2003) (see Figure 1.11).

Example 19

A study of the needs of professional dance teachers in dance schools. The first exploratory step involved interviews (QUAL) to gather the opinions of dance teachers (both qualified and non-qualified but with sufficient experience, for example, at least ten years teaching) about their professional difficulties. This was followed by the construction of a taxonomy that enabled systematic observations (QUAN) to be made of their classes, thereby determining the obstacles they faced. The interpretation was based on contrasting the two types of data (QUAL → quan).

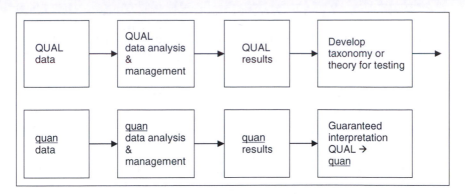

Figure 1.11   Variant of the exploratory sequential design: the taxonomy development model (emphasis on QUAL) (adapted from Creswell and Plano Clark 2007: 76).

The initial qualitative phase gives rise to specific categories which serve to guide the second, quantitative phase of the study. It is also possible to identify emergent categories on the basis of the qualitative data, and then use the quantitative phase to explore the prevalence of these categories in different samples (Morse 1991).

Advantages and challenges in using the exploratory sequential design

The exploratory sequential design has a number of advantages over other designs (Creswell and Plano Clark 2007), for example:

- The two phases are implemented separately.
- Although the design emphasises the qualitative aspect, the inclusion of a quantitative component makes it more likely to be accepted by audiences with a bias towards the quantitative model.
- This design is easy to apply in studies with different pilot stages and for instrument development.

However, it also presents a number of challenges:

- The two-phase approach is time consuming.
- Researchers need to decide which data from the qualitative phase will be used in developing the instrument, and how they will be employed to generate quantitative measures.
- Appropriate steps need to be taken to ensure that the instruments developed are valid and reliable with respect to the corresponding qualitative decisions and findings.

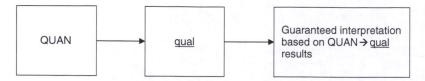

Figure 1.12 Explanatory sequential design (adapted from Creswell and Plano Clark 2007: 73).

Explanatory sequential designs

This is another two-phase design in which qualitative data are used to help explain and expand upon the quantitative results obtained initially (Creswell 1999; Creswell *et al*. 2003; Creswell and Plano Clark 2007) (see Figure 1.12). Although this design begins with a quantitative phase, researchers generally place greater emphasis on the qualitative aspect.

Example 20

A study of anthropometric and personality parameters among different athletes and their relationship to the specific sport being practised. The first stage would involve collecting data about the athletes' stature (QUAN) and personality using standardized tests so that they could be classified according to their measurements and personality traits. They would then be grouped together for the purpose of interviews (qual) aimed at detecting the reasons behind their sporting preferences.

In the context of physical activity this kind of design is used in studies with relatively large samples, especially when the researcher wants to begin by gathering quantitative data and, on the basis of this, form study groups which will be then be subjected to a qualitative analysis. Thus, the quantitative characteristics of participants guide the sampling process in the qualitative phase (Morgan 1998; Tashakkori and Teddlie 2003).

Variants of the explanatory sequential design

There are two variants of the explanatory sequential design: the *follow-up* model (emphasis on QUAN) and the *participant selection* model (emphasis on QUAL). Both begin with a quantitative phase that is followed by a qualitative phase, but they differ in how these two phases are connected, as well as in the relative emphasis placed on each.

The follow-up explanatory design places greater emphasis on the quantitative data, which are used by the researcher to identify significant statistical differences between groups of participants, between individuals with extreme test scores, or in the case of unexpected results (see Figure 1.13).

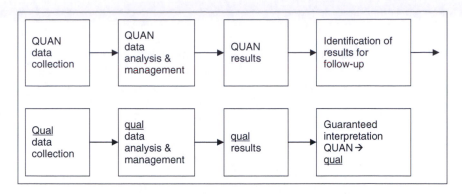

Figure 1.13 Variant of the explanatory sequential design: the follow-up explanatory model
(emphasis on QUAN) (adapted from Creswell and Plano Clark 2007: 73).

Example 21

A study of fitness levels among retired adults. The first step would involve
gathering quantitative survey data (QUAN) from a stratified, random sample
in order to identify factors related to their exercise preferences. In the second
phase, multiple case studies (QUAL) would be conducted in order to explain
why some of the factors identified in the first phase were significant predic-
tors of adherence to physical activity programmes among retired adults.

The participant selection design, which emphasizes the QUAL aspects, is
used when the researcher needs quantitative information to identify and adequately select participants for a subsequent, in-depth qualitative study (see Figure
1.14).

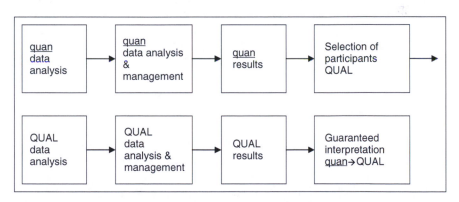

Figure 1.14 Variant of the explanatory sequential design: the participant selection model
(emphasis on QUAL) (adapted from Creswell and Plano Clark 2007: 73).

Example 22

A study about talent spotting in sport and the influence of family on an individual's success. The first step involved collecting quantitative survey data (QUAN) in order to identify types of families associated with elite sportsmen and women. A sample of these was then selected in order to conduct in-depth interviews (QUAL) and interpret the results (QUAN qual).

Advantages and challenges in using the explanatory sequential design

The advantages of the explanatory sequential design are:

- Its two-phase structure makes it easy to implement and there is no need for a team of researchers.
- The final report can be written in two stages.
- It is suitable for both multi-phase and single mixed methods research.
- It is appealing to quantitative researchers as studies usually begin with the collection of quantitative data.

The challenges faced by these designs are:

- Implementation of the two phases is time consuming. This is especially the case of the qualitative phase, although fewer participants are required here.
- Researchers need to decide whether to use the same participants for both phases, or if the two phases should draw their participants from the same sample or population.
- It may be difficult to gain approval from the local research review board as the number of participants required by the second phase cannot be specified until after the first set of results have been obtained.
- The researcher who collects the qualitative data is often the best placed to understand in greater detail the results obtained.

ADVANTAGES AND CHALLENGES RESULTING FROM THE USE OF MIXED METHODS

Having described the various designs that result from the application of mixed methods it would now seem appropriate to try to consider objectively the overall benefits and drawbacks of this approach. As regards the specific context of research on sport, physical education and dance it should be said that the verdict is a positive one, and this should encourage researchers to promote the use of mixed methods so as to achieve more efficient results and applications in this field.

The main advantages or benefits of using mixed methods designs have been widely discussed by various authors (Creswell *et al*. 2003; Todd *et al*. 2004) and can be summarized as follows:

- They offer a fuller, more holistic view of the behaviour or episode under study, with various levels or dimensions of the research problem being explored. As stated by Lincoln and Guba (2000) this implies a more objective and comprehensive view or snapshot of reality, while remaining close to the study context (Harré and Crystal 2004) and offering greater explanatory power (Miles and Huberman 1994).
- The approach pays specific attention to problem formulation and the conceptual framework (Brannen 1992), which must be sensitive to the competing perspectives and establish connections between them. This contrasts with the more simplistic approach that involves just one way of considering the research question (Todd *et al*. 2004).
- The data obtained are much richer as there are no limits in terms of their source or the nature of the information.
- Mixed methods designs foster theoretical creativity through the use of numerous critical evaluation procedures (Clarke 2004).
- The enormous complexity of the real world can be better studied, taking into account the dynamic relationships that are established and the changing nature of reality. The combination of different methods (Mingers and Gill 1997) makes researchers better equipped.
- The combination of methods offers greater opportunities to extend the scope of a study (Morse 2003; Newman *et al*. 2003).
- Mixed methods designs can offer more robust support for scientific inferences than would be the case if the methods were used in isolation.
- A greater and better exploration and exploitation of data can be achieved (Todd *et al*. 2004).
- They enable a more suggestive presentation of results (Todd *et al*. 2004), as more than just numerical tables are used.

Both individually and as a whole, the above aspects clearly illustrate the enormous benefits of mixed methods designs. However, there are also a number of important challenges that remain to be met through future developments:

- Conducting mixed methods research requires training in both qualitative and quantitative methods, something which is still not common given that the research tradition in recent decades has clearly distinguished between the two (Todd and Nerlich 2004).
- Clear criteria need to be established for evaluating mixed methods studies. To date, the criteria for evaluating quantitative studies have been much more clearly defined than those for qualitative research, although work on the latter has developed in recent years (Sandín 2000, 2003; Onwuegbuzie and Johnson 2006).

- There is a need to 'demystify' those aspects which have been considered taboo or controversial so that they are accepted as valid issues within the field. Researchers should revise their criticisms of these aspects and seek to resolve complex dilemmas (Yardley 2000; Todd and Nerlich 2004). Examples in this regard include sampling versus loading and generalization versus transfer of results.

In the broad context of physical activity, human behaviour is enormously heterogeneous as there are numerous facets which can serve as the focus for its analysis. Researchers in this field must therefore be prepared to contemplate a wide range of problems, theoretical frameworks and methodological approaches. At all events, the variety of situations which may be faced when conducting research on sport, physical education and dance makes the use of mixed methods designs both a suitable and highly interesting approach.

Acknowledgements

We gratefully acknowledge the support of the Spanish government project *Avances tecnológicos y metodológicos en la automatización de estudios observacionales en deporte* (Dirección General de Investigación, Ministerio de Ciencia e Innovación) [Grant number PSI2008-01179].

We gratefully acknowledge the support of the Generalitat de Catalunya government project GRUP DE RECERCA E INNOVACIÓ EN DISSENYS (GRID). Tecnología i aplicació multimedia i digital als dissenys observacionals, Departament d'Innovació, Universitats i Empresa, Generalitat de Catalunya [Grant number 2009 SGR 829].

References

Anguera, M.T., Blanco, A. and Losada, J.L. (2001). Diseños observacionales, cuestión clave en el proceso de la metodología observacional. *Metodología de las Ciencias del Comportamiento, 3* (2), 135–160.

Bergman, M.M. (2010). On concepts and paradigms in mixed methods research. *Journal of Mixed Methods Research, 4* (3), 171–175.

Brannen, J. (ed.) (1992). *Mixing methods: Qualitative and quantitative research.* Aldershot: Avebury.

Bryk, A.S. and Raudenbush, S.W. (1992). *Hierarchical linear models.* Newbury Park, CA: Sage.

Camerino, O. (1995): *Integració metodològica en la investigació de l'educació física.* Lleida: INEFC. Col.lecció Recerca n° 1.

Campbell, D.T. and Fiske, D.W. (1959). Convergent and discriminant validation by the multitrait-multimethod matrix. *Psychological Bulletin, 54,* 297–312.

Castañer, M. (1999). Elaboración de un sistema de categorías para la observación de la conducta cinésica no-verbal de los docentes. In M.T. Anguera (Coord.) (1999), *Observación en deporte y conducta cinésico-motriz: aplicaciones* (pp. 71–105). Barcelona: EUB.

Castañer, M., Torrents, C., Anguera, M.T., Dinušová, M. and Jonsson, G. (2009). Identifying and analyzing motor skill responses in body movement and dance. *Behavior Research Methods, 41* (3), 857–867.

Clarke, D. (2004). Structured judgement methods. In Z. Todd, B. Nerlich, S. McKeown and D. Clarke (eds), *Mixing methods in psychology* (pp. 81–100). Hove, East Sussex: Psychology Press.

Creswell, J.W. (1999). Mixed-method research: Introduction and application. In G.J. Cizek (ed.), *Handbook of educational policy* (pp. 455–472). San Diego, CA: Academic Press.

Creswell, J.W., Fetters, M.D. and Ivankova, N.V. (2004). Designing a mixed methods study in primary care. *Annals of Family Medicine 2* (1), 7–12.

Creswell, J.W. and Plano Clark, V.L. (2007). *Designing and conducting mixed methods research.* Thousand Oaks, CA: Sage.

Creswell, J.W., Plano Clark, V.L., Gutmann, M.L. and Hanson, W.E. (2003). Advanced mixed methods research designs. In A. Tashakkori and C. Teddlie (eds) (2003), *Handbook of mixed methods in social and behavioral research* (pp. 209–240). Thousand Oaks, CA: Sage.

Denzin, N.K. (1978). The logic of naturalistic inquiry. In N.K. Denzin (ed.), *Sociological methods: A sourcebook.* New York: McGraw-Hill.

Denzin, N.K. (1989). *The research act.* Englewood Cliffs, NJ: Prentice-Hall.

Denzin, N.K. and Lincoln, Y.S. (eds) (1994). *Handbook of qualitative research.* Thousand Oak, CA: Sage.

Fernández, J., Camerino, O., Anguera, M.T. and Jonsson, G. (2009). Identifying and analyzing the construction and effectiveness of offensive plays in basketball by using systematic observation. *Behavior Research Methods, 41* (3), 719–730.

Fielding, N.G. and Fielding, J.L. (1986). *Linking data.* Newbury Park, CA: Sage.

Greene, J.C. and Caracelli, V.J. (2003). Making paradigmatic sense of mixed methods practice. In A. Tashakkori and C. Teddlie (eds) (2003), *Handbook of mixed methods in social and behavioral research* (pp. 91–110). Thousand Oaks, CA: Sage.

Greene, J.C., Caracelli, V.J. and Graham, W.F. (1989). Toward a conceptual framework for mixed-method evaluation designs. *Education Evaluation and Policy Analysis, 11*, 255–274 [Reprinted in V.L. Plano Clark and J.W. Creswell (eds) (2008). *The mixed methods reader* (pp. 119–148). Thousand Oaks, CA: Sage.]

Grinnell, R.M. and Unrau, Y.A. (eds) (2005). *Social work: Research and evaluation. Quantitative and qualitative approaches.* New York: Oxford University Press.

Harré, R. and Crystal, D. (2004). Discursive analysis and the interpretation of statistics. In Z. Todd, B. Nerlich, S. McKeown and D. Clarke (eds), *Mixing methods in psychology* (pp. 61–80). Hove, East Sussex: Psychology Press.

Heinemann, K. (2003). Introducción a la metodología de la investigación empírica en las ciencias del deporte. Barcelona: Paidotribo.

Hernández-Mendo, A. and Anguera, M.T. (2002). Behavioral structure in sociomotor sports: Roller-hockey. *Quality & Quantity. European Journal of Methodology, 36*, 347–378.

Jick, T.D. (1979). Mixing qualitative and quantitative methods: Triangulation in action. *Administrative Science Quarterly, 24*, 602–611 [Reprinted in V.L. Plano Clark and J.W. Creswell (eds) (2008). *The mixed methods reader* (pp. 105–118). Thousand Oaks, CA: Sage.]

Johnson, R.B., Onwuegbuzie, A.J. and Turner, L.A. (2007). Toward a definition of mixed methods research. *Journal of Mixed Methods Research, 1* (2), 112–133.

Jonsson, G.K., Anguera, M.T., Blanco-Villaseñor, A., Losada, J.L., Hernández-Mendo, A.,

Ardá, T., Camerino, O. and Castellano, J. (2006). Hidden patterns of play interaction in soccer using SOF-CODER. *Behavior Research Methods, 38* (3), 372–381.

Jonsson, G.K., Anguera, M.T., Sánchez-Algarra, P., Olivera, C., Campanico, J., Castañer, M., Torrents, C., Dinušová, M., Chaverri, J., Camerino, O. and Magnusson, M.S. (2010): Application of T-pattern detection and analysis in sports research. *The Open Sports Sciences Journal, 3*, 62–71.

Lincoln, Y.S. and Guba, E.G. (2000). Paradigmatic controversies, contradictions, and emerging confluences. In N.K. Denzin and Y.S. Lincoln (eds), *Handbook of qualitative research* (pp. 163–188). Newbury Park, CA: Sage.

Mertens, D.M. (2005). *Research and evaluation in education and psychology: Integrating diversity with quantitative, qualitative, and mixed methods*. Thousand Oaks, CA: Sage.

Miles, M.B. and Huberman, A.M. (1994). *Qualitative data analysis: An expanded sourcebook*. Thousand Oaks, CA: Sage.

Mingers, J. and Gill, A. (1997). *Multimethodology: The theory and practice of combining management science methodologies*. Winchester: Wiley.

Morgan, A. (1998). Practical strategies for combining qualitative and qualitative methods: Application to health research. *Qualitative Health Research, 8* (3), 362–376.

Morse, J.M. (1991). Approaches to qualitative-quantitative methodological triangulation. *Nursing Research, 40* (2), 120–123.

Morse, J.M. (2003). Principles of mixed methods and multimethod research design. In A. Tashakkori and C. Teddlie (eds) (2003), *Handbook of mixed methods in social and behavioural research* (pp. 189–208). Thousand Oaks, CA: Sage.

Newman, I., Ridenour, C.S., Newman, C. and De Marco, G.M. (2003). A typology of research purposes and its relationship to mixed methods. In A. Tashakkori and C. Teddlie (eds) (2003), *Handbook of mixed methods in social and behavioural research* (pp. 167–188). Thousand Oaks, CA: Sage.

O'Cathain, A. (2009). Mixed methods research in health sciences: A quiet revolution. *Journal of Mixed Methods Research, 3* (3), 3–6.

Onwuegbuzie, A.J. and Johnson, R.B. (2006). The validity issue in mixed research. *Research in the Schools, 131*, 48–63. Retrieved March 23, 2008, from http://www.msera.org/Rits_131/Onwuegbuzie_Johnson_131.pdf [Reprinted in V.L. Plano Clark and J.W. Creswell (eds) (2008). *The mixed methods reader* (pp. 271–298). Thousand Oaks, CA: Sage.]

Patton, M.Q. (1990). *Qualitative evaluation and research methods*. Newbury Park, CA: Sage.

Riba, C.E. (2007). *La metodologia qualitativa en l'estudi del comportament*. Barcelona: UOC.

Sandín, M.P. (2000). Criterios de validez en la investigación cualitativa: De la objetividad a la solidaridad. *Revista de Investigación Educativa, 18* (1), 223–242.

Sandín, M.P. (2003). *Investigación cualitativa en Educación: Fundamentos y tradiciones*. Madrid: McGraw-Hill.

Smith, H.W. (1975). *Strategies of social research: The methodological imagination*. Englewood Cliffs, NJ: Prentice-Hall.

Stenner, P. and Rogers, R.S. (2004). Q methodology and qualiquantology: The example of discriminating between emotions. In Z. Todd, B. Nerlich, S. McKeown and D. Clarke (eds), *Mixing methods in psychology* (pp. 101–121). Hove, East Sussex: Psychology Press.

Tashakkori, A. and Creswell, J. (2007). The new era of mixed methods. *Journal of Mixed Methods Research, 1* (1), 3–7.

Tashakkori, A. and Creswell, J. (2008). Mixed methodology across disciplines. *Journal of Mixed Methods Research, 2* (1), 3–6.

Tashakkori, A. and Teddlie, C. (1998). *Mixed methodology: Combining qualitative and quantitative approaches.* Thousand Oaks, CA: Sage Publications.

Tashakkori, A. and C. Teddlie (eds) (2003). *Handbook of mixed methods in social and behavioural research* (pp. 3–50). Thousand Oaks, CA: Sage.

Teddlie, C. and Tashakkori, A. (2003). Major issues and controversies in the use of mixed methods in the social and behavioural sciences. In A. Tashakkori and C. Teddlie (eds) (2003), *Handbook of mixed methods in social and behavioural research* (pp. 3–50). Thousand Oaks, CA: Sage.

Teddlie, C. and Tashakkori, A. (2006). A general typology of research designs featuring mixed methods. *Research in the Schools, 13* (1), 12–28.

Todd, Z. and Nerlich, B. (2004). Future directions. In Z. Todd, B. Nerlich, S. McKeown and D. Clarke (eds), *Mixing methods in psychology* (pp. 231–237). Hove, East Sussex: Psychology Press.

Todd, Z., Nerlich, B. and McKeown, S. (2004). Introduction. In Z. Todd, B. Nerlich, S. McKeown and D. Clarke (eds), *Mixing methods in psychology* (pp. 3–16). Hove, East Sussex: Psychology Press.

Torrents, C., Castañer, M., Dinušová, M. and Anguera, M.T. (2010). Discovering new ways of moving: Observational analysis of motor creativity while dancing contact improvisation and the influence of the partner. *Journal of Creative Behavior, 44* (1), 45–61.

Vann, K. and Cole, M. (2004). Method and methodology in interpretative studies of cognitive life. In Z. Todd, B. Nerlich, S. McKeown and D. Clarke (eds), *Mixing methods in psychology* (pp. 149–167). Hove, East Sussex: Psychology Press.

Wolcott, H.F. (2009). *Writing up qualitative research.* Los Angeles, CA: Sage.

Yardley, L. (2000). Dilemmas of qualitative research. *Psychology and Health, 15,* 215–228.

Part II
Team and individual sports

2 Detecting hidden patterns in the dynamics of play in team sports

- • **Case Study 2.1: Temporal pattern analysis and its applicability in sport: illustrative data from an attack session in rugby**
  Gudberg K. Jonsson

- • **Case Study 2.2: Influence of the use of space on the dynamics of play in basketball**
  Oleguer Camerino, Javier Chaverri, Gudberg K. Jonsson, Pedro Sánchez-Algarra and M. Teresa Anguera

- • **Case Study 2.3: The dynamics of play and defensive systems in handball**
  António Lopes and Oleguer Camerino

One important area in the field of sports science concerns the need to explain, predict and even control the factors that determine success in competitive team sports. In our view, this is a key aspect when it comes to helping coaches to make decisions regarding the management of both training and competitive situations, as well as for increasing player motivation in high-level performance. Recently, sports performance has begun to be considered as a dynamical system (Davids *et al.* 2008), and attempts have been made to apply concepts from dynamical systems theory to the study of emergent game structure and tactical patterns in team sport (McGarry *et al.* 2002). In this regard, understanding profiles of play and how they are learnt cognitively in team sports is a new and interesting approach to the optimization of effective performance.

Given the above there is a growing need for the rigorous collection of sport-related data that provide empirical evidence about the complex reality they refer to. Key aspects in this regard include the presence of regularities that are not detectable through visual inference or traditional methods of data analysis, as well as the lack of standard observation instruments and the priority need to develop powerful, computerized coding systems, all of which must form part of an approach that is suitable for natural exercise environments (Kerr *et al.* 2006).

This second chapter presents a range of ideas related to how the dynamics of team play might be understood by detecting repeated patterns and other parameters. Specifically, it discusses the results obtained from *mixed methods research* with three different team sports: rugby, basketball and handball. We believe that the findings can be used to improve coaching and performance in team sports.

CASE STUDY 2.1: TEMPORAL PATTERN ANALYSIS AND ITS APPLICABILITY IN SPORT: ILLUSTRATIVE DATA FROM AN ATTACK SESSION IN RUGBY

Introduction

Skilled behaviour is central to all sports and requires a dynamic co-coordinated process of perception, cognition and action. Research has demonstrated that skill acquisition and skilled performance share underlying mechanisms across the perceptual, cognitive and motor domains (Williams and Ericsson 2005). In order to produce and develop skilled behaviour it is important to identify the discrete requirements of sporting activities, as skilled behaviour can be improved through the processes of learning, acquisition and physical conditioning. However, it has been shown that coaches are unable to observe and recall all of the discrete incidents and activities that are required for a complete understanding of sport performance (Franks and Miller 1986).

In the search for success, each sport favours specific biological strategies based on the rules of the game and its physiological and biomechanical demands (McCall *et al.* 1999). However, in order to apply this principle to physical conditioning it is first necessary to identify specific movement and physiological patterns. Although the physiological responses to performance and the biomechanical analysis of several critical skills have been widely reported, it can be argued that more specific and detailed knowledge about physical demands is required.

The physical demands of rugby

Rugby has been under scientific investigation for a number of years now in an attempt to understand and improve the sport. Indeed, numerous studies have been conducted in areas such as physiology, biomechanics, psychology, sociology and kinanthropometry, the key aim being to establish the demands of the competitive game.

What is clear is that today's rugby players have to be powerful (to compete for the ball when there is a breakdown in play and to burst through tackles), strong (in the maul or scrummage drive), quick in attack and defence, agile (to dodge and dart through gaps in the opposition's defence), and physically fit (to play at high intensity for 80 minutes). If players are to make the most of their natural abilities they need to start working on their fitness from an early age (around 11 or 12 years old), and as they get older they will need to develop specific aspects of their fitness, particularly if they are aiming to play professional rugby. In this context, one of the challenges for rugby players is to develop the necessary fitness attributes required to play the game successfully, the problem being that some of these attributes do not complement one another. For example, whereas no-one expects a hammer thrower to make a good middle distance runner, or vice-versa, a successful rugby player has to combine aspects of the two.

In light of the above the challenge for the performance analyst is to find methods or techniques of data analysis that can generate more complete, and therefore more complex, quantitative and qualitative representations of performance (Lebed 2006). Before moving on to the case study itself, it will be useful to look at one of the key aspects in this regard, namely the analysis of temporal patterns.

Studies of temporality within sports performance

Research on this topic has traditionally investigated the time spent in different modes of motion (time-motion analysis), with the first studies being conducted in soccer (Brookes and Knowles 1974; Reilly and Thomas 1976). The main advantages of using a time-based methodology to assess physical and physiological demands are that it offers a non-intrusive way of analysing performance during play, and that the distances covered provide a measure of energy expended (Reilly and Thomas 1976). Furthermore, the distances covered by a player can be broken down into discrete motion categories that can be classified according to type, intensity, quality, duration, distance and frequency (Reilly 1994). The data obtained can then be used to build research models and for the purposes of physical conditioning. However, there is a need for continued research of this kind so as to assess the demands of sports as they are played today (Rienzi *et al.* 1998; Strudwick and Reilly 2001; Araújo *et al.* 2006). In this regard, one aspect of performance that has not been adequately studied thus far is its temporal structure and the inter-relationships between the different events that go to make up a given piece of play.

Analysis of temporal patterns

A temporal pattern (T-pattern) is essentially a combination of events that occur in the same order, with the consecutive time distances between consecutive pattern components remaining relatively invariant, it being assumed, as a null hypothesis, that each component is independently and randomly distributed over time (Magnusson 1996, 2000, 2006). As we can see in Figure 2.1 the temporal relationship between A and B, thus defined as a critical interval, lies at the heart of the algorithms used to detect T-patterns (Magnusson 2005).

The software package THEME (www.noldus.com) is designed to detect statistically significant T-patterns among sequences of behaviours, and can thus provide new insights into the structure of behaviour that cannot be observed with the naked eye or with any other method. Timing and order are crucial to the effectiveness of nearly any kind of action, but they are often hard to capture in statistics. THEME 6.0 was especially developed to meet this challenge.

A number of studies (Borrie *et al.* 2002; Camerino *et al.* 2012) have analysed T-patterns in soccer matches using a computerized video method to transcribe ball and player pitch locations and selected match events. The data show that there are

Figure 2.1 Even with extremely simple data the most regular T-patterns may be hard to spot. The T-pattern on the lower axis is present in the upper axis, where the occurrences of w and k make it hard to see. The defining characteristics of T-patterns are apparent: fixed order of components occurring with similar distances between them at each pattern occurrence. The binary tree structure indicates the bottom-up detection strategy, which may or may not reflect an inherent hierarchical structure (Borrie *et al.* 2002).

a high number of temporal, interactive patterns of play in soccer, with the number, frequency and complexity of the detected patterns indicating that sport behaviour is more synchronized than the human eye can detect. The study by Borrie *et al.* (2001) also investigated the correlation between the performance rating given by coaches and the degree of structure in team and player performance. Several professional soccer coaches were asked to rate the performance of players from both teams on a simple ten-point Likert scale. The data showed that the coaches' ratings of team performance were significantly correlated with the number of patterns identified for each team ($r = 0.81$, $p < 0.05$).

The following case study presents data from an attack session in rugby, the aim being to confirm whether the detection of T-patterns is indeed a useful analytical method in relation to performance analysis.

Aims and the mixed methods approach: triangulation design

We use here the most common design, the *triangulation design*, in which the investigator applies quantitative and qualitative methods (QUAN+QUAL) simultaneously, giving them equal weight and importance (see Chapter 1, Figure 1.1).

This case study presents a method of data analysis that detects temporal structures in time-based data sets and illustrates how it can be applied to sport performance. The method can identify consistent temporal patterns of behaviour in relation to physical activity, thus providing a more detailed picture of the complex inter-relationships between the discrete events involved therein.

The case study has a dual purpose. On the one hand, as the first case study in this book, it provides an initial demonstration of the power and applicability of T-pattern detection analysis. This is important since several of the other case studies described in the book make use of the same instrument for mixed methods research. The second purpose is to present a specific analysis of data derived from an attacking session in rugby. The aim of the study was to search for mixed patterns of physiological measurements, speed and location by using the software package THEME 6.0 (www.noldus.com) to detect T-patterns.

This case study is the only one in the book that does not correspond fully to a mixed design involving qualitative and quantitative data. This is because the data analysed are actually categorized quantitative data regarding location (coordinates and zones), heart rate and heart rate zone monitored in an attacking situation. Nonetheless, the case study is of interest as it shows how quantitative information can be obtained regarding different parameters related to the same event. It will be argued that this approach is highly useful in terms of identifying specific patterns of movement which can then be reproduced to enhance physical conditioning and coaching practices.

Method

The analysis is based on a 13-minute sample of training data derived from the observation of one player during an attack session in rugby. The player wore a wireless GPS unit throughout, thereby enabling data to be collected on heart rate, heart rate zone, speed, pitch location zones and GPS coordinates. In addition, the player's behaviour was also transcribed using an observation system designed specifically for rugby (Hughes and Franks 2008), one which is able to notate positions of play in different pitch zones, offensive and defensive formations (i.e. man-on-man, drift defence, standard backline and flat backline attack), runs, scrums, tackles (i.e. front, side and back) and passes (i.e. dive, dummy, flicks, pop, scrum half and spiral pass).

The raw data obtained were first imported into the SPORTSCODE software (Anguera and Jonsson 2003; Jonsson *et al.* 2009), which enables the synchronized observation of recorded data and the corresponding video footage. SPORT-SCODE also allowed the data to be processed into heart rate zones, location zones, speed and distance covered (see Figure 2.2).

These data were then exported into an Excel file and categorized manually before being imported into the THEME software (see Table 2.1). All the data were then analysed using the THEME software package.

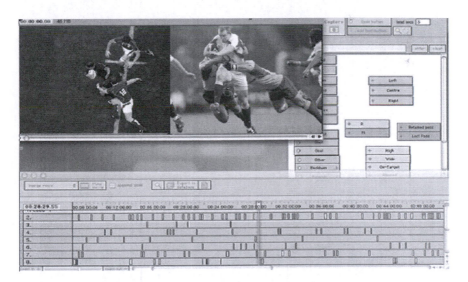

Figure 2.2 The SPORTSCODE interface (www.sportstec.com).

Table 2.1 Heart rate data

RAW DATA						CATEGORIZED DATA FOR THEME			
Clock Time	Heart Rate	HR Zone	Speed (km/h)	X (m)	Y (m)	Heart Rate	HR Zone	Speed (km/h)	X&Y Coordinates
11:35:21.6	114	2	0.398	35.7	65	x,b,hr114	x,b,hrz2	x,b,Sp0	x,b,xy36_65
11:35:21.8	114	2	0.074	35.8	64.9				
11:35:22.0	114	2	0.131	35.8	64.9				
11:35:22.2	113	2	0.061	35.8	64.9	x,b,hr113			
11:35:22.4	112	2	0	35.8	64.9	x,b,hr112			
11:35:22.6	110	2	0	35.8	64.9	x,b,hr110			
11:35:22.8	109	2	0.317	35.8	64.9	x,b,hr109			
11:35:23.0	108	2	0.148	35.8	64.9	x,b,hr108			
11:35:23.2	108	2	0.28	35.8	64.9				
11:35:23.4	109	2	0.093	35.9	65	x,b,hr109			
:	:	:	:	:	:	:	:	:	:
11:37:29.0	140	3	15.003	54.1	97.1	x,b,hr140	x,b,hrz3	x,b,Sp15	x,b,xy54_97
11:37:29.2	140	3	14.916	54.8	96.6				x,b,xy55_97
:	:	:	:	:	:	:	:	:	:

Note: The raw data columns to the left are examples from the data record. The categorized data columns are examples of events transformed from the raw data for the analysis by THEME. The 'x' stands for actor, in this case the rugby player monitored, 'b' stands for beginning of event, 'hr' refers to heart rate, 'hrz' to heart rate zone, 'sp' to speed and 'xy' to the coordinates. The raw data figures are rounded-up.

Table 2.2 The variable and value table transformed from the raw data with examples of player locations

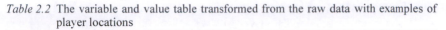

	X& Y Coordinates	Speed	Heart Rate	HR Zone
	X range: 0 to 70	**0**	95	1
		1	96	2
	Y range: 54 to 154	..	..	3
	—			
	Examples of	..	..	4
	locations	27	165	5
	x,b,xy15_113			
	x,b,xy35_65			

This variable and value table, derived from a transformation of the raw data, includes X and Y coordinates of the pitch and shows the player's movement tracked from X 0 to 70 and from Y 54 to 154. By grouping coordinates into pitch zones (see Table 2.2) it is possible to obtain information about different activities between zones, thereby enabling the tracing of inter-zone movement and movement patterns, as well as a more detailed (micro) analysis of exact coordinates.

Results

The results provide a combined analysis of distance, speed, location and physiological measurements. According to the analysis of GPS data (see Figure 2.3), 84 per cent of the distance covered by the player corresponded to running in speed zone

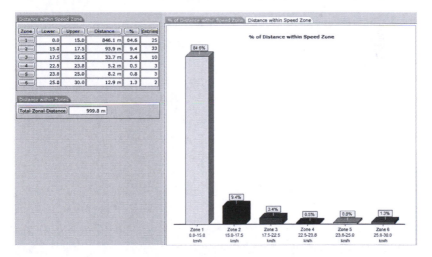

Figure 2.3 Distance covered and number of sprints for each speed zone.

1 (0–15 km/h) and 9.4 per cent to running in speed zone 2 (15–17.5 km/h). During the 13-minute attack session the player covered a distance of 846.1 m in 25 sprints at 0–15 km/h, and a distance of 93.9 m in 33 sprints at 15–17.5 km/h. Overall, his speed ranged from 0 to 27 km/h. Figure 2.3 shows the distribution of distances across zones for the total 999.8 m the player ran during the observation period.

Figure 2.4 shows the heart rate measurements (beats per minute, bpm) obtained across the observation period. Overall heart rate ranged between 95 and 165 bpm (see Figure 2.4), with values being clustered into heart rate (HR) zones 2 to 4. Specifically, the player's heart rate corresponded to HR zone 3 (120–150 bpm) for 52 per cent of the period, to HR zone 2 (90–120 bpm) for 28.5 per cent and to HR zone 4 (150–165 bpm) for 19.1 per cent of the period.

Figure 2.5 provides an overview of speed and heart rate changes during the 13-minute attack session. These changes, along with those in heart rate zones, pitch zones and GPS coordinates, constitute the data exported for T-pattern analysis (see Figure 2.5).

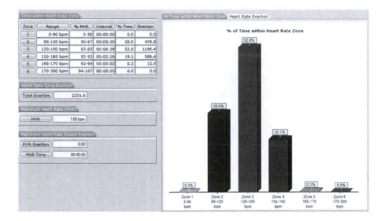

Figure 2.4 Time spent within each heart rate zone.

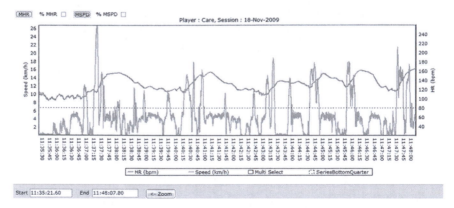

Figure 2.5 Graphical overview of speed and heart rate changes during the observation period.

Discussion

A large number of temporal patterns were detected in the synchronized embedded data. These patterns related to repeated changes in heart rate, heart zone, speed, location and GPS coordinates. Figure 2.6 is an example of a very complex and highly significant pattern and it should be read as follows. The upper-left box shows the events occurring within the pattern, listed in the order in which they occur within the pattern. Note that they are presented in the form of a tree diagram, with the first event in the pattern appearing at the top and the last at the bottom.

All the tree diagrams that appear in this book should be read in this way, i.e. from top to bottom. The upper-right box in Figure 2.6 shows the frequency of events within the pattern, and each dot means that an event has been coded. The pattern diagram (the lines connecting the dots) shows the connection between events. The number of pattern diagrams illustrates how often the pattern occurs. Sub-patterns also occur when some of the events within the pattern occur without the whole of the pattern occurring. The lower box illustrates the real-time of the pattern. The lines show the connections between events, when they take place and how much time passes between each event. The T-pattern shown in Figure 2.6 occurred five times during the observation period and involves 14 changes in the player's location and heart rate. These occur in the same order with significantly similar time intervals between each occurrence, and cover 15 per cent of the observation period.

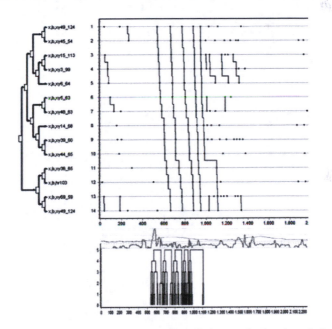

Figure 2.6 The pattern describes 14 event types of changes in the player's location and heart rate, occurring five times in the same order with significantly similar time intervals between events during the first five minutes of the observation period. The speed and heart rate changes from Figure 2.5 are superimposed on the time line showing their relationship to the T-patterns.

Figure 2.7 is an example of the most complex pattern detected. This pattern occurs three times during the first five minutes of the observation period and involves 31 changes in the player's location and heart rate. These occur in the same order with significantly similar time intervals between each occurrence, and cover 15 per cent of the observation period (see Figure 2.7).

Conclusions

The purpose of this case study has not been to suggest that an analysis of temporal structure is better than other analytical approaches, but merely that the detection of T-patterns provides an additional and fresh perspective as regards the study of sport performance. Traditional frequency analyses of performance have provided, and continue to provide, valuable information that coaches and players use to enhance the coaching process. However, such methods are unable to identify temporal patterns of the kind described here.

This study of an attack session in rugby, like previous research on soccer (Bloomfield *et al.* 2005), handball (Lopes *et al.* 2011), and basketball (Fernández

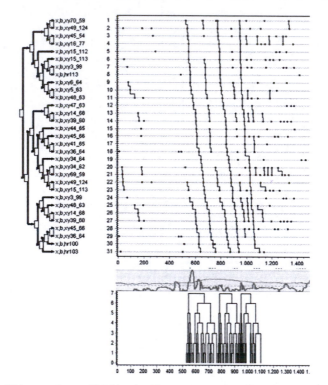

Figure 2.7 This complex and highly significant pattern describes changes in the player's location and heart rate occurring in the same manner and on three occasions during the first five minutes of the observation period. The speed and heart rate changes from Figure 2.5 are superimposed on the time line showing their relationship to the T-patterns.

et al. 2009), has shown that temporal patterns do exist in team sports, and the data highlight the potential for T-pattern analysis to make a significant contribution to a deeper understanding of sports performance. Indeed, the results suggest that there is a very real possibility of discovering new kinds of profiles (complex intra- and inter-individual patterns) for both individuals and teams using the detected behavioural patterns in combination with elementary statistics.

It is difficult to imagine coaching situations in which the type of information identified in the figures above, and the further analyses they might stimulate, would not be of value in terms of enhancing the knowledge of coaches and players. At the very least, such analyses provide a perspective on team and/or individual performance that is unattainable using traditional frequency counts of discrete events within a match. Therefore, if such analyses are not conducted as a complement to traditional methods, then both coaches and players are being deprived of meaningful information, and this may mean that performance is not being optimized. In this regard, the analysis of T-patterns has the potential to be an effective research and support tool in relation to performance analysis.

CASE STUDY 2.2: INFLUENCE OF THE USE OF SPACE ON THE DYNAMICS OF PLAY IN BASKETBALL

Introduction

Studies of the dynamics of play in team sports or opposition/collaboration situations consider that their structure is determined by parameters concerning technique, rules and the type of motor communication. Various models have been developed to describe the dynamics of play: structural models, based on the existence of a changing, uncertain and variable context that requires cognitive operations in order to evaluate, anticipate and adapt oneself to the new circumstances of the game; decision-making models, which consider the players' creativity and abilities in responding to new learning situations; and analysis of the dimensional kinematics of play (Okubo and Hubbard 2006).

In the context of basketball most research has focused on factors which might have a determining influence: technical skills, the physical/coordination abilities required of players during the game, factors that affect the style of play (Sampaio *et al.* 2006; Castellano 2008b), the effect of rule changes (Miller and Bartlett 1993, 1996; Romanowich *et al.* 2007), the detection of behavioural patterns revealed in free throws (Hamilton and Reinschmidt 1997; Al-Abood *et al.* 2002; Lonsdale and Tam 2007) or the technical/tactical structure of play during training periods (Ortega *et al.* 2006). Following this line of research the case study described below examines the effect which the use of space may have on the dynamics of play in basketball.

Aims and the mixed methods approach: convergent triangulation

This case study presents a rigorous and scientific analysis of basketball that was conducted in order to determine the influence of players' spatial distribution on the dynamics of play. Two sets of data, obtained by means of the same observation instrument, were analysed: qualitative data (QUAL), derived from the detection of temporal patterns (T-patterns) and quantitative data (QUAN), based on the detection and analysis of correspondences.

The design used was *convergent triangulation* (see Chapter 1, Figure 1.4), which implies, firstly, the independent capture of two kinds of data: qualitative (QUAL) and quantitative (QUAN). In a second stage these data are then combined (QUAL+QUAN) in order to enable an integrated interpretation (Creswell 2003).

Observational methods applied to sporting contexts

Traditional analytic methods have used frequency of event occurrence as their index of performance, for example, recording the number of passes made from particular zones or how many times a team makes a mistake. However, if one accepts that sport performance consists of a complex series of inter-relationships between wide arrays of performance variables, then simple frequency data can only provide a relatively superficial view of performance. There is therefore a growing demand for data analysis methods or techniques that can generate more complete, and therefore more complex, quantitative representations of performance.

Observational methods are scientific procedures that reveal the occurrence of perceivable behaviours, allowing them to be formally recorded and quantified (Anguera *et al.* 2001). They also enable analysis of the relationships between these behaviours, such as sequentiality, association and covariation. However, when it comes to a sport such as basketball the extraordinary diversity of situations that can be systematically observed means that we cannot rely on standard tools, and it becomes necessary to develop ad hoc instruments for each particular study.

The observation instrument

The observation system SOBL-1 chosen for this case study combines different criteria with different categories (Jonsson *et al.* 2006). The SOBL-1 (see Table 2.3) is multidimensional in nature and has the following criteria structure:

* The *fixed criteria* only apply at the start of the game.
* The *mixed criteria* are applied each time there is a change in the score.
* The *changing criteria* are applied in a continuous recording of the whole game.

Each of these criteria gives rise to respective category systems that fulfil the conditions of exhaustiveness and mutual exclusivity (E/ME).

The changing criteria related to space and the dynamics of play were: laterality, the zone of play, and the interaction contexts. These criteria were defined as follows:

* Laterality: referring to three lanes or spatial strips: right (Ri), centre (Ce) and left (Le) (see Figure 2.8).

Table 2.3 The SOBL-1 observation system

FIXED CRITERIA	Team	Observed Team	Opposing Team	
	Level	Club	National Team	
	Context	National	International	
	Competition	League	Cup	Friendly
	Venue	Home	Away	Neutral
	Quarter	First quarter		
		Second quarter		
		Third quarter		
		Fourth quarter		
MIXED CRITERIA	Momentary score			
	Accumulated score			
	Laterality	Right		Ri
		Centre		Ce
		Left		Le
	Zone	Ultra-defensive		UD
		Defensive		D
		Offensive		O
		Ultra-offensive		UO
CHANGING CRITERIA	Possession	Initial	Ball in play — Recovery	IR
			By observed team / In	IFD
			Interruptions (ball stopped) — By observed team/ Out / Out	IFFA
			By observed team/ Out / Rule	IFFB
		Final	Ball in play — Throw	FT
			Lost	FP
			By observed team/ In	FFD
			By observed team/ Out	FFF
			Interruptions (ball stopped) — Against observed team / In	FCD
			Against observed team / Out	FCF
			Basket for observed team	FC
	Interaction contexts	Attacking line-Rear line		A ⚽ R
		Attacking line-Middle line		A ⚽ M
		Attacking line-Empty zone		A ⚽ 0
		Rear line-Attacking line		R ⚽ A
		Rear line-Middle line		R ⚽ M
		Middle line-Rear line		M ⚽ R
		Middle line-Middle line		M ⚽ M
		Middle line-Attacking line		M ⚽ A

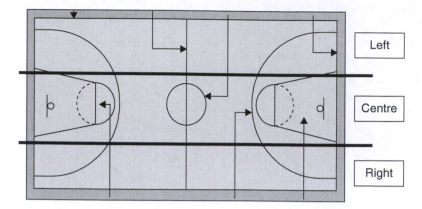

Figure 2.8 Laterality of the court as regards the observed team.

- Zone: related to the area in which play occurs and defined according to four pitch zones or spatial strips: ultra-defensive, defensive, offensive and ultra-offensive (see Figure 2.9).
- Interaction contexts: momentary ball position in relation to the spatial configuration of the two teams and their lines, expressed by two letters which correspond to the lines that are performing the strategic action: 'R' is the rear line, 'M' is the middle line, 'A' is the attacking line and 'O' is the empty zone behind the rear line. The first letter in each pair corresponds to the line of the observed team that is nearest to the ball, while the second letter corresponds to the line of the opposing team that is nearest to the ball (see Figure 2.10). The nine possible interaction contexts are therefore defined as follows:

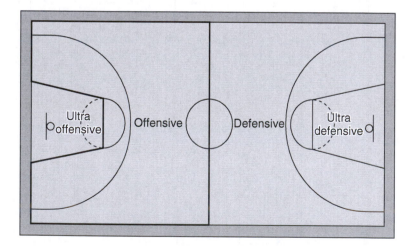

Figure 2.9 Zone of the court as regards the observed team.

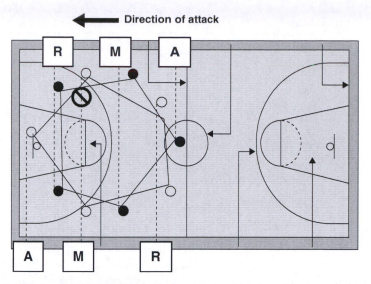

Figure 2.10 Example of an MR interaction context in which the ball is situated between the midline of the observed team and the rear line of the opposing team.

- A ⊕ R: The ball is located between the *attacking* line of the observed team and the *rear* line of the opposing team;
- A ⊕ M: The ball is located between the *attacking* line of the observed team and the *middle* line of the opposing team;
- A ⊕ O: The ball is located between the *attacking* line of the observed team and the *empty* zone of the opposing team;
- R ⊕ A: The ball is located between the *rear* line of the observed team and the *attacking* line of the opposing team;
- R ⊕ M: The ball is located between the *rear* line of the observed team and the *middle* line of the opposing team;
- M ⊕ R: The ball is located between the *middle* line of the observed team and the *rear* line of the opposing team;
- M ⊕ M: The ball is located between the *middle* line of the observed team and the *middle* line of the opposing team;
- M ⊕ A: The ball is located between the *middle* line of the observed team and the *attacking* line of the opposing team.

Procedure and participants

We randomly selected ten games from the Spanish ACB League and the Final Four of the Euro-league played during the 2005–2006 season. All these games were broadcast on public television, and the results are based on data obtained from recordings of these broadcasts. In Table 2.4 the team observed in each game is shown in capital letters. This table also groups the results according to whether the observed team won or lost, and indicates whether they were playing at home or away.

Table 2.4 List of basketball games observed (the team observed in each game is shown in capital letters)

	Result	Venue	Teams
	73–75	Away	Akasvayu – UNICAJA
	73–69	Home	CSKA – Maccabi Tel Aviv
	73–76	Away	Panathinaikos – EFES PILSEN
Won	84–78	Home	REAL MADRID – Barcelona
	86–73	Home	REAL MADRID – Dkv
	72–76	Away	Tau – UNICAJA
	83–78	Home	UNICAJA – Tau
	66–57	Away	Cska – EFES PILSEN
Lost	62–73	Home	REAL MADRID – Tau
	70–66	Away	Tau – BARCELONA

The recording instrument used was the Lince software (Gabin *et al.* 2012a, b), a flexible software package that enables the digital recording of games to be viewed on a screen (see Figure 2.11). While viewing the recording the observer introduces all the codes corresponding to each criterion considered by the SOBL-1 instrument (i.e. laterality, zone of play and interaction contexts). When changes are observed in any of these criteria the video is paused and the corresponding data are entered into the observational record. So as to enable the analysis of patterns or sequences of play the software records all the co-occurrences of codes, each of which occurs in a frame (the time unit used). This produces a recording composed of successive co-occurrences. Table 2.12 shows how Lince can be used not only for observational purposes but also for exporting data to other software packages.

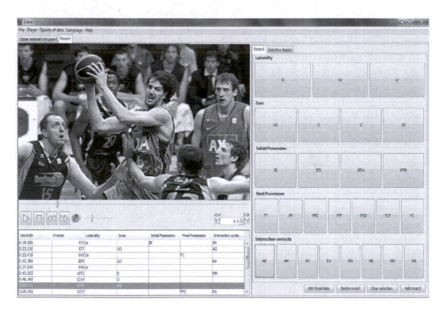

Figure 2.11 Recording instrument: Lince (Gabin *et al.* 2012a, b).

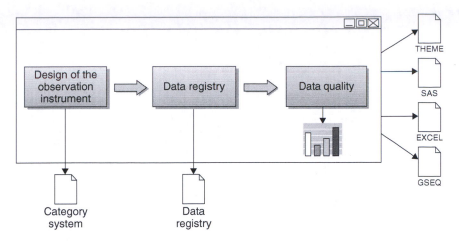

Figure 2.12 Diagram showing the different functions of Lince (Gabin *et al.* 2012a, b)

In this case study, different observers used Lince software (Gabin *et al.* 2012a, b) to transcribe the recordings of the ten games according to the codes of the SOBL-1, thereby obtaining the corresponding event frequencies. Data quality (Blanco-Villaseñor and Anguera 2000; Jansen *et al.* 2003) was controlled by calculating the Kappa coefficient (Cohen 1960). The values obtained ranged between 0.75 and 0.85, which provides a satisfactory guarantee of inter-observer reliability.

After recording each quarter, or at the end of a game, the resulting data file is exported to an Excel file such as that shown in Table 2.5. Here each row corresponds to a configuration of codes that refer to a specific observation of play and also shows the time at which they occurred and their duration expressed in frames (25 frames is equivalent to 1 second). Each new row indicates a change in the codes, such that the table, read from top to bottom, shows the successive configurations of changing codes. The total number of configurations registered with the Lince software for the ten games observed was 7357, an average of 735.7 per game.

Having obtained these data from the SOBL-1 observation instrument the use of space and its effect on the dynamics of play was then studied through two successive procedures: the detection of temporal patterns (T-patterns) and a correspondence analysis.

Results derived from the detection of temporal patterns (T-patterns)

As noted above, the data obtained from each game analysed with Lince yield a series of Excel files that show the successive configurations of changing codes (i.e. groups of codes referring to laterality, zone of play and interaction contexts, for example [Ce, C, MM] or [Le, D, MA]), along with the time at which they occurred and their duration expressed in frames (see Table 2.5).

Table 2.5   Recording obtained using Lince (Gabin *et al.* 2012).

	A	B	C
1	DATANAME	TIME	EVENT
2	Record	474	:
3	Record	475	Le,IR,AR
4	Record	577	UO,AO
5	Record	645	Ce,FC
6	Record	809	UO,RA
7	Record	946	Le
8	Record	1075	D,MM
9	Record	1214	O
10	Record	1375	UO
11	Record	1727	FFD,RA
12	Record	1925	IFFB,AR
13	Record	2166	MM
14	Record	2266	O,RA
15	Record	2470	UO,MM
16	Record	2658	O,RA
17	Record	2847	Ce
18	Record	2966	Ri,UO,MM
19	Record	3234	AR
20	Record	3235	&

In order to explore in greater depth the differences between the interaction contexts and the laterality of games won versus those of games lost, we then conducted a T-pattern analysis (Magnusson 1996, 2000, 2005) of the two data sets using the THEME software (http://www.noldus.com/content/theme-0). As we saw in Case Study 2.1, this software presents the data in the form of tree diagrams in which each branch corresponds to a specific configuration of codes and is linked to another branch that represents a different set of codes. These diagrams also indicate the temporal distance between the occurrence of these events or sets of codes (Anguera 2005). As mentioned in the previous case study, the THEME software enables the user to search for patterns (temporal configurations) that occur across all games as well as those occurring exclusively in a group of games, i.e. based on independent variables.

Figures 2.13 to 2.20 show eight examples of detected patterns and reveal repeated configurations of game events that occur not only in the same order but also with significantly similar time intervals between each event occurrence. Specifically, the analysis detected 773 T-patterns in the subset of games won (see examples in Figures 2.13, 2.15, 2.16 and 2.17) and 677 T-patterns in the subset of games lost (see examples in Figures 2.14, 2.18, 2.19 and 2.20). Some of these patterns only appeared in games won, while others were only detected in games lost. However, other patterns were found regardless of the game result.

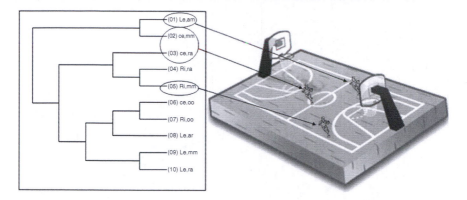

Figure 2.13 Example of a T-pattern detected in all games won. The attack begins (01) in the left-hand lane with the attacking line of the observed team and with opposition from the middle line (le,am). Next (02), the ball moves to the central lane and is played between the middle line and rear line of the attacking team and (03) the middle line and attacking line of the opponent (ce,mm) (ce,ra). The attack begins again (04) in the right-hand lane (ri,ra), moving forward (5) through the middle line (ri,mm), before ending in the left-hand lane (from 08 to 010).

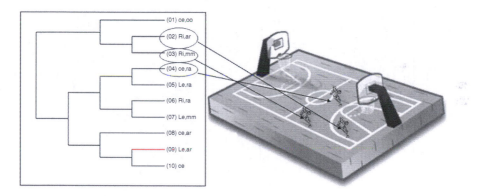

Figure 2.14 Example of a T-pattern detected in all games lost. The attack begins (from 01 to 02) with the attacking line of the observed team in the central lane, moving to the right-hand lane with opposition from the opposing team's rear line (ri,ar). It continues in this right-hand lane (03), retreating to the middle lines of both teams (de,mm), and then back (04) through the central lane with the rear lines (ce,ra), before shifting (05 and 06) between the left-hand lane (le,ra) and the right-hand lane (ri,ra) with penetrations from the attacking line, and with the move finishing in the centre (010).

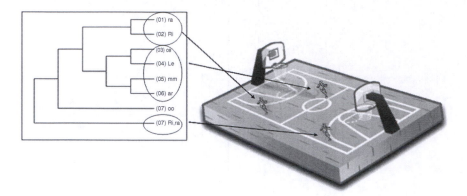

Figure 2.15 Example of a T-pattern detected in all games won. The attack begins
(from 01 to 02) in the central defensive lane with the rear line of the observed
team, and with opposition from the attacking line of the opponent (ra,ri). It
moves forward (from 03 to 06) through the central lane (ce) to the left-hand
lane (le), with the middle lines of both teams opposing one another (m,m),
and then shifts to the attacking line (ar) of the observed team. It ends (08) in
the right-hand lane with all the attacking team's lines forward (ri, ra).

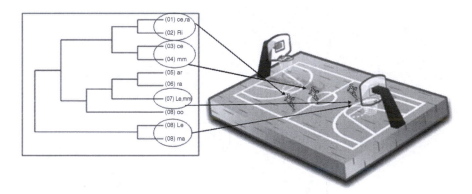

Figure 2.16 Example of a T-pattern detected in all games won. Play starts (01 and 02) in
the central/right lane, through the line behind the forward line of attackers
and the defenders (ce, ra, ri). In the same central lane (03 and 04) the ball is
passed by the middle line of the observed team, who are opposed by the other
team's middle line (ce, mm). (07) These players then move the ball to the left
(le, mm), and (09 and 10) in moving forward they eventually link up with the
forward line of attacking players (le, ma).

Results derived from the correspondence analysis

The correspondence analysis is a statistical skill that is applied to the analysis of
stage of risk by means of a Cartesian diagram based on the association between the
analyzed variables. In the above mentioned graph there are represented jointly the

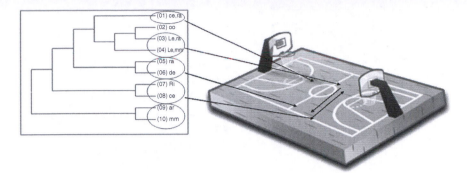

Figure 2.17 Example of a T-pattern detected in all games won. Play starts (01) in the central zone with a line of attackers and defenders (ce, ra). It then moves (03 and 04) through the same central area to the left-hand side, involving the attacking and rear lines (le, ra), having passed through the middle lines of both teams (le, mm). (05, 06, 07 and 08) The ball is switched from the left to the right-hand lane, before being returned to the left and moved through the centre by the line of attacking players, who are opposed by the defenisve line (ra) (ri) (le) (ce) (ar). Finally (10), play moves back between the middle lines of both teams (m,m).

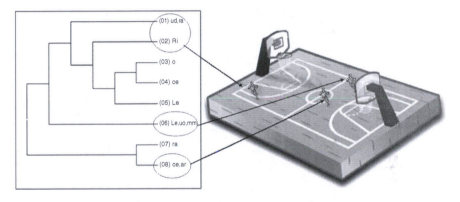

Figure 2.18 Example of a T-pattern detected in all games lost. The attack begins (01 and 02) in the ultra-defensive zone with the observed team located very deep due to the other team's defence being very forward (ud,ra) (d). They then (04, 05 and 06) move forward through the central lane, developing play along the left as far as the ultra-offensive zone, the move involving the middle lines of both teams (le,uo,mm). Finally (07), play moves back (ra) and then forward again, with the attacking lines penetrating through the central lane, where they are opposed by the other team's defenders in a deep position (ce,ar).

different forms of the table of risk, so that the proximity between the represented points is related at the association level between the above mentioned forms.

The correspondence analysis was performed using SPSS (version 14.0) and was based on the frequencies of all the co-occurrences of interaction contexts and

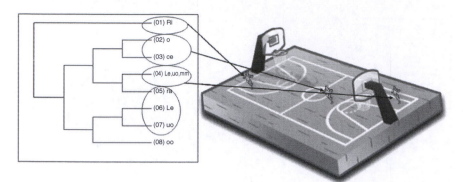

Figure 2.19 Example of a T-pattern detected in all games lost. The counterattack (01) starts on the right-hand side (ri) and progresses through the central area into the offensive zone (o, ce). (04) Play moves to the left and the ultra-offensive zone by means of middle-line attacking players, and is stopped by defenders of the middle line (le, uo, mm). (05, 06 and 07) The attacking team then moves its lines back, such that play is located between this deeper attacking line and the forward line of defenders, who reorganize their positions (ra, le, uo).

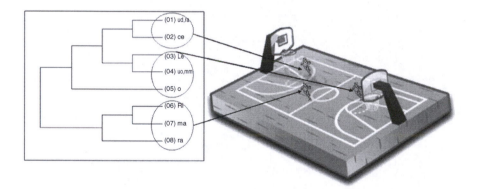

Figure 2.20 Example of a T-pattern detected in all games lost. Play starts (01 and 02) in the central area by means of the ultra-defensive line behind the forward line of attackers and the defenders (ud, ra, ce). (03 and 04) Play moves quickly through the left-hand lane as far as the ultra-offensive zone between the middle line of both teams (le) (uo,mm), and then (06, 07 and 04) back to the defensive zone, where it is reorganized before being moved forward again, this time with the attacking players slightly deep and the defenders in a more advanced position (d)(mm)(ra).

laterality. Tables 2.6 and 2.7 show the results of simple correspondence analyses for interaction contexts and laterality, respectively.

The first column in these tables represents the code of the nine interaction contexts and the three lanes of laterality, respectively. The second column shows the frequency of each interaction context and each lane of laterality, respectively

Table 2.6 Examination of row scores in the simple correspondence analysis for interaction contexts (using SPSS, version 14)

Interaction Context	Score in Dimension				Relation				
					The points of the inertia dimensions		Dimension of the inertia points		
	%	1	2	Inertia	1	2	1	2	Total
AM	.105	.651	.555	.008	.359	.423	.691	.309	1.000
AO	.063	.075	.166	.000	.003	.023	.252	.748	1.000
AR	.126	.075	.166	.000	.006	.045	.252	.748	1.000
MA	.126	.075	.166	.000	.006	.045	.252	.748	1.000
MM	.126	.075	.166	.000	.006	.045	.252	.748	1.000
MR	.095	.483	.508	.005	.177	.320	.594	.406	1.000
OO	.126	.075	.166	.000	.006	.045	.252	.748	1.000
RA	.126	.075	.166	.000	.006	.045	.252	.748	1.000
RM	.105	.715	.081	.007	.432	.009	.992	.008	1.000
Total active	1.000			.021	1.000	1.000			

Table 2.7 Examination of column scores in the simple correspondence analysis for laterality (using SPSS, version 14)

Laterality	Score in Dimension				Relation				
					The points of the inertia dimensions		Dimension of the inertia points		
	%	1	2	inertia	1	2	1	2	Total
Ri	.326	.349	.289	.007	.319	.355	.703	.297	1.000
Ce	.358	.124	.358	.004	.044	.598	.164	.836	1.000
Le	.316	.501	.107	.010	.637	.047	.973	.027	1.000
Total active	1.000			.021	1.000	1.000			

(referred to in statistical terms as the relative marginal frequency). The next two columns give the scores on the dimensions (coordinates of each point). The fifth column indicates the inertia of each point. The next four columns show the absolute and relative contributions to the axes (factors). The final column shows the quality of the representation in the sub-space considered (plane of the two axes).

The results in Tables 2.6 and 2.7 can then be used to plot the graph of the most important absolute contributions as regards interpreting the two factor axes:

A. With respect to the first factor axis (Figure 2.21):
    For laterality: 31.9 per cent of the inertia is due to the right lane (Ri), situated at the positive and negative ends of the axes; 4.4 per cent of the inertia corresponds to the central lane (Ce), situated in the central and positive part; and 63 per cent of the inertia is accounted for by the left lane (Le), situated at the negative ends of both axes.

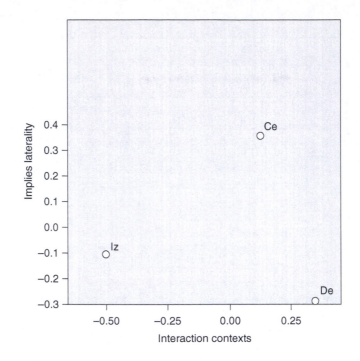

Figure 2.21 Plot of the column points. Dimension 1 refers to interaction contexts and Dimension 2 to laterality.

With respect to interaction contexts: there is an opposition between the interaction context AM, situated at the negative end and which accounts for 35.9 per cent of the explained inertia for the first axis, and the interaction contexts RM and MR, situated at the positive end and which account for 60.9 per cent of the axis inertia.

With regard to the best represented interaction contexts and laterality, i.e. those which have the highest relative contributions, the results corroborate the above description: the most important interaction contexts are RM (69.1 per cent) and MR (59.4 per cent), while the most important lanes are Le (97.3 per cent) and Ri (70.3 per cent).

Therefore, this factor axis identifies positions of equilibrium between defensive strategies (RM) and attacking ones (MR), and also shows that the left lane is more important than the right lane.

B. As regards the second factor axis (Figure 2.22):
The interaction contexts MA, AO, MM and AR are situated at the negative end and account for 16.6 per cent of the axis inertia. By contrast, the interaction contexts AM, RM and MR are situated at the positive end, although they only account for 1.3 per cent of the axis inertia. With respect to laterality,

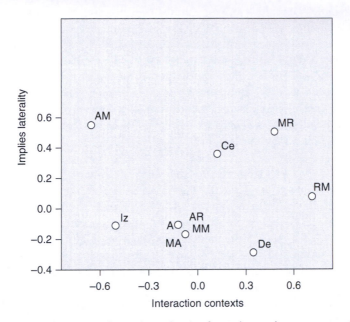

Figure 2.22 Plot of the row points. Dimension 1 refers to interaction contexts and Dimension 2 to laterality.

there is a noteworthy negative contribution of the right lane, which accounts for 0.7 per cent of the axis inertia, and a positive contribution of the central lane, accounting for 0.4 per cent of the axis inertia.

The best represented points on this second factor axis are the interaction contexts AO, AR, MA, MM, OO and RA, each of which yield a value of 74.8 per cent, and the central lane, with 83.6 per cent.

Therefore, the second factor axis identifies outside positions of a clearly attacking (AR and MA) and conservative (MA and RA) nature, as well as some atypical positions (AO and OO) and an equilibrium position (MM) in the central lane.

Consequently, the factor plane formed by the two factor axes comprises the following interaction contexts: AM, which occupies a more isolated position, equidistant from the left and central lanes; MR, which is more clearly associated with the central lane; RM, which is closer to the right lane; and the interaction contexts AO, AR, MA and MM, at a position equidistant from the left and right lanes.

Discussion

Two factor axes were extracted from the analysis of simple correspondences. The first identified positions of equilibrium between defensive (RM) and attacking (MR) strategies, and also showed that the left lane was more important than the right. The second showed outside positions of a clearly attacking (AR and MA) and conservative (MA and RA) nature, as well as some atypical positions (AO and OO) and an equilibrium position (MM) in the central lane.

The factor plane formed by the two factor axes included the following interaction contexts: AM, which occupies a more isolated position, equidistant from the left and central lanes; MR, which is more clearly associated with the central lane; RM, which is closer to the right lane; and the interaction contexts AO, AR, MA and MM, at a position equidistant from the left and right lanes.

The results indicate that the profiles of play for the team that is ahead are determined by the following aspects of laterality:

a. In the *left lane* with the observed team forward and the opposing team in the rear zone (interaction context AR) there is: (1) a predominance of play in positions very close to the opposing team's basket, such that the inside players on the left side (low post) tend to go toward the centre, throwing with the hand on the far side of the defender; and (2) the possibility of generating more disequilibrium options through a player receiving the ball on the left side close to the hoop, which enables him to score or pass the ball to another more central zone that is more favourable.

b. In the *central lane*: (1) with the observed team forward and without an opponent (interaction context AO) there appear good defences that generate effective counterattacks; and (2) with the observed team in the rear zone and the opposing team forward (interaction context RA), ball possession is held by the player furthest back (who could be the baseline player) rather than the most forward player of the opponent, and he wins the more favourable central lane to either change the ball direction or play the ball into the zone that most favours an attack.

c. The *right lane* with the observed team in a mid-court position and the opponent in either a rear, mid-court or forward position (interaction contexts MR, MM, MA), showing strength in the middle line and seeking to generate advantageous situations through trying to obtain numerical superiority in play prior to the endpoint of a given move. The MM positions show a pairing of the attacker and his defender, but the objective is to create MR or MA disequilibrium situations in which the attacker beats his defender, creating help from the inside players (MR) or outside players (MA).

The winning team is strong in dominating the central lane, which enables it to make good easy shots and counterattacks. In the left lane, play predominantly occurs close to the hoop, while the right lane is characterized by situations of static attack by outside players.

Depending on technical and tactical characteristics, the team in possession of the ball seeks to create a situation of equilibrium during a phase of effective scoring which is revealed through: (a) counterattack with quick transitions; (b) dominating inside play close to the opponent's basket; and (c) dominating outside play that favours either the play of shooters or penetration into the opponent's zones.

Obviously, each game has its own pace and style according to the technical and tactical characteristics of the players. However, during the game the contest arises from a team's attempts to impose itself in one of the above-mentioned three situations (i.e. the three lanes of laterality), and subsequently to shift play to one of the other two. The ability to maintain variability between these three situations that favour disequilibrium produces disorganization in the opponent, thus enabling a playing advantage to be obtained. Overall, the results suggest that when team tactics can be detected in the form of repeated T-patterns, which have qualitative significance as regards the team's performance, it is possible to distinguish between successful playing strategies, which are worth pursuing, and unsuccessful ones, which could be rejected for future games.

Conclusions

The results obtained in this case study show that the observation of basketball based on a comparison of the result, the dynamics of play (interaction contexts) and laterality helps to understand the optimum equilibrium achieved during play. Specifically, the study offers a precise description of the relationships between interaction contexts and laterality (the three lanes of the court) in professional basketball games from the Spanish ACB league and the Euro-league Final Four 2005–2006, these relationships being distinguished according to a team's performance in a particular game. We believe that these findings provide a starting point for further research, not only into the relationships between interaction contexts and laterality in professional basketball but also into the temporal patterning of team and player behaviour.

CASE STUDY 2.3: THE DYNAMICS OF PLAY AND DEFENSIVE SYSTEMS IN HANDBALL

Introduction

By analysing the dynamics of play it is possible to describe and understand the factors and critical events that determine the performance of teams and individual players in team sports. Although a team's actions, and the shift from one kind of play to another, is influenced by many factors, the present case study focuses particularly on the relationship between defensive players and the formations used by their attacking opponents (Schmidt *et al.* 1999; Araújo 2006).

The theory of dynamic and complex systems is now an emerging research paradigm as regards the analysis of performance in team sports. According to this theoretical perspective the dynamics of play show the following characteristics: degrees of freedom, integration of the different levels of the system, and the capacity to create a stable and self-organized nonlinear system (Handford *et al.* 1997; Davids *et al.* 2008). In this context, research has considered how teams seek to redress disequilibrium and achieve stability in opposition collective sports (Nevill *et al.* 2002), how performance may be optimized through self-regulation based on visual feedback (Hodges and Franks 2002; Hodges *et al.* 2007; Horn *et al.* 2002), and how the theory of dynamic neural networks may be used to identify tactical structures in handball (Pfeiffer and Perl 2006).

The self-organizing aspect of the dynamics of play has been described in terms of the following characteristics (McGarry *et al.* 2002):

- stability manifested in an ordered organization;
- control of and adaptation to different states;
- stability of different states of change;
- variability in transitions (nonlinear changes).

In light of the above, sports play should be regarded as a dynamical system characterized by self-organization based on dynamic principles. Consequently, an understanding of individual and team performance that takes into account the internal interaction of the team and the structure of play may therefore help coaches to make decisions.

In order to respect the dynamic nature of play, and to capture the frequency, order and complexity of events as it unfolds, this case study uses observational methodology to record the wide variety of interactive, collaborative and oppositional situations that arise during the organized defensive play of an elite handball team. The specific aim is to identify strategic defensive patterns and highlight their key features (Dumangane *et al.* 2009).

Aims and mixed methods: explanatory sequential design

An increasing number of observational studies of handball have begun to consider the defensive factors that enable a team to be more effective at breaking up an attack. This is consistent with the greater attention paid to the defensive process by coaches in recent international competitions. However, research on this issue remains scarce (Gomes and Volossovitch 2008).

The present case study analyses the organized defensive play (involving six outfield players per side – 6 × 6 situations) of the Spanish national handball team during the 2008 Beijing Olympics, the focus being on:

- the ways in which ball possession was recovered;
- the defensive structures that precede ball recovery.

The aim was to study the tactical defensive behaviour that begins when the team which loses the ball adopts a structured defensive system[1] based on previously defined defensive principles and strategies and which ends when the ball is recovered.

The *explanatory sequential design* used (see Chapter 1, Figure 1.12) consists of the successive use of the observational instrument (QUAN) and an interview to gather opinions (QUAL) (Creswell 2003). Thus, the analysis of defensive play begins by applying observational methodology (QUAN), which provides the first set of data about the organized defensive tactics used by the Spanish team in the two matches observed (Nevill *et al.* 2008). This data is then complemented with information obtained through an interview with one of the players involved (QUAL).

Instrument 1: Observation system of organized defensive phase (SODMO)

Construction of the instrument

An ad hoc observation instrument based on a system of categories was developed to record the tactical behaviours associated with the organized defensive systems of elite handball teams involving six outfield players per side (6 × 6 situations). The Observation System of Organized Defensive Phase (SODMO) was constructed in four stages, three preliminary and one involving active recording:

a. First preliminary stage (deductive/theoretical): we began by defining a repertory of the criteria (fundamental variables) that are considered relevant to an event of organized defence (from its start to its completion): score, defensive system, defensive organization, ball position, position of the pivot, group actions of the attacking players, defensive opposition and ball recovery.

b. Second preliminary stage (inductive/exploratory): we then drew up an open-ended list (in the form of a catalogue) of the categories to be observed (objective, exhaustive and mutually exclusive behaviours) in relation to each criterion when viewing the matches played in the 2008 Beijing Olympics. This constituted a first draft of the SODMO (see Table 2.8 and Figures 2.23, 2.24 and 2.25).

c. Third preliminary stage (validation/reliability): in order to ensure that the instrument (SODMO) would actually enable users to observe the target behaviours (validation) we gathered the opinions and suggested corrections from a panel of experts/coaches. This information was then used to develop an observation manual, which made it easier to train observers and to assess the degree of agreement between them. The credibility and quality of the observational data thus obtained was then evaluated by calculating Cohen's kappa coefficient of inter-observer reliability, whose value had to be greater than or equal to 0.8 (Cohen 1960; Jansen *et al.* 2003; Sheskin 2004).

d. Fourth stage (systematic recording): having thus developed a reliable instrument (SODMO) that was able to provide a global view of the dynamics of defensive play, the SODMO was then applied to match recordings in order to produce a register of the above-mentioned criteria: ball position, position of the attacking pivot, the actions of attacking players, the defensive actions of the observed team, and how the sequence of play comes to an end in the context of an organized defensive strategy.

The SODMO observation instrument has nine criteria, with the following codes and categories:

Table 2.8 SODMO observation instrument

Criteria	Start	Score	Defensive System	Defensive Organization	Court Positions (ball position)	Pivot Position	Group Actions of Attacking Players	Defensive Opposition	Ball Recovery
Codes	On	W1	Zonal	ZA	LD	PM	Perb	Stop	Dcb
		W2	One	ZP	LDC	P23E	Perm	Desl	Dsc6
		W3	Two	Press	C	P23D	Cz	Apr	Dsc9
		W4	Three		LE	P12E	Blq	Cont	Rec
		W5	Four		LEC	P12D	Ecr	Blc	GS
		T	Five		ZT	2P23	Pee	Flt	GS7m
		L1	Six		PD	2P12	PeSu	F7m	I
		L2	Seven		PiD	2P1ME		TInter	BL
		L3	Eight		PiC	2P1MD		TDes	Dsm
		L4	Nine		PiE	2P1E23			Res
		L5	Man-marking		PE	2P1D23			PDB
						OPiv			Pb
									MPR
									Vio
									Fa
									Jp
									ROR
									ROO
									Out

1. Start – used to initiate a sequence.
2. Score – used to describe the scoreboard goal difference between teams when the Spanish team is:

   - winning by one (W1), two (W2), three (W3), four (W4) and five or more goals (W5);
   - losing by one (L1), two (L2), three (L3), four (L4), and five or more goals (L5);
   - tied (T).

3. Defensive system – used to identify the defensive system used by the Spanish team: 6:0 (Zonal), 5:1 (One), 4:2 (Two), 2:4 (Three), 3:3 (Four), 1:5 (Five), 5 + 1 (Six), 4 + 2 (Seven), 3 + 3 (Eight), 3:2:1 (Nine) and M × M (Man-Marking) (see an example of 6:0 and 5:1 defensive systems in Figure 2.23).
4. Defensive organization – used to identify how the defensive system is interpreted:

   - passive (ZP) when the defenders don't actively try to recover the ball;
   - active (ZA) when there's active opposition on the ball possessor and passing lines; and
   - pressing (Press) when the defenders seek to recover the ball using great depth to cut passing lines and pressure the ball possessor.

5. Ball position – refers to the attacking player with the ball in the marked zones in the handball field (see Figure 2.24).
6. Pivot position – used to identify where the attacking pivots are in the defensive system (for an example, see Figure 2.25):

   - pivot was in the middle of the defensive system (PM);
   - pivot was between the second and the third defenders on the left side (P23E) or on the right side (P23D);

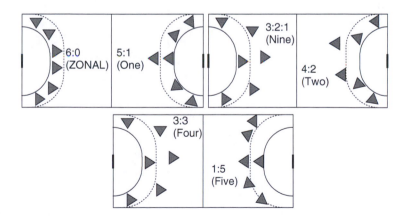

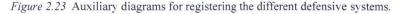

Figure 2.23 Auxiliary diagrams for registering the different defensive systems.

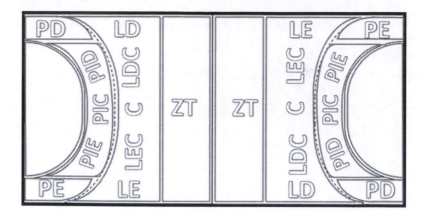

Figure 2.24 Auxiliary diagram for registering the position of the player with the ball.

- pivot was between the first and the second defenders on the left side (P12E) or right side (P12D);
- two pivots used between the second and the third defenders on the (2P23);
- two pivots used between the first and the second defenders (2P12);
- two pivots used one between the first and the second defenders on the left side (2P1ME) or on the right side (2P1MD) and the second in the middle;
- two pivots used, one between the second and the third defenders on the left side (2P1E23) or on the right side (2P1D23) and the second in the middle; or
- other pivot positions besides the above (OPiv).

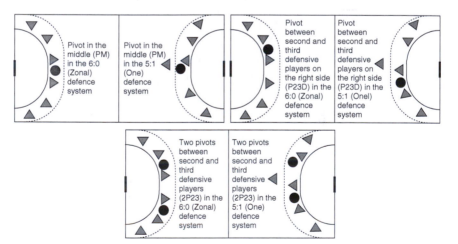

Figure 2.25 Example of auxiliary diagrams for registering the position of the attacking team's pivot.

7.   Defensive players opposition – used to identify the type of opposition that the direct defender take against the ball possessor:

- stand still or not attempt any opposition (STOP);
- lateral defensive displacement (DESL);
- approach the ball possessor (APR);
- contact the ball possessor (CONT);
- block (BLC);
- foul (FLT);
- foul that results in a seven meters throw (F7M);
- try to recover the ball by an interception (TINTER);
- try to recover the ball by a disarming move (TDES).

8.   Group action of attacking players, registered as they occurred:

- an exchange of position between attacking players with the ball (PERB) or without it (PERM);
- a cross between two attacking players in which one of those was the ball possessor (Cz);
- an offensive blockade by an attacking player without the ball near the ball possessor zone (Blq);
- a pass and go situation (PEE);
- a successive and consecutive fixation of a second defender beside the direct defender (PeSu).

9.   Ball recovery – used to end a sequence with one of the following actions:

- goalkeeper defends by controlling the ball completely (Dcb), inside his area (Dsc6), outside it (Dsc9), after an attacking throw that goes directly out by the back court line (Rec), or takes a goal in a play (GS) or in a 7 meters throw (GS7m); defenders get the ball by an interception (I), by a block (BL), by disarming the opponent (Dsm), by winning a rebound (Res), by a technical fault like dribbling or travelling (PDB), lose ball (Pb), bad pass or reception (MPR), goalkeeper area violation (Vio) or an offensive foul (FA).

Figure 2.24 shows a diagram with the handball field divided into zones which were used to register the position of the player with the ball when the Spanish team was defending using the organized method (one half field per game part). The first line of defence is represented by the zones near the goalkeeper area, from one wing player zone to another (from left (PE) to the right (PD) side), passing by the pivots' area that was divided into three zones: central (PIC), left (PIE) and right (PID). The second defensive line was from the 9 m limit to the transition zone (ZT), and was represented by five areas normally used by first line attacking players, like the player maker, and the outside throwers between the central zone (C) and the side line on the left (LE, LEC) and on the right (LD, LDC).

In this figure we show an example of how we registered the position of the Spanish pivots' opponents, taking into consideration the different defence system. The example represents the 6:0 (Zonal) and 5:1 (One):

- when the pivot was in the middle of the defence (PM);
- when he/she was between the second and the third Spanish defensive players on the left side (P23D);
- and when the opposite team used two pivots between the second and third defensive players.

Participants

This case study forms part of a research project concerning the defensive play of the Spanish handball team during the 2008 Beijing Olympics. The analysis focuses on two matches (recorded from televised broadcasts): the group-stage match between Spain and Croatia, which Spain lost 31–29, and the third place play-off between the same two teams, which Spain won 35–29 (see Table 2.9).

Since these matches were the first and last played by the Spanish team during the tournament it is possible to study the evolution of the team's defensive play.

Procedure

The recording instrument used was Match Vision Studio 3.0 (Castellano *et al.* 2008a), the same as that used in Case Study 2.2 of this chapter. As we have already seen, this is a flexible software package that, by means of an intuitive graphical interface, enables the observer to introduce the codes corresponding to each of the criteria featured in the observation instrument. In the case of the SODMO these are: start, score, defensive system, defensive organization, court ball position, position of the attacking team's pivot, group actions of attacking players, defensive opposition and ball recovery. These codes can be recorded at the same time as viewing the video. Specifically, the software enables the user to code the observed behaviours, pausing the image when a given behaviour occurs and selecting the corresponding category from the list of codes. The digital video files can be

Table 2.9 Matches played by the Spanish handball team during the 2008 Beijing Olympic Games

Round	Teams	1st half	2nd half	Result	
Group stage	Croatia–Spain	16–11	15–18	31–29	Lost
	China–Spain	12–16	10–20	22–36	Won
	France–Spain	16–10	12–11	28–21	Lost
	Spain–Brazil	20–17	16–18	36–35	Won
Quarter finals	Korea–Spain	13–14	11–15	24–29	Won
Semi-final	Iceland–Spain	17–15	19–15	36–30	Lost
Third placement game	Croatia–Spain	14–12	15–23	29–35	Won

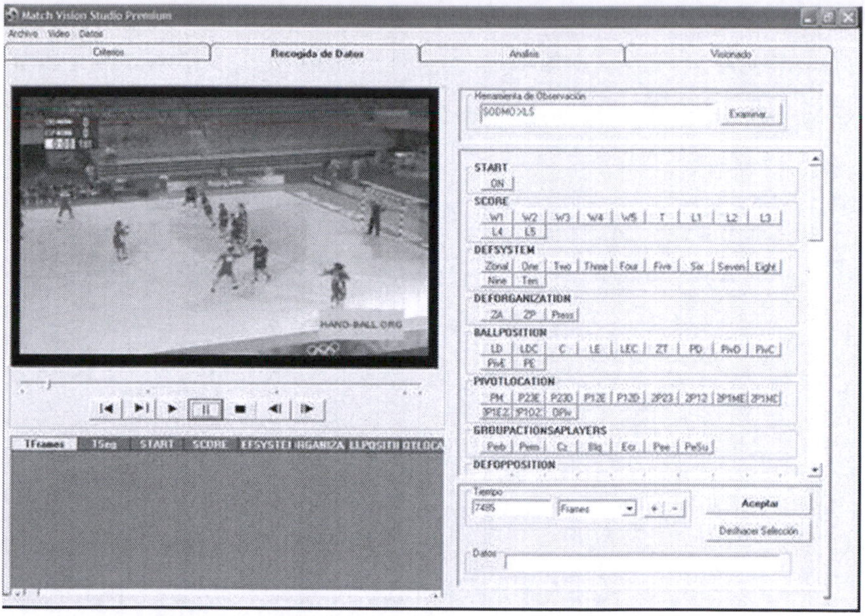

Figure 2.26 The recording instrument: MATCH VISION STUDIO 3.0 (Castellano *et al.* 2008a).

reproduced in a range of formats (avi, mpeg and wmv), and the software records all the occurrences of behaviour, the corresponding sequence and the duration of each sequence (see Figure 2.26).

The resulting data are automatically saved in an Excel file (.xls) that includes columns referring to the time, the duration of the event (in frames and seconds) and the behaviours observed. Each row in the Excel file corresponds to a configuration or group of behaviours (Table 2.10).

Results

Detecting temporal patterns (T-patterns)

In order to study the defensive behaviour of the Spanish handball team in the 2008 Beijing Olympics we analysed the sequences of behaviour that were identified through the application of the observation instrument (SODMO). This sequential analysis enabled us to obtain temporal patterns (T-patterns) for each game and each game half. T-patterns are important as they can help to reveal hidden structures and non-observable aspects of sports techniques (Magnusson 1996, 2000, 2005).

As noted above, each row of the Excel file produced by the Match Vision Studio 3.0 software corresponds to a configuration or group of behaviours. Specifically,

Table 2.10 Data file produced by the MATCH VISION STUDIO 3.0 software

	E	F	G	H	I	J	K	L
	Score	Defensive System	Defensive Organization	Court positions	Pivot Position	Group Actions Attacking Players	Defensive opposition	Ball Recovery
1								
2	T	zonal	ZP	LE	P23E	o	Desl	o
3	T	zonal	ZP	PE	P23E	o	Desl	o
4	T	zonal	ZP	LE	P23E	o	Desl	o
5	T	zonal	ZP	C	P23E	o	Desl	o
6	T	zonal	ZP	LD	P23E	o	Desl	o
7	T	zonal	ZP	C	P23E	o	Desl	o
8	T	zonal	ZP	LE	P23E	o	Desl	o
9	T	zonal	ZP	C	P23E	o	Desl	o
10	T	zonal	ZP	LEC	P23E	Cz	Cont	o
11	T	zonal	ZP	C	P23E	o	Flt	o
12	T	zonal	ZP	C	OPiv	o	Stop	o
13	T	zonal	ZP	C	PM	o	Stop	o
14	T	zonal	ZP	LE	PM	o	Cont	o
15	T	zonal	ZP	LEC	PM	Blq	Apr	o
16	T	zonal	ZP	C	PM	o	Blc	o

each configuration or row refers to a set of codes that have changed with respect to the previous row, and the data file also shows their corresponding temporality and duration, expressed in frames (25 frames is equivalent to 1 second). The total number of events configuration registered by Match Vision Studio 3.0 for the two matches observed (and based on the changing criteria of the SODMO) was 1016, an average of 508 per match.

These data were then imported into the THEME v.5 software (www.noldus. com) in order to detect any T-patterns. In what follows we present the results obtained by analysing each of the two matches between Spain and Croatia independently. For the first match we describe a descriptive analysis of the distribution of configurations in a plot, accompanied by a sequential analysis of T-patterns by means of tree diagrams. For the second match we present results of the descriptive analysis only, as no T-patterns were detected.

Descriptive analysis of the group-stage match between Spain and Croatia

In this first match of Group A, Spain was behind in 36 of the 42 (85.71 per cent) defensive sequences registered, and tied up in the remaining six (14.29 per cent). Overall, therefore, the score during this match was rarely a draw, although the Spanish team was only losing by five or more goals in two defensive sequences (see Table 2.11).

The plot shown in Figure 2.27 represents a way of describing the defensive

Table 2.11 Number of defensive sequences and the momentary scores in the group-stage match between Spain and Croatia

Momentary score	1st half	2nd half	Total	%
Tie	3	3	6	14.29
Losing by 1 goal	6	4	10	23.81
Losing by 2 goals	6	3	9	21.43
Losing by 3 goals	4	5	9	21.43
Losing by 4 goals	3	3	6	14.29
Losing by 5 or more goals	2	0	2	4.76

sequences and ball recovery methods that were observed according to the match score at a given point.

The strip labelled with the letter (a) represents those points in the match when the Spanish team was losing by four or more goals (i.e. L4 and L5). The rectangle formed by a dashed line (b) indicates a period during which Spain conceded ten goals. The circles labelled with the letter (c) refer to five sequences of ball recovery without conceding a goal. The defensive sequences inside the

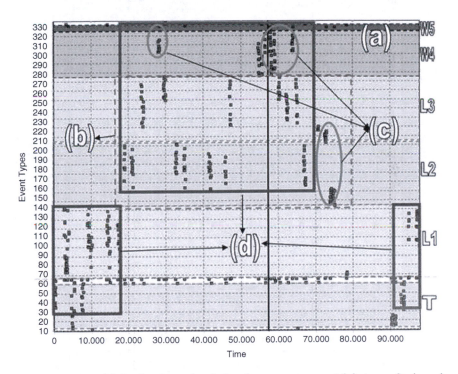

Figure 2.27 Plot of defensive dynamics during the group-stage match between Spain and Croatia.

square formed by a solid line (d) are those in which the team used the defensive system 6:0, taking into account the score at that time. The 6:0 is a zonal system in which all six outfield players form a single defensive line at the edge of the goal keeper area.

Sequential analysis of the group-stage match between Spain and Croatia

The analysis of all the configurations (rows in the Excel file) revealed four stable T-patterns, with some variations (Figures 2.28, 2.29, 2.30 and 2.31). These T-patterns show that when the Spanish team was losing by two goals it was highly likely to adopt a passive defensive strategy with respect to the player with the ball, while the opposing team's pivot was between the second and third defender on the right-hand side of the court. This was done using the 6:0 defensive system.

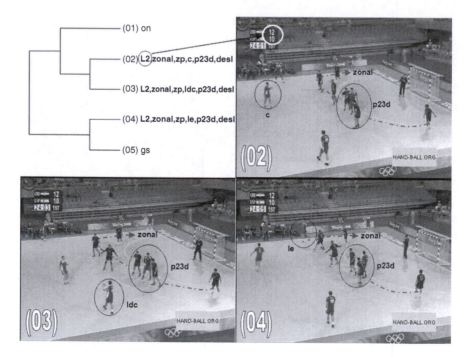

Figure 2.28 Defensive sequence comprising five configurations: When the Spanish team was (02) losing by two goals (L2) it used a 6:0 system (zonal) with a passive defensive strategy (zp), with the opposing team's pivot between the second and third defenders on the right-hand side (p23d); the defender marking the player with the ball makes a defensive displacement (desl) when the ball is moved through (03) the central zone (c) to the (04) right-hand side of the court that is closest to the centre (ldc), and then immediately to the left-hand side (le).

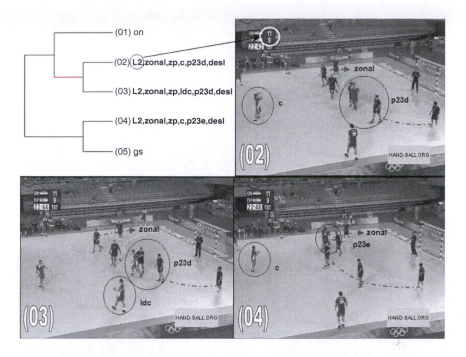

Figure 2.29 Second significant T-pattern: When the Spanish team was (02) losing by two goals (L2) it used defends using a 6:0 system (zonal) passive defensive strategy (zp), with the opposing team's pivot between the second and third defenders on the right-hand side (p23d); the defender marking the player with the ball makes a defensive displacement (desl) when the ball is moved through (03) the central zone (c) to the right-hand side of the court closest to the centre (ldc), and continues to do so when (04) it returns to the central zone (c) with the opposing team's pivot between the second and third defenders on the left-hand side (p23e).

Descriptive analysis of the third placement match between Spain and Croatia

The second match between Spain and Croatia was the play-off for the bronze medal, and the analysis revealed 42 defensive situations distributed across eight categories of momentary score (Table 2.12).

The Spanish team was ahead in 21 of the 42 (50 per cent) defensive sequences detected, although this aspect only became more apparent during the second half of the match, as can be seen in the chronology of the plot in Figure 2.32.

The Spanish team conceded a high number of goals at two points during the match: in the first half, each time the teams were drawing [(a) in the plot]; and during the last fifteen minutes of the match, when they were winning by five or more goals [(b) in the plot]. After the opening fifteen minutes of the match,

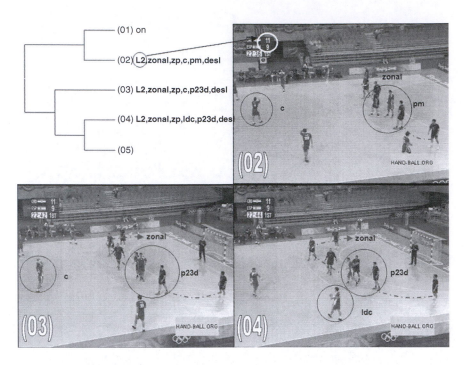

Figure 2.30 Third significant T-pattern: When the Spanish team was (02) losing by two goals (L2) it used defends using a 6:0 system (zonal) passive defensive strategy (zp), with the opposing team's pivot in the middle of the defence (pm); the defender marking the player with the ball makes a defensive displacement (desl) when the ball is in the central zone (c) and (03) continues to do so (desl) when the opposing team's pivot positions himself between the second and third defenders on the right-hand side (p23d) and the ball (04) is moved through the same area (c) to the right-hand zone of the court that is closest to the centre (ldc).

Table 2.12 Number of defensive sequences and the momentary scores in the third placement match between Spain and Croatia

Momentary score	1st half	2nd half	Total	%
Tie	10	1	11	26
Losing by 1 goal	6	1	7	16
Losing by 2 goals	2	1	3	7
Winning by 1 goal	2	1	3	7
Winning by 2 goals	0	4	4	9
Winning by 3 goals	0	2	2	7
Winning by 4 goals	0	4	4	9
Winning by 5 or more goals	0	8	8	19

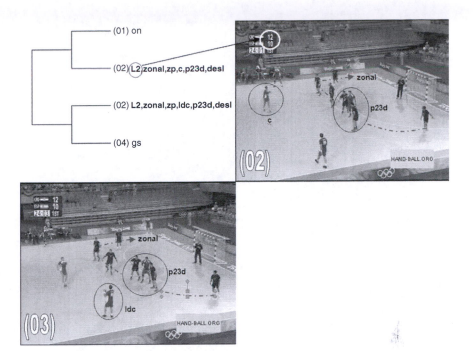

Figure 2.31 Fourth significant T-pattern: When the Spanish team was (02) losing by two goals (L2) it used defends using a 6:0 system (zonal) passive defensive strategy (zp), with the opposing team's pivot between the second and third defenders on the right-hand side (p23d); the defender marking the player with the ball makes a defensive displacement (desl) when the ball (03) is moved through the central zone (c) to the right-hand zone of the court that is closest to the centre (ldc).

and during almost the whole of the second half, their defensive game improved and they recovered the ball on more occasions without the opposing team having scored: 17 ball recoveries without conceding a goal.

As in the first match against Croatia, and despite the fact that scores were more often level in the play-off, the Spanish team continued to use the 6:0 defensive system (zonal) and a passive defensive strategy (zp) in both halves of this second match.

Descriptive analysis of the first half

At half-time the Spanish team was losing by two goals (14–12). With respect to the twenty defensive sequences detected during the first half of the match the plot in Figure 2.33 shows that there were four different types of sequence depending on the momentary score (drawing (T), losing by one goal (L1), losing by two goals (L2) or winning by one goal (W1).

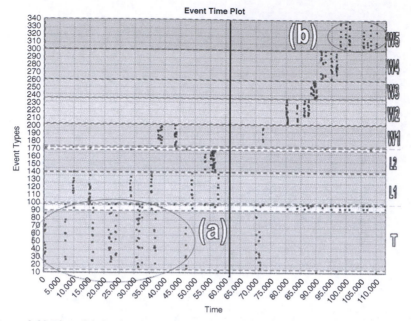

Figure 2.32 Plot of defensive dynamics during the third placement match between Spain and Croatia.

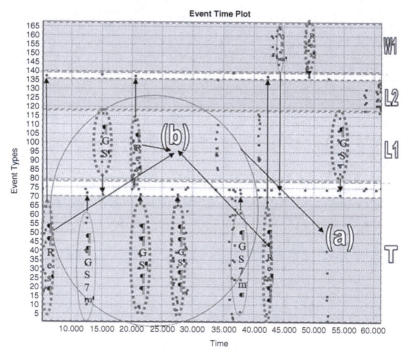

Figure 2.33 Plot of defensive dynamics during the first half of the third placement match between Spain and Croatia.

During the opening minutes of the match, and despite adopting a 6:0 defensive system (zonal), it can be seen that the Spanish team conceded the greatest number of goals (gs) and goals from 7 m (gs7m) each time the two teams were drawing (a). There were also four instances of ball recovery without having conceded a goal (b), with defensive rebound (res). None of the ball recovery events involved the direct intervention of the goalkeeper.

Descriptive analysis of the second half

Spain ended up winning the match (35–29) by successfully stifling the Croatian attack through its defensive system, and Figure 2.34 shows the effect and distribution of this during the second half.

The Spanish team was clearly ahead during the last eight defensive sequences detected, and were winning by five or more goals during the final ten minutes of the match (see the circle labelled with (a) in Figure 2.34). This means that when the Spanish team was ahead it tended to recover the ball more often after having conceded a goal (gs), possibly because the Croatian team adapted itself to Spain's defensive system and strategy of play. Among the different ways in which the ball

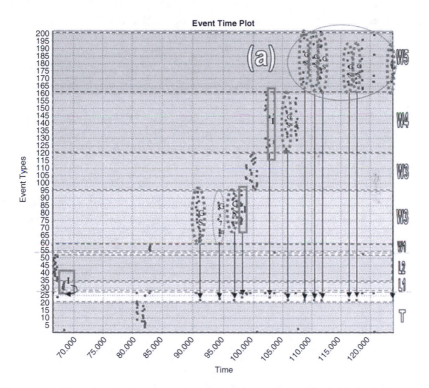

Figure 2.34 Plot of defensive dynamics during the second half of the third placement match between Spain and Croatia.

was recovered it is worth highlighting three interventions in which the defence intercepted the ball (see the squares labelled with (I) in the plot), as together with the opposing team's errors this could be the reason for Spain's advantage in the score.

Overall, it appears that the observed events are more stable when the Spanish team is ahead by five or more goals, while there was greater variability when the teams' score was tied. At all events, the Spanish team's defensive strategy was effective and the players managed to organize their defence quickly in order to protect their lead as the match went on.

Instrument 2: Retrospective interview and video recordings

The purpose of using this second instrument was to confirm the observations and interpretations made regarding the defensive tactics of the Spanish handball team in the two matches observed. To this end, the quantitative data obtained from the descriptive analysis and the sequential analysis of T-patterns were compared with the opinions of a player from the Spanish Olympic team. The specific method was based on the use of video recordings and a retrospective interview (Hauw and Durand 2007). The technique, known as a self-confrontation interview, consisted in showing the player a video recording of the match in order to refresh his memory and then invite him to answer specific questions arising from our quantitative analysis. His responses would therefore confirm or challenge our findings.

The player's responses were subjected to a content analysis (qualitative procedure) using the N-VIVO 8.0 software package, taking into account three criteria and their respective categories: (1) understanding of the observed play, which included correct understanding, correct description and complementary explanations; (2) justifications, which included an explanation of the opposing team's response, the reasons for his own team's defence, and a comparison of the two matches; and (3) differences in interpretation, which included doubts over the interpretation and deductions of no consequence. The initial results of the content analysis are shown in Table 2.13.

Table 2.13 Criteria and categories for the content analysis of the retrospective interview

Criteria	Category	Number of references in the transcript	Percentage of references in the transcript	Average percentage
	Correct description	30	92.46	
Understanding	Correct understanding	25	67.36	80.09
	Complementary explanations	17	80.45	
Justifications	Reasons for own defence	12	18.11	15.40
	Explanation of the opposing team's response	17	26.12	
	Comparison between matches	1	1.99	
Differences in	Doubts over the interpretation	5	5.65	5
interpretation	Deductions of no consequence	1	4.35	

Results of the retrospective interview

Correct understanding of defensive play

The player interviewed agreed with most of the conclusions reached by our descriptive analysis of the defensive strategy used by the Spanish team in the two matches played against Croatia. His complementary explanations extended the initial quantitative information and helped us understand better the reasons why certain defensive tactics were adopted during the two matches:

> The comments and interpretations seem appropriate to me. The changes in defensive tactics were made in an attempt to turn things around, as we were losing by three goals and it didn't look like we able to close the gap using the 6:0 system.

The player makes constant reference to the importance of good defensive systems, and this supports our conclusions in relation to how this aspect of play is the first step in breaking down an attack:

> You are most likely to get the ball back, whether directly or indirectly, through good defensive play. Even when it is the goalkeeper who blocks a throw on goal, the defence is involved by closing down certain angles so as to give the goalkeeper a better chance of making a save.

The player's tactical knowledge about the strategies used by the team lead him to offer important theoretical interpretations and explanations:

> Apart from variations in defence that are influenced by the score there are other changes in the defensive system that are due to lots of factors that the coach weighs up when deciding which system to use. For instance, adapting it to the skill level of the other team, matching your defence to the attacking system they use, how effective your team is in switching from attack to defence, or variations in how you approach a counterattack.

These explanations support and enrich our quantitative analysis.

Justifications and clarifications

The quantitative analysis of T-patterns provided a chronological snapshot of the defensive sequences that appeared in the two matches, and this information was also compared with the player's views regarding why each team reacted in the way it did. In his opinion the defensive strategy of the Spanish team in relation to an opponent such as Croatia was based on maintaining the 6:0 system:

> One of the objectives of the 6:0 defensive system is to close down the space available to the second line of attack, which is very effective in the Croatian team. The quality of their players, who are very quick and skilled in a

one-on-one, made us adopt a more closed defensive system, and the 6:0 gaves us more protection.

The player also explained that this system was adopted due to certain features of the Spanish team:

Moreover, the nature of Spanish goalkeepers is such that this kind of defence is the best approach in most matches, because they're specialists when it comes to blocking throws from the outside zones.

Knowledge about the Croatian players was another argument used in the retrospective interview to justify why the Spanish team adopted the 6:0 system:

As we have argued, the quality of their players made us opt for a more closed defensive system, one that wouldn't leave so much open space.

The interview also revealed factors related to the Olympic tournament itself, of which we had been unaware, but which were of importance when it came to comparing the effectiveness of defence in the two matches analysed:

In the first match, in the group stage, the fitness factor did not really come into it as both teams had just begun the Games. However, in the play-off, where we won the bronze medal, the Croatians were more tired than we were, and I think that's why we came out on top. The Croatians were a great team, but their whole game depended on seven players. Their substitutes weren't of the same level, and so these seven players had played throughout most of the tournament. Therefore, they were much more tired than we were because we had a bigger squad of quality players.

Differences in interpretation

There were some differences between our interpretation and that of the player interviewed, and this obliged us to modify some of our conclusions. For example, we did not understand why the Spanish team conceded more goals when they were losing by two goals, but the player regarded this as a superfluous observation:

It's anecdotal. They were ahead and we weren't managing to balance the game. We were behind and we weren't being effective in defence or attack. They took a two-goal lead and we managed to limit them to that, but we couldn't catch them as they were dictating the pace of the game. So eventually we changed our defence.

Doubts over how to interpret the observed behaviour can also arise due to random factors that may influence the game but which cannot be fully accounted for:

This type of match, when an Olympic medal is at stake, produces a kind of heightened motivation among players and coaches. What's more, you've got the world's best players facing one another, and in that sort of situation anything can happen.

Conclusions to be drawn from the retrospective interview

The analysis of the interview shed light upon why the Spanish team maintained a 6:0 zonal system with a passive defensive organization and closed lines. The player interviewed stated that the team's knowledge of its rival led the coach to adopt this system as the most suitable one to use against the Croatian team, which was very effective coming forward and included quick, attacking pivots who were skilled at losing their markers by taking up positions between the defensive lines; furthermore, the Croatians had powerful throwers, who were capable of making highly effective throws from 9 m. However, changes were made to this system when the coach felt it was a good moment to surprise the opponents and attempt to turn the score around before the Croatian team could adapt its own strategy. This is what occurred in the final minutes of the first match.

In relation to the second match, in which the bronze medal was at stake, the player interviewed stated that the Spanish team was able to recover the ball more often as a result of its good zonal 6:0 defensive system, and also that it sought to avoid player suspensions so as not to lose the advantage it had gained. The fact that the Spanish team was ahead forced the Croatians to adopt a more risky defensive strategy, pressuring its opponent in order to get the ball back as quickly as possible. In addition, being behind led the Croatian team to make rapid and less accurate attacking moves. In the opinion of the player interviewed, the Spanish defence was able to break down the Croatian attack due to being less tired in the final minutes of this decisive match.

Tactical and strategic knowledge about a rival team can have a decisive influence. Indeed, in the case of the two matches analysed here, an awareness of the opponent's range of strategies and how they might be alternated proved to be of vital importance in relation to the Spanish team's victory, as well as in terms of understanding how it was achieved.

Discussion

This case study has examined the defensive strategy used by the Spanish handball team in the 2008 Beijing Olympics, and has discussed how this might have been influenced by the score at a given point in the match, as well as by the stage of the tournament. The quantitative results obtained from a descriptive analysis of observational data and the sequential analysis of T-patterns have been compared with qualitative information derived from a retrospective interview with one of the players from the Spanish team. This mixed methods approach to understanding behaviour in sporting contexts generates a richer set of information, which may then help coaches in their future decision making (Macquet 2009).

Although, in the context of sports psychology, interviews in general have proved to be a useful tool in relation to improving performance (Rhea *et al.* 1997; Tenenbaum *et al.* 2002), the specific value of the retrospective interview is that it confronts players or athletes with their own behaviour. As such, it is one of the best ways of capturing players' understanding and thought processes regarding their experience of the strategic events that occurred during a match. Indeed, by being combined with a viewing of the match video the retrospective interview can be of enormous help in describing how players' behaviour and actions evolved in the context of those dynamic systems that we commonly refer to as play.

In summary, the explanatory sequential design (see Chapter 1) used here has enabled us to enrich the interpretation of the quantitative results by complementing them with the meaning ascribed to the observational data by one of the players involved.

Acknowledgements

We gratefully acknowledge the support of the Spanish government project *Avances tecnológicos y metodológicos en la automatización de estudios observacionales en deporte* (Dirección General de Investigación, Ministerio de Ciencia e Innovación) [Grant number PSI2008-01179]. We also gratefully acknowledge the support of the Generalitat de Catalunya government project GRUP DE RECERCA E INNOVACIÓ EN DISSENYS (GRID). Tecnología i aplicació multimedia i digital als dissenys observacionals, Departament d'Innovació, Universitats i Empresa, Generalitat de Catalunya [Grant number 2009 SGR 829].

Note

1   A defensive system may refer to the number of players occupying different positions in each line of defence, indicating the initial distribution of the players on the court.

References

Al-Abood, S.A., Bennett, S.J., Moreno, F., Ashford, D., and Davids, K. (2002). Effect of verbal instructions and image size on visual search strategies in basketball free throw shooting. *Journal of Sports Sciences, 20* (3), 271–278.

Anguera, M.T. (2005). Microanalysis of T-patterns: Analysis of symmetry/asymmetry in social interaction. In L. Anolli, S. Duncan, M. Magnusson and G. Riva (eds), *The hidden structure of social interaction: From Genomics to Culture Patterns* (pp. 51–70). Amsterdam: IOS Press.

Anguera, M.T., Blanco-Villaseñor, A., and Losada, J.L. (2001). Diseños Observacionales, cuestión clave en el proceso de la metodología observacional. *Metodología de las Ciencias del Comportamiento, 3* (2), 135–161.

Anguera, M.T., and Jonsson, G.K. (2003). Detection of real-time patterns in sport: Interactions in football. *International Journal of Computer Science in Sport (e-Journal), 2* (2), 118–121.

Araújo, D. (2006). *Tomada de decisão no desporto.* Cruz Quebrada: Edições FMH.

Araújo, D., Davids, K., and Hristovski, R. (2006). The ecological dynamics of decision-making in sport. *Psychology of Sport and Exercice, 7*, 653–676.

Blanco-Villaseñor, A., and Anguera, M.T. (2000). Evaluación de la calidad en el registro del comportamiento: Aplicación a deportes de equipo. In E. Oñate, F. García-Sicilia, and L. Ramallo (eds), *Métodos Numéricos en Ciencias Sociales* (pp. 30–48). Barcelona: Centro Internacional de Métodos Numéricos en Ingeniería.

Bloomfield, J., Jonsson, G.K., Polman, R., Houlahan, K., and O'Donoghue, P. (2005). Temporal patterns analysis and its applicability in soccer. In Anolli, L., Duncan, S.,

Magnusson, M., and Riva, G. (eds), *The hidden structure of social interaction: From genomics to culture patterns* (pp. 237–251). Amsterdam: IOS Press.

Borrie, A., Jonsson, G.K. Anguera, T., and Magnusson, M.S. (2001). Application of t-pattern detection and analysis in sports research. *Metodología de las Ciencias del Comportamiento, 3* (2), 215–226.

Borrie, A., Jonsson, G.K., and Magnusson, M.S. (2002). Temporal pattern analysis and its applicability in sport: An explanation and preliminary data. *Journal of Sport Science. 20* (10), 845–852.

Brookes, J.D., and Knowles, J.E. (1974). A movement analysis of player behaviour in soccer match performance. Paper presented at the British Society of Sports Psychology Conference, Salford, 1974.

Camerino, O., Chaverri, J., Anguera, M.T., and Jonsson, G.K. (2012). Dynamics of the game in soccer: Detection of T-patterns. *European Journal of Sport Science, 12* (3), 216–224.

Castellano, J., Perea, A., Alday, L., and Hernández-Mendo, A. (2008a). The Measuring and Observation Tool in sports. *Behavior Research Methods, 40* (3), 898–905

Castellano, J., Perea, A., and Hernández-Mendo, A. (2008b). Análisis de la evolución del fútbol a lo largo de los mundiales. *Psicothema, 20* (4), 928–932.

Cohen, J. (1960). A coefficient of agreement for nominal scales. *Educational and Psychological Measurement, 20* (1), 37–46.

Creswell, J.W. (2003). *Research design: Qualitative, quantitative and mixed methods approaches*. Thousand Oaks, CA: Sage.

Davids, K., Button, C., and Bennet, S. (2008). *Dynamics of skill acquisition*. Champaign, IL: Human Kinetics.

Dumangane, M., Rosati, N., and Volossovitch, A. (2009). Departure from independence and stationarity in a handball match. *Journal of Applied Statistics, 36* (7), 723–741.

Fernández, J., Camerino, O., Anguera, M.T., and Jonsson, G.K. (2009). Identifying and analyzing the construction and effectiveness of offensive plays in basketball by using systematic observation. *Behavior Research Methods, 41* (3), 719–730.

Franks, I.M., and Miller, G. (1986). Eyewitness testimony in sport. *Journal of Sport Behaviour, 9,* 39–45.

Gabin, B., Camerino, O., Castañer, M. and Anguera, M. Teresa (in press, 2012a) Lince: new software to integrate registers and analysis on behavior observation. *Procedia Computer Science Technology.*

Gabín, B., Camerino, O., Anguera, Mª.T. & Castañer, M. (in press, 2012b). Lince: multiplatform sport analysis software. *Procedia – Social and Behavioral Sciences.*

Gomes, F., and Volossovitch, A. (2008). The defensive performance in handball analysis of the three first placed teams in men's European Championship 2006. *Proceedings of the 13th Annual Congress of the European College of Sport Science – Sport by the Sea,* Estoril - Portugal, pp. 450–451.

Hamilton, G.R., and Reinschmidt, C. (1997). Optimal trajectory for the basketball free throw. *Journal of Sports Sciences, 15* (5), 491–504.

Handford, C., Davids, K., Bennett, S., and Button, C. (1997). Skill acquisition in sport: Some applications of an evolving practice ecology. *Journal of Sports Sciences, 15,* 621–640.

Hauw, D., and Durand, M. (2007). Situated analysis of elite trampolinists' problems in competition, *Journal of Sports Sciences, 25* (2), 173–183.

Hodges, N., and Franks, I. (2002). Modelling coaching practice: The role of instruction and demonstration. *Journal of Sports Sciences, 20,* 1–19.

Hodges, N., Williams, A. Hayes, S. and Breslin, G. (2007). What is modelled during observational learning? *Journal of Sports Sciences, 25*, 531–545.

Horn, R., Williams, A., and Scott, M. (2002). Learning from demonstration: The role of visual search from video and pointlight displays. *Journal of Sports Sciences, 20,* 253–269.

Hughes, M., and Franks, M. (2008). *The essencial of performance analysis an introduction.* New York: Routledge.

Jansen, R.G., Wiertz, L.F., Meyer, E.S., and Noldus, L.P.J.J. (2003). Reliability analysis of observational data: Problems, solutions, and software implementation. *Behavior Research Methods, Instruments, and Computers, 35* (3), 391–399.

Jonsson, G.K., Anguera, M.T., Blanco-Villaseñor, A., Losada, J.L., Hernández-Mendo, A., Ardá, T., Camerino, O., and Castellano, J. (2006). Hidden patterns of play interaction in soccer using SOF-CODER. *Behavior Research Methods, Instruments and Computers, 38* (3), 372–381.

Jonsson, M., Anguera, M.T., Sánchez. P., Olivera, C., Santos, J., Campanico, J., Castañer, M., Torrents,C., Dinušová, M., Chaverri, J., Camerino O., and Magnusson, M. (2009). Application of T-pattern detection and analysis in sport research. *Sports Sciences Journal 3*, 62–71.

Kerr, J.K., Fujiyama, H., Sugano, A., Okamura, T., Chang, M., and Onouha, F. (2006). Psychological responses to exercising in laboratory and natural environments. *Psychology of Sport and Exercise, 7* (4), 345–359.

Lebed, F. (2006). System approach to games and competitive playing. *European Journal of Sports Sciences, 6* (1), 33–42.

Lonsdale, C., and Tam, J.T.M. (2007). On the temporal and behavioural consistency of pre-performance routines: An intra-individual analysis of elite basketball players' free throw shooting accuracy. *Journal of Sports Sciences, 26* (3), 259–266.

Lopes, A., Camerino, O., Anguera, M. T., and Jonsson, G.K. (2011). Ball recovery in the handball tournament of the 2008 Beijing Olympic Games: Sequential analysis of positional play as used by the Spanish team's defence. *ACM Digital Library. Measuring Behavior* '10. Proceedings of the 7th International Conference on Methods and Techniques in Behavioral Research Proceedings.

Macquet, A. C. (2009). Recognition within the decision-making process: A case study of expert volleyball players, *Journal of Applied Sport Psychology, 21* (1) 64–79.

Magnusson, M.S. (1996). Hidden real-time patterns in intra- and inter-individual behavior: Description and detection. *European Journal of Psychological Assessment, 12* (2), 112–123.

Magnusson, M.S. (2000). Discovering hidden time patterns in behavior: T-patterns and their detection. *Behavior Research Methods, Instruments, and Computers, 32* (1), 93–110.

Magnusson, M.S. (2005). Understanding social interaction: Discovering hidden structure with model and algorithms. In L. Anolli, S. Duncan, M. Magnusson and G. Riva (eds), *The hidden structure of social interaction: From genomics to culture patterns* (pp. 51–70). Amsterdam: IOS Press.

Magnusson, M.S. (2006). Structure and communication in interaction. In G. Riva, M.T. Anguera, B.K. Wiederhold, and F. Mantovani (eds), *From communication to presence: Cognition, emotions and culture towards the ultimate communicative experience.* Amsterdam: IOS Press.

McCall, G.E., Byrnes, W.C., Fleck, S.J., Dickinson, A., and Kraemer, W.J. (1999). Acute and chronic hormonal responses to resistance training designed to promote muscle hypertrophy. *Canadian Journal of Applied Physiology, 24* (1), 1999, 96–107.

McGarry, T., Anderson, D.I., Wallace, S.A., Hughes, M.D., and Franks, I.M. (2002). Sport competition as a dynamical self-organizing system. *Journal of Sports Sciences, 20* (10), 771–781.

Miller, S., and Bartlett, R.M. (1993). The effects of increased shooting distance in the basketball jump shot. *Journal of Sports Sciences, 11* (4), 285–293.

Miller, S., and Bartlett, R.M. (1996). The relationship between basketball shooting kinematics, distance and playing position. *Journal of Sports Sciences, 14* (3), 243–253.

Nevill, A.M., Atkinson, G., Hughes, M.D., and Cooper, S. (2002). Statistical methods for analysing discrete and categorical data recorded in performance analysis. *Journal of Sports Sciences, 20* (10), 829.

Nevill, A.M., Atkinson, G., and Hughes, M. (2008). Twenty-five years of sport performance research in the *Journal of Sports Sciences*. *Journal of Sports Sciences, 26* (4), 413.

Okubo, H., and Hubbard, M. (2006). Dynamics of the basketball shot with application to the free throw. *Journal of Sports Sciences, 24* (12), 1303–1314.

Ortega, E., Cárdenas, D., Sainz de Baranda, P., and Palao, J.M. (2006). Analysis of the final actions used in basketball during formative years according to player's position. *Journal of Human Movement Studies, 50* (6), 421–437.

Pfeiffer, M., and Perl, J. (2006). Analysis of tactical structures in team handball by means of artificial neural networks. *International Journal of Computer Science in Sport, 5* (1), 4–14.

Reilly, T. (1994). Physiological aspects of soccer. *Biology of Sport, 11* (1), 1994, 3–20.

Reilly, T., and Thomas, V. (1976). A motion analysis of work-rate in different positional roles in professional football match-play. *Journal of Human Movement Studies, 2*, 87–89.

Rhea, D.J., Mathes, S.A., and Hardin, K. (1997). Video recall for analysis of performance by collegiate female tennis players. *Perceptual and Motor Skills, 85*, 1354.

Rienzi, E., Drust, B., Reilly, T., Carter, J.E.L., and Martin, A. (1998). Investigation of anthropometric and work-rate profiles of elite South American international soccer players. *Journal of Sports Medicine and Physical Fitness, 40*, 162–169.

Romanowich, P., Bourret, J., and Vollmer, T.R. (2007). Further analysis of the matching law to describe two- and three-point shot allocation by professional basketball players. *Journal of Applied Behavior Analysis, 40* (2), 311–315.

Sampaio, J., Janeira, M., Ibáñez, S., and Lorenzo, A. (2006). Discriminant analysis of game-related statistics between basketball guards, forwards and centres in three professional leagues. *European Journal of Sport Science, 6* (3), 173–178.

Schmidt, R., O'Brien, B., and Sysko, R. (1999). Self-organization of between-person cooperative tasks and possible applications to sport. *International Journal of Sport Psychology, 30*(4), 558–579.

Sheskin, D.J. (2004). *Handbook of parametric and nonparametric statistical procedures* (3rd edition, pp. 563–566). Boca Raton, FL: Chapman and Hall/CRC.

Strudwick, T., and Reilly, T. (2001). Work-rate profiles of elite Premier League football players. *Insight, 2* (2), 28–29.

Tenenbaum, G., Lloyd, M., Pretty, G., and Hanin, Y.L. (2002). Congluence of actual and retrospective reports of precompeticion emotion in equestrian. *Journal of Sport and Exercise Psychology, 24*, 217–288.

Williams, A.M., and Ericsson, K.A. (2005). Perceptual-cognitive expertise in sport: Some considerations when applying the expert performance approach. *Human Movement Science, 24* (3), 283–307.

3 Optimizing techniques and dynamics in individual sports

- **Case Study 3.1: The influence of environmental factors in the context of elite fencing**
  Xavier Iglesias and M. Teresa Anguera

- **Case Study 3.2: Errors in the judo throw *Ippon Seoi Nage* and their consequences for the learning process**
  Iván Prieto, Alfonso Gutiérrez and Oleguer Camerino

- **Case Study 3.3: Analysis of specific technical behaviour in freestyle swimming.**
  Jorge Campaniço

This third chapter presents three case studies that consider ways of optimizing performance in individual sports, specifically, fencing, judo and swimming. Each case study uses observational methodology (Anguera 2003; Anguera and Blanco-Villaseñor 2003) to develop specific observation and recording instruments which, in combination with other tools, are applied in order to analyse certain parameters: temporal parameters in fencing, biomechanical parameters in judo and physiological parameters in swimming.

Individual sports are not subject to the same contextual factors as are team sports, and this affects the technical aspects which coaches need to focus on, doing so on an individualized basis that reflects the particular characteristics of each athlete. In this regard, the first case study shows how factors such as the available space, the time remaining and the score at any given point may influence the actions of competitors. The second case study, which focuses on judo, highlights the need for coaches to be aware of the basic errors or sequences of errors that combatants may commit when performing a throw, as this can help them plan their teaching strategies. Finally, the third case study shows how an analysis of the aerobic and technical capacity of swimmers can be used to improve their performance in freestyle swimming.

CASE STUDY 3.1: THE INFLUENCE OF ENVIRONMENTAL FACTORS IN THE CONTEXT OF ELITE FENCING

Introduction

In combat sports such as fencing it is possible to identify the influence of different factors on the performance of competitors. Although coaches usually focus on technical preparation and on developing an optimal tactical approach; factors such as the available space, the time remaining and the score at any given point may also determine the behaviour of competitors and their interaction with one another. These three elements constitute what can be termed the 'environmental pressure', i.e. the influence of space, time and score on the possibility of success, which in fencing would be scoring a touché or touch (Gasset and Iglesias 2010).

Combat sports are characterized by situations of constant interaction in which the two rivals move back and forth between attacking and defensive moves, and it is these behaviours that are influenced not only by the rules of combat but also by the above-mentioned environmental factors: space, time and score. In the specific context of fencing, the competitive space, i.e. the size of the strip or *piste*, is defined by the rules, and stepping behind the back edge of the *piste* incurs a penalty point. Similarly, the bout time is finite and both competitors will be seeking victory before the time is up. Therefore, the effect of time may show an inverse and exponential relationship, with the competitors' behaviour changing as time begins to run out. Finally, the score at any given moment may also influence behaviour. In fencing the winner in a direct elimination is the first to post fifteen touches, or five touches in the pool stages, and this will determine the extent to which the competitors are prepared to take risks, since only a finite number of touches can be received while attempting to touch the opponent. For example, if the score is 2–1 a competitor will be prepared to risk much more than if the score is 13–14, where one more touch by the opponent would mean losing the contest.

All these factors may affect the way in which two rivals interact in each of the actions that make up a bout. Indeed, the various technical and tactical moves will be associated with different behaviours, such as seeking to regain the initiative or pressuring the opponent by adopting a more attacking attitude. These behavioural patterns may be modified by a fencer during a bout, and may also vary from one contest to another depending on the rival, on the type of interactions between two opponents, and on the environmental pressure at any given moment.

The use of observational methodology in combat sports

In fencing, elite coaches, or fencing masters, have for many years based their teaching on observation and intuitive analysis, but without the help of suitable observation instruments. However, in recent years observational methodology (Hernández *et al.* 2000) has become one of the main tools for analysing sport, not least because of the complexity that derives from its multidimensional viewpoint (Lago and Anguera 2003). Observational studies have been conducted in relation to a number of combat sports such as judo (Gutiérrez *et al.* 2009; Gutiérrez *et al.* 2011; Heinisch 1997) and taekwondo (Fernández Fonseca 2004), and in the context of fencing, research has examined the temporal distribution of different actions during bouts (Iglesias 1997; Lavoie *et al.* 1985; Marini 1984) and vari-ability in the techniques used in competition (Iglesias *et al.* 2008). This work has demonstrated how observational methodology, especially when applied in combi-nation with other procedures in the context of a mixed methods design, can help to produce more systematic analyses and more precise and objective studies, thereby increasing the reliability of the research process.

Aims and the mixed methods approach: triangulation design

This case study had two main aims: (1) to analyse the influence of environmental pressure on the frequency and effectiveness of the actions performed in competi-tive fencing; and (2) to detect sequential patterns among behaviours that serve as catalysts for the actions used in combat.

We use here the most common design, the *triangulation design*, in which the investigator applies quantitative and qualitative methods (QUAN+QUAL) simul-taneously, giving them equal weight and importance.

These aims were met by applying systematic observational methodology (Anguera *et al.* 2001) to a series of video recordings of professional fencing bouts. This observational material was then subjected to a mixed analysis based on descriptive statistics and lag sequential analysis of the contingency of observed behaviours.

Participants

Participants were eighteen elite male fencers in the épée category. The systematic observation involved video recordings of nine bouts from either the semi-finals or finals of fencing world cups or the Olympic Games (during the period 2005 to 2008), with a total of 353 combat actions being analysed.

Observation instrument

An open-ended observation instrument was developed ad hoc so that it could be specifically adapted to the circumstances of fencing. The instrument was based on a series of criteria (see Table 3.1) comprising different categories that represented exhaustive and mutually exclusive behaviours and situations which are found in fencing. The validity of the instrument was determined according to its conceptual consistency and robustness within the corresponding theoretical framework, as well as through the consensus opinion of fencing experts.

The criteria used refer to the interaction between two fencers (PRESS, INI-TIAT, PREP), to the environmental pressure resulting from the factors space, time and score (PISTE, TIME, PERIOD, SCORE), and to the number and effectiveness of the actions analysed (EFFECT, TOUCH).

Table 3.1 Criteria and categories used in the ad hoc instrument for the observation of fencing

Criterion	Category	Description
PRESS		**Clear pressure at the start of the action**
	LPRE	*Clear pressure from the fencer on the LEFT*
	RPRE	*Clear pressure from the fencer on the RIGHT*
	NPRE	*No pressure from the fencers*
INITIAT		**Taking initiative in the action**
	INIL	*Initiative in the action from the fencer on the LEFT*
	INIR	*Initiative in the action from the fencer on the RIGHT*
	INI2	*Initiative from BOTH fencers*
PREP		**Preparation by the fencer**
	RPREP	*Preparation by the fencer on the RIGHT*
	LPREP	*Preparation by the fencer on the LEFT*
PISTE		**Piste zone in which the action takes place**
	2LEF	*Left end zone (2 m)*
	3LEF	*Left intermediate zone (3 m)*
	CENT	*Central zone (4 m)*
	3RIG	*Right intermediate zone (3 m)*
	2RIG	*Right end zone (2 m)*
TIME		**Time remaining to end of bout**
	TEN	*Ten seconds remaining (10–0 s)*
	TWENT	*Twenty seconds remaining (20–10 s)*
	1MIN	*Sixty seconds remaining (60–20 s)*
	2MIN	*2 minutes remaining (2–1 min)*
	3MIN	*3 minutes remaining (3–2 min)*
	2PER	*Two periods remaining (6–3 min)*
	3PER	*Three periods remaining (9–6 min)*
PERIOD		**Period of the bout**
	PER1	*Period 1*
	PER2	*Period 2*
	PER3	*Period 3*
	MIN	*Additional minute*
SCORE		**Difference in score (numerical)**
EFFECT		Effectiveness of the action
	YES	*Action effective. Achieves touch*
	NO	*Action not effective. Fails to achieve touch*
TOUCH		
	TLEF	*Touch achieved by the fencer on the LEFT*
	TRIG	*Touch achieved by the fencer on the RIGHT*
	TT	*DOUBLE touch*
	NT	*No valid TOUCH*

Recording instrument

Match Vision Studio 3.0 software (Castellano *et al.* 2008) was used to code the different criteria and categories defined in the observation instrument and to register the data derived from observation of the video recordings of the competitive fencing bouts (see Figure 3.1).

Having thus registered the observational data they were then exported to an Excel file (Microsoft® Office Excel, v. 2007) in which each row corresponded to an action, and where the different co-occurrences of actions could be indicated. This file was then used for data processing and to prepare data matrices for subsequent analysis.

Procedure

Data were registered by analysing digital files of televised fencing bouts from world cups and the Olympic Games (semi-finals and finals, 2005–2008). The recorded images capture the spatial evolution of the bout, and always show both fencers. The observational unit considered was any combat action in which one or both competitors sought to score a point, regardless of whether this action was simple or complex. Data quality was assessed according to general criteria set out in previous observational studies (Lago and Anguera 2003; Prudente *et al.* 2004). Inter- and intra-observer reliability was determined in relation to two bouts by calculating Cohen's kappa coefficient for the observational data produced by two experts who had been previously trained in how to use the observation instrument. This analysis was performed using the software package SDIS-GSEQ for Windows 4.1.5 (Bakeman and Quera 2001), and yielded kappa values above 0.90 in all cases.

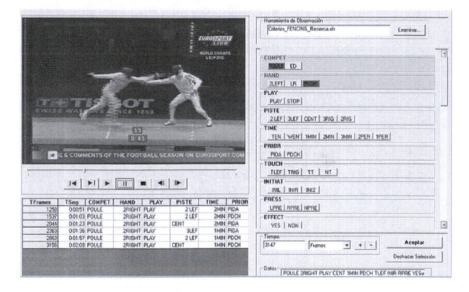

Figure 3.1 An example screen from the Match Vision Studio 3.0 software when applied to fencing (Castellano *et al.* 2008a).

The resulting data were then subjected to two different analyses through two complementary procedures:

1. A descriptive statistical analysis of the relationship between the effectiveness of the observed actions and the three environmental criteria: space, time and score. SPSS v. 15.0 was used to determine bivariate relationships between effectiveness (scoring a point) and the influence of each of these three criteria.
2. A sequential analysis of the interaction between the behaviour of the two opponents. The software package SDIS-GSEQ for Windows 4.1.5 (Bakeman and Quera 2001) was used to conduct a prospective and retrospective sequential analysis, which involved calculating the contingency relationship between behaviours at different lags.

Results for procedure 1: descriptive statistics

The relationship between the three criteria (space, time and score) and the frequency and effectiveness of actions was studied by means of contingency tables, applying the chi-square test in a bivariate analysis (SPSS v. 15.0). Table 3.2 shows the distribution of the 353 fencing actions observed across the different bout stages, as well as the effectiveness of each one.

Figure 3.2 plots the number and effectiveness of actions performed in the observed bouts. There was a significant reduction in the number of actions performed as the bouts progressed across the three periods ($p < 0.001$), but this was not matched by a significant loss of effectiveness (see Figure 3.2).

Figure 3.3 presents the data obtained when analysing the number and effectiveness of actions performed in each 10 s of the bout (actions/10 s). It can be seen that the number of actions increases exponentially towards the end of the bout as time is running out ($p < 0.001$). However, despite the concomitant increase in effectiveness as the bout comes to an end the trend for differences in effectiveness across these 10 s periods was not significant (see Figure 3.3).

Figure 3.4 plots the number of actions and their effectiveness according to the difference in score. There was a significant reduction in the number of actions as the difference in score increased ($p = 0.006$), while there a inverse trend between the effectiveness of actions and the difference in score (see Figure 3.4).

Table 3.2 Number of actions and their effectiveness for each period of the fencing bouts

Bouts (n=9)	Actions		Effective		Not effective		Effectiveness
1st Period	160	(45.3%)	81	(46.6%)	79	(44.1%)	51%
2nd Period	112	(31.7%)	60	(34.5%)	52	(29.1%)	54%
3rd Period	74	(21.0%)	31	(17.8%)	43	(24.0%)	42%
Additional minute	7	(2.0%)	2	(1.1%)	5	(2.8%)	29%
Total	353	(100%)	174	(100%)	179	(100%)	49%

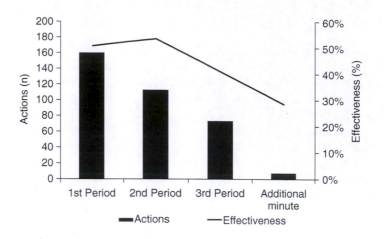

Figure 3.2 Distribution of the actions (n = 353) observed in the fencing bouts (men's épée) for each of the three-minute periods.

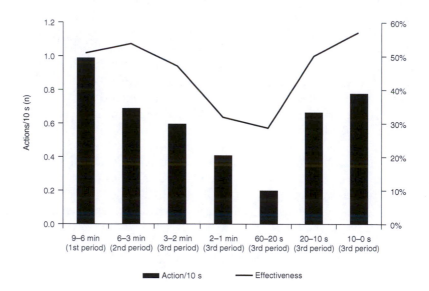

Figure 3.3 Mean number and effectiveness of actions in each 10 s period of the fencing bouts according to the amount of time remaining.

Finally, Figure 3.5 shows the frequency and effectiveness of actions according to the different *piste* zones in which they take place (p < 0.001). It can be seen that the fencers' behaviour was relatively symmetrical in this regard, which is consistent with the type of bout studied (épée).

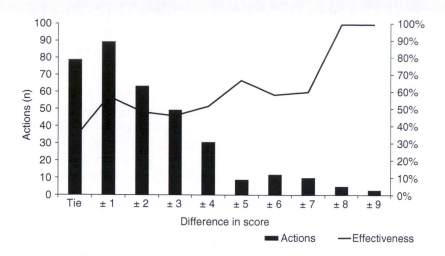

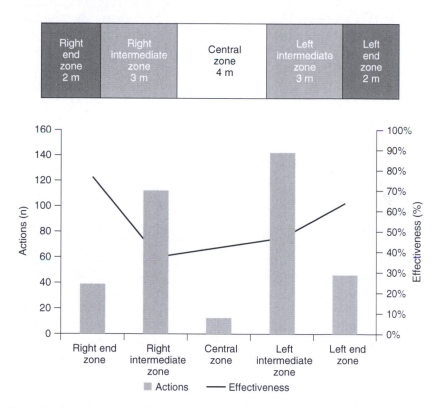

Figure 3.4 Number and effectiveness of actions in the fencing bouts according to the difference in score.

Figure 3.5 Frequency and effectiveness (%) of actions (n = 353) in the fencing bouts according to the *piste* zone in which they take place.

Results for procedure 2: lag sequential analysis

Patterns among behaviours that served as catalysts for combative actions were detected by means of lag sequential analysis (Bakeman 1978). The purpose of this analysis was to observe, across the duration of the bouts, the influence of criterion behaviours (such as taking the initiative or pressuring the opponent) on conditioned behaviours (i.e. the techniques used or the actions which proved to be effective). Figure 3.6 shows both the prospective (from 0 to +15) and retrospective (from 0 to −15) lag sequential patterns, in which one can observe the associative relationships between different behaviours that occur sequentially. The significant adjusted residuals between lags −12 and +12 disappear symmetrically and progressively (Anguera 2005), and disappear completely after lag ±13. Figure 3.6 shows the excitatory and inhibitory behaviours that are significant at the 0.05 level (values > 1.96).

The analysis of lag 0, which would indicate co-occurrence among fencing actions, is interesting due to the possibility of revealing significant relationships between criterion behaviours and conditioned behaviours. By way of an example, Figure 3.7 shows the relationships that are significant at the 0.05 level (values > 1.96) for both excitatory and inhibitory behaviours when studying each fencing bout individually. It can be seen that when one of the fencers took the initiative, reflected in the variables INIR and INIL, this led to the opponent scoring a touch (TRIG) or double touch (TT), respectively. This suggests, perhaps counterintuitively, that taking the initiative can be a risky strategy.

Discussion

The descriptive statistics by means of bivaried analysis of double frequencies show that environmental pressure has an effect on the frequency and effectiveness

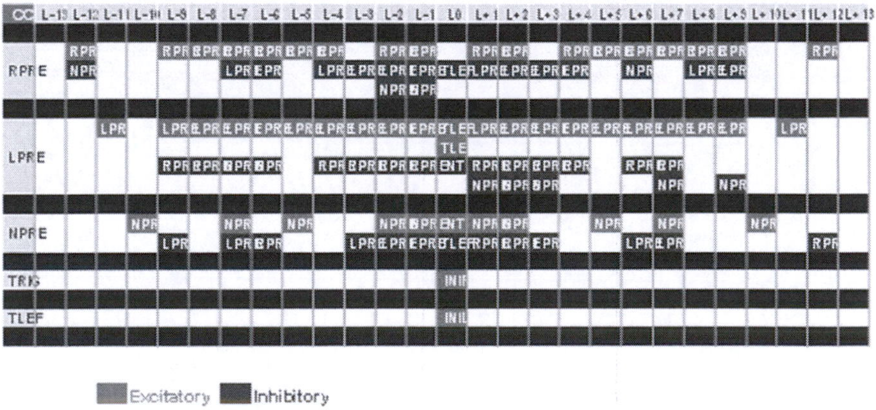

Figure 3.6 Prospective (0 to +15) and retrospective (0 to −15) lag sequential patterns for the actions observed in fencing. The figure shows the excitatory and inhibitory behaviours that are significant at the 0.05 level (values > 1.96).

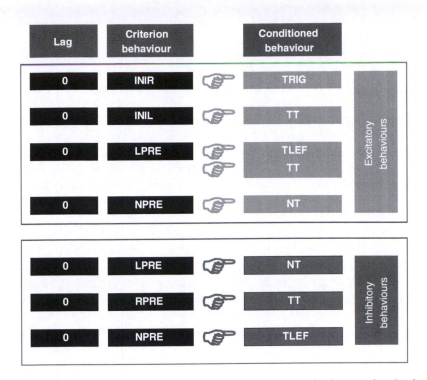

Figure 3.7 Relationships between criterion and conditioned behaviours at lag 0 when studying each fencing bout individually. The figure shows the excitatory and inhibitory behaviours that are significant at the 0.05 level (values > 1.96).

of fencing actions. As regards the time factor, the results presented in Figures 3.2 and 3.3 illustrate the value of considering time from an inverse and exponential perspective, i.e. the time remaining in the bout, studied here in 10 s intervals, rather than simply focusing on the arithmetic distribution of homogeneous intervals, i.e. the three regulation periods. Specifically, the results depicted in Figure 3.3 show that as the end of the bout approaches there is an exponential rise in the number of actions (due to the time factor) and a concomitant increase in their effectiveness.

With respect to the use of space, the results show that the number and effectiveness of actions are clearly related to *piste* zones. Figure 3.5 shows that the épée bouts studied here contained very few actions in the central zone, and also that the effectiveness of actions was greater in the right and left end zones (final 2 m of the strip). In the latter zones the fencers are more pressured in terms of space and have limited options in terms of retreating as a defensive strategy.

The relationship between the number of actions and the difference in score followed a logical trend, with more actions being performed when the score was closer. The corresponding analysis of effectiveness (Figure 3.4) shows that effectiveness increases as the difference in score widens, which may be due to a difference in the fencers' ability, or to a progressive reduction in competitive tension as those who are losing realize they have little chance of success.

Application of the scientific method to performance and behaviour in sport offers coaches a robust opportunity to optimize their training procedures on the basis of significant research findings. In this regard the present results could be used by fencing masters to design specific strategies that take account of the three environmental factors studied (space, time and score). For instance, they could develop training drills in which fencers are subject to temporal and/or spatial pressure, but where the score is close. An example would be a combat situation in which two fencers are level on points, are located in the end zone of the *piste*, and where there are only 10 or 20 seconds remaining. Yet whatever combination of these three factors is used, the aim would always be to increase the effectiveness of actions by giving fencers the opportunity to prepare for such situations in training.

The second analytic method used in this case study sought to detect behavioural patterns by means of lag sequential analysis. The analysis of behaviours that implied putting pressure on the opponent or taking the initiative showed, unsurprisingly, that the pressure of one fencer is incompatible with pressure from the opponent (RPRE vs. LPRE). This means that across a bout the two competitors will vary their strategies in terms of applying more pressure or letting the opponent take the initiative. The lag data also confirm that behaviours which imply pressuring the opponent are incompatible with the absence of pressure (NPRE). The fact that these behaviours persist until lag ± 12, coupled with their progressive disappearance, suggests a degree of homogeneity in the strategies used by competitors: those fencers who pressure their opponent maintain this attitude throughout most of the bout (Figure 3.6). In line with other studies of team sports (Lago and Anguera 2003), the sequential analysis revealed patterns in the behavioural interactions between competitors. Excitatory criterion behaviours related to putting pressure on the opponent (RPRE, LPRE, NPRE) showed absolute symmetry between the prospective and retrospective adjusted residuals, while the corresponding inhibitory criterion behaviours showed considerable symmetry between their adjusted residuals (prospective and retrospective).

Finally, the analysis of lag 0 for the actions observed in each bout could be enormously useful for coaches as regards their strategic analysis of a fencer's performance. The example in Figure 3.7 shows how such an analysis can identify whether behaviours such as taking the initiative or pressuring the opponent will be beneficial or prejudicial for a fencer. This kind of analysis could be used to evaluate a fencer's behaviour in relation to an opponent in a specific bout or, alternatively, it could be applied longitudinally to monitor the fencer's performance and assess whether his/her behaviour has the same effect with different opponents.

Conclusions

The combination of mixed methods and observational research can make a highly interesting contribution to the field of sports coaching, since the kind of results produced can help coaches to optimize their training procedures and decision making in relation to tactical and strategic aspects.

As regards this study of fencing the following specific conclusions can be drawn:

- Environmental pressure is determined by the influence of the space available, the time remaining and the extent to which a competitor is prepared to take risks.
- The observed trend for the time factor shows that it influences the behaviours which determine the performance of actions.
- The amount of space available (*piste*) affects the frequency of actions and their effectiveness.
- The score at any given point in the bout influences the effectiveness of the actions performed.
- The effect of time on specific behaviours should be analysed from an inverse and exponential perspective, i.e. in relation to the time remaining in the bout and how this affects the number and effectiveness of actions.
- Sequential analysis can reveal behavioural patterns in the interactions between competitors.

CASE STUDY 3.2: ERRORS IN THE JUDO THROW *IPPON SEOI NAGE* AND THEIR CONSEQUENCES FOR THE LEARNING PROCESS

Introduction

Although knowledge of results has been a key element in the field of motor learning, greater importance has increasingly been paid to knowledge of performance (Salmoni *et al.* 1984; Swinnen 1996). The main reason for this is that knowledge of results becomes less useful as tasks become more complex, since participants do not know where their performance went wrong or how to improve it (Newell and Walter 1981). Hence, knowledge of results is sufficient when the task is simple, but it is unable to rectify errors in complex tasks (Gutiérrez *et al.* 2011b; Wulf and Shea 2002), such as performance of the judo technique studied here.

In novices the learning process benefits enormously if their attention is drawn to the most relevant aspects of performance (Kernodle and Carlton 1992). Indeed, this knowledge of performance provides information about how best to perform the next action. Various studies have focused on knowledge of performance in relation to sports technique (Brison and Alain 1996; Schmidt 1988; Weeks and Kordus 1998) and, in particular, on the technical errors that are often committed in this context (Badets *et al.* 2006; Bruechert *et al.* 2003). This approach has proved to be a valuable and novel tool, since correcting a technical move or gesture from the perspective of error is, when information is available about the nature of those errors, more useful than simply indicating the result of the performance (Schmidt and Lee 2005).

The present study reports a detailed examination of knowledge of perform-ance in the context of judo technique. Specifically, it uses a method of system-atic observation to identify patterns of motor behaviour (in the form of errors and sequences) that remain hidden to the naked eye, the aim being to develop an optimal tool that could be used by various professionals as a technical comple-ment to the process of teaching and learning. Although this approach has been described in other fields (Lai and Shea 1999; Lai *et al.* 2000) it has yet to be applied to judo. It is possible, therefore, that coaches are missing key aspects in their teaching of judo throws, and they may be unaware of the basic errors or sequences of errors that are committed when performing such throws. In this context the present case study uses an analysis of temporal patterns (T-patterns) and descriptive statistics to identify the most common errors and the most important sequences of errors when performing the judo throw *Ippon Seoi Nage*.

Aims and the mixed methods approach: convergent triangulation

The most important obstacles to studying knowledge of performance have been at the methodological level (Zubiaur 1998). Here, therefore, we use observational methodology (Anguera and Jonsson 2003; Black *et al.* 2005; Bloomfield *et al.* 2005), which offers the rigor and flexibility required to study the episodes that emerge naturally in the process of teaching and learning judo. The type of obser-vation conducted can be described as systematic, open and non-participant (Bor-rie *et al.* 2001, 2002). By video recording the judo bouts it was possible to obtain descriptive statistics and to conduct a sequential analysis of the temporal relation-ship between the errors made when performing the *Ippon Seoi Nage*. The findings could then be used to propose ways of improving the teaching and learning proc-ess in combat sports.

The mixed methods approach used was *convergent triangulation* (see Chapter 1, Figure 1.4), which implies, firstly, the independent capture of two kinds of data: quantitative (QUAN) and qualitative (QUAL). In a second stage these data are then combined (QUAN + QUAL) in order to enable an integrated interpretation (Creswell and Plano Clark 2007).

Participants

Participants were physical education students (n = 42, 18 men and 24 women) who were studied over a period of five academic years (from 2003/2004 to 2007/2008). They all gave their written informed consent to be filmed on video.

Observation instrument

The observation instrument developed for this study was the SOBJUDO-IP (see Table 3.3), which combines field formats with category systems (Fernández *et al.*

2009; Jonsson *et al.* 2006). The criteria on which the SOBJUDO-IP is based are consistent with the object of this study, i.e. technical errors in performance of the *Ippon Seoi Nage*. Specifically, the criteria used are as follows: grip, off-balance,

Table 3.3 The observation instrument SOBJUDO-IP

Criterion	Code	Description
GRIP	FAGR	*Tori*, while performing the technique, grips *Uke's judogi* with his left hand, around the midpoint of the forearm.
OFF-B	NOB	*Tori* does not put *Uke* off balance in the first part of the technique. His arms maintain the initial grip and only serve to accompany the action.
	DOB	The frontal off-balancing action and the subsequent initial displacement are performed in a discontinuous way.
RFP	IRFP	*Tori* incorrectly positions his right foot in the *Tsukuri* of the technique, after turning in the vertical axis.
RAP	LAC	*Tori* takes control of *Uke's* right arm during the second stage of the *Ippon Seoi Nage*, but is late in doing so.
	ACMF	*Tori* positions his right arm correctly over *Uke's* upper right arm, but does so with minimal force, such that the control is insufficient.
	AG	*Tori*, with his back to his adversary following the initial displacement and trapping his opponent's arm with his own, grips *Uke's* right arm with his right hand at the level of the brachial biceps.
	SHAP	*Tori* places his right shoulder in *Uke's* right armpit while performing the *Ippon Seoi Nage*.
HP	IHP	There is a gap (sagittal plane) between the posterior part of *Tori's* left hip/trunk and the anterior part of the left-hand side of *Uke's* body during the second stage of the throw.
LFP	ILFP	*Tori* incorrectly positions his left foot in the *Tsukuri* of the technique, after turning in the vertical axis.
LEA	INSQ	*Tori* fails to bend his knees sufficiently, as his hip is not located at the level of *Uke's* thighs during the leg squat.
LOA	NLHL	During the second stage of the throw *Tori* fails to take *Uke's* weight on his back, or instead does so over his hip.
	NSIM	*Tori* first bends and straightens his knees, and then bears *Uke's* weight with his body, in other words, the two actions are not simultaneous.
TS	STH	*Tori* throws *Uke* around the side of his body instead of over the top and toward the front of his shoulder (following a linear trajectory perpendicular to *Tori's* frontal plane).
	IAT	During the final stage of the throw *Tori's* arms produce insufficient force when throwing *Uke's* body to the floor.
	ITFL	Insufficient trunk flexion at the end of the throw (*Tori* maintains a position of between 10° and 60°).
	ITTU	*Tori* fails to turn his trunk enough in the *Kake* stage of the technique.
CS	FNC	During the final stage of the technique *Tori* performs no action with his left hand and therefore fails to control the fall of his adversary's body.
	KTB	*Tori* bends his trunk, between 90° and 110° with respect to the vertical axis, during the final stage of the throw and maintains this position once the technique is complete.
REB	RRF	After performing the throw *Tori* loses his balance. In order to regain it he steadies himself with his right foot.
	RLF	Upon completion of the technique *Tori* loses his balance, which he regains by steadying himself with his left foot.

right foot position, right arm position, hip position, left foot position, leg action, load action, throw stage, control stage and rebalancing. Each of these dimensions gives rise to a system of categories that fulfil the requirements of exhaustiveness and mutual exclusivity.

In terms of judo technique the *Ippon Seoi Nage* was taught according to the approach of the Kodokan School (Kodokan, no date).

Recording instrument

The performance of the *Ippon Seoi Nage* was filmed after a training period lasting approximately four months. Data were recorded by means of two digital video cameras (JVC GZ-MG21E). The recordings of the throws were then edited using the video editing software Pinnacle Studio v.12.

The recording instrument used for the observation was the software package Match Vision Studio Premium v.1.0 (Castellano *et al.* 2008). This is an interactive multimedia program that enables the user to visualize and register digitalized video recordings on the same computer screen. The program is highly flexible and allowed us to introduce all the codes corresponding to each of the changing criteria of the SOBJUDO-IP observation instrument, thereby producing a record of their successive appearance.

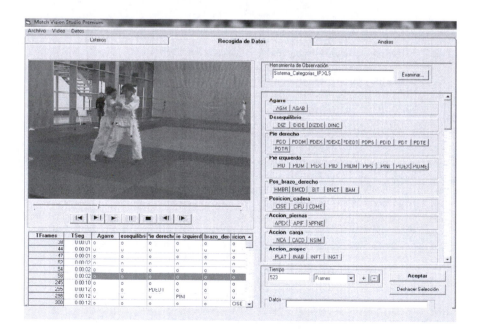

Figure 3.8 The recording instrument Match Vision Studio Premium v.1.0 (Castellano *et al.* 2008).

Procedure

After recording all the relevant technical moves produced during the observation period we obtained an Excel file containing the successive configurations formed by the lines of codes that have changed, with their temporality and duration expressed in frames (25 frames is equivalent to 1 s). The quality of the data was assessed by means of Cohen's kappa, with values of this coefficient above 0.8 being regarded as indicative of reliability. This test was conducted using the software SDIS-GSEQ v.4.2 (Bakeman and Quera 1992, 2001), and yielded a kappa value of 0.9. Having ensured the quality of the recorded data we then conducted an initial descriptive analysis (in SPSS v.12) of the frequency and percentage of occurrence of technical errors. The resulting .xls files, which provide frequencies for all the occurrences of recorded codes, were then transformed successively in order to enable various analyses to be carried out. Finally, the codes of the SOBJUDO-IP observation instrument were exported to the THEME software (Magnusson 1996, 2000, 2005) with the aim of detecting temporal patterns (T-patterns). T-patterns, which were obtained by means of the algorithm incorporated within THEME v.5 (Magnusson 2000), can help to reveal hidden structures and unobservable aspects in sports techniques. The application of this software has proved to be highly effective for studying team, individual and combat sports (Fernández *et al.* 2009; Gutiérrez *et al.* 2009; Louro *et al.* 2010).

Results

Descriptive analysis

In accordance with the above list of technical errors (Table 3.3), Table 3.4 shows the frequency and percentage of these errors in the *Ippon Seoi Nage* performed by the study sample (n = 42). These data were calculated using SPSS v.12.

The most common errors were: the lack of an initial action using both arms to put the adversary off balance (NOB); inadequate positioning of the hip (IHP) and feet (IRFP and ILFP) after turning in the vertical axis; a sub-optimal leg bend (INSQ); the failure of *Tori* to take *Uke's* weight on his back (NLHL); throwing the adversary's body around the side (STH); and the rebalancing manoeuvre which the participant has to make with his right foot in order to keep his balance upon completion of the technique (RRF).

Comparison of means according to gender

The possibility of differences between male and female participants as regards the observed performance errors was tested by comparing means with a Mann-Whitney U test. This showed that none of the differences was statistically significant ($p < 0.05$).

Table 3.4 Frequency and percentage of technical errors when performing the *Ippon Seoi Nage*

	Error	*Frequency*	*Percentage*
Grip	FAGR	19	45.2
Off-balance	NOB	26	61.9
	DOB	2	4.8
Right foot position	IRFP	25	59.5
Right arm position	LAC	1	2.4
	ACMF	4	9.5
	AG	4	9.5
	SHAP	2	4.8
Hip position	IHP	18	42.9
Left foot position	ILFP	31	73.8
Leg action	INSQ	34	81
Load action	NLHL	28	66.7
	NSIM	1	2.4
Throw stage	STH	36	85.7
	IAT	20	47.6
	ITFL	9	21.4
	ITTU	2	4.8
Control stage	FNC	19	45.2
	KTB	11	26.2
Rebalancing	RRF	26	61.9
	RLF	18	42.9

Detecting temporal patterns (T-patterns)

In order to examine in greater depth the errors produced when performing the *Ippon Seoi Nage*, the THEME software (Magnusson 1996, 2000) was used to conduct an analysis of T-patterns among the data, which in this case were sequential. This analysis revealed a series of important relationships associated with the emergence of sequential errors.

By way of an example, let us consider the T-pattern shown in Figure 3.9. The upper-left box shows the events occurring within the pattern, listed in the order in which they occur, i.e. the first event (01) in the pattern appears at the top and the last (012) at the bottom. As was noted in Chapter 2, all such tree diagrams should be read from top to bottom in this way. The T-pattern shown here reveals that an incorrect foot position (IRFP and ILFP) is closely related to the group of categories that represent the incorrect hip position (IHP), while the latter is linked to the category group that refers to a sub-optimal knee bend (INSQ), an error which itself is strongly related to *Tori's* subsequent failure to take *Uke's* weight on his back (NLHL). Furthermore, this failure to take *Uke's* weight on the back, or to do so over the hip (NLHL), derives from a side throw (STH). The absence of an initial off-balancing action (NOB) is also related to this set of categories, which are strongly linked with one another. It can therefore be assumed that all the above-mentioned errors follow from a failure to put the adversary off balance in the correct way at the beginning of the throw sequence.

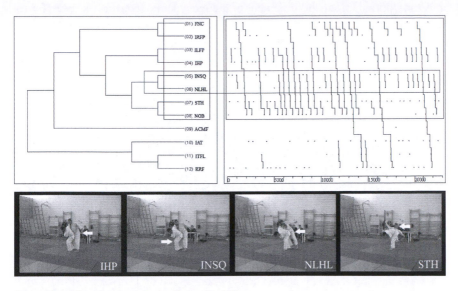

Figure 3.9 First T-pattern in the *Ippon Seoi Nage.*

Also noteworthy is the strong relationship between a sub-optimal leg action and the subsequent failure to take *Uke's* weight on the back (INSQ-NLHL), this being important insofar as it directly influences the motor action of the throw. The results show that this occurred in 26 of the 28 occasions in which the hip was observed to take an inadequate load.

Discussion

Although there is a lack of scientific research on technical errors in judo, the most prestigious authors associated with the sport (Carmeni 1989; Daigo 2005; FFJDA 1967; Mifune 2004; Ohlenkamp 2006) do, in their descriptions of judo technique, reflect upon the key aspects or the most common errors made. Interestingly, the points they make, which are no doubt based on their personal and professional experience, coincide on many occasions with the typical errors revealed by this case study.

As regards one of the most common errors made by our participants, i.e. failing at the outset to put their opponent off balance in the correct way, the expert literature is clear about the importance of using both arms in the direction of the right anterior diagonal in order to perform this off-balancing manoeuvre (Carmeni 1989; Daigo 2005; FFJDA 1967; Kolychkine 1989; Ohlenkamp 2006). We also observed that most of the students positioned both their left and right foot incorrectly after turning in the vertical axis. Once again, the majority of the most prestigious authors agree that *Tori's* feet should ideally be placed inside and in parallel to the position of the opponent's feet (Daigo 2005; Kawaishi 1964; Kimura 1976; Ohlenkamp 2006).

A sub-optimal knee bend is another of the most common errors when performing this throwing technique, with the importance of correct leg flexion being another aspect that is highlighted by many of the classical authors on judo (Daigo 2005; Kimura 1976; Koizumi 1965; Mifune 2004).

Another error committed by many of our participants, and which is easily observed when performing an *Ippon Seoi Nage*, is throwing *Uke's* body to the side rather than over the shoulder. When discussing key points in judo technique some authors highlight the importance of this technical aspect and stress the need to throw *Uke* over and toward the front of one's shoulder (Gleeson 1977; Mifune 2004; Uzawa 1970). Most of the time, this error, which appeared on numerous occasions, follows from a failure by *Tori* to take *Uke's* weight on his back, or to bear it on his hip instead. In this regard, Daigo (2005) explicitly recommends that the load be borne by *Tori's* back, not his hip.

As regards the sequences of technical errors observed here it should be noted that some judo experts have paid attention to the aspects revealed by the tree diagram shown in Figure 3.9. For example, the most important combination of errors found in the *Ippon Seoi Nage* (minimal leg bend → no load bearing or taking *Uke's* weight on the hip → a side throw) is discussed by Uzawa: '*Tori* must not seek to lift *Uke* as if it were merely a question of taking a weight on his back. He must lower his head and raise his hips, using his bent knees as if they were a spring before throwing *Uke's* body forwards, the whole manoeuvre being founded on the principle of a balance' (Uzawa 1970: 62).

The sequential analysis also revealed an important relationship between an inadequate hip position and either a lack of load bearing or taking *Uke's* weight on the hip. The concurrence of these events can easily be understood in biomechanical terms, but it has also been noted by judo experts such as Daigo, who warns that 'if *Tori* does not maintain firmness in this state, a space will open between them, and he will not be able to execute the loading action' (Daigo 2005: 14).

Finally, the latter author also highlights the importance of ensuring that arm movements are continuous from the initial off-balancing of *Uke* until the point at which he hits the floor. Failure to do so is likely to produce obvious imperfections in the performance of the throw. Both these errors can be observed in the tree diagram above (Figure 3.9).

Conclusions

The results obtained from the analysis of T-patterns confirm the presence of sequences of typical errors. In terms of teaching and learning judo these results enable us to propose motor tasks and drills based on the errors detected, to suggest movement sequences that would ensure a successful throw, and to make recommendations about the use of feedback. The most common errors observed with the *Ippon Seoi Nage* are a side throw (instead of over and towards the front of the shoulder), an insufficient knee bend by *Tori* prior to bearing the weight of *Uke's* body, and a failure to bear *Uke's* weight or doing so over the hip rather than on the back. Similarly, many participants failed to use their arms properly during the *Kake* of the technique, or positioned their feet incorrectly after the initial displacement in the throw sequence. Other errors made by a large percentage of the students involved an off-balancing manoeuvre with minimal force or in inappropriate directions, an incorrect hip position, a failure to control the final stage of the opponent's fall, and the need to use one or both feet in order to keep their balance after performing the throw.

The tree diagrams show that the lack of appropriate leg flexion leads to a failure to bear *Uke's* weight, or to doing so over the hip instead of the back, which in turn results in a throw around the side of *Tori's* body rather than over and towards the front of the shoulder. An inadequate hip position prior to leg flexion on the part of *Tori*, which follows from incorrect placement of the left foot, may lie behind this error and, therefore, could be partly responsible for the failure to bear *Uke's* weight or to do so over the hip.

Based on the knowledge of performance derived from this analysis there are a number of strategies which judo professionals could use to optimize both the teaching and learning of the *Ippon Seoi Nage* technique. In general terms these strategies would include the following:

- Drills or exercises that directly avoid the most important errors and sequences of errors detected here.
- Motor tasks using general methods but which help students to focus their attention on the most significant errors and/or sequences described above.
- When explaining the technique, focus attention on those parts most susceptible to technical errors.
- Optimize the communication between teacher and student by means of more precise feedback (based on the sequences detected).

There are also a number of specific recommendations that can be made in order to avoid errors when performing the *Ippon Seoi Nage*: (1) using the left hand *Tori* must grip *Uke's* right sleeve at the level of the elbow or triceps; (2) put *Uke* off balance from the front, pulling him towards you with both hands; (3) place both feet inside the adversary's feet (frontal plane) and more or less at the same level (sagittal plane); (4) close contact should be established between the posterior part of *Tori's* hip and the anterior part of *Uke's*; (5) bend the knees during the *Tsukuri* stage; (6) bear the weight of the adversary's body on the back; (7) throw *Uke* over and towards the front of the shoulder; and (8) control *Uke's* fall with the left arm, maintaining an upright position without moving the feet.

In order to improve the teaching and learning of this technique, special attention should also be paid to the movement sequences which ensure that a throw is successful: (1) bending the knees makes it easier for *Tori* to take *Uke's* weight on his back, which in turn enables him to throw *Uke* over and towards the front of his shoulder; and (2) correct placement of the left foot after turning in the vertical axis enables close contact to be established between the posterior part of *Tori's* hip and the anterior part of *Uke's*, which subsequently makes it easier for Tori to bear Uke's weight on his back.

CASE STUDY 3.3: AN ANALYSIS OF EFFECTIVENESS IN FREESTYLE SWIMMING

Introduction

In order to understand the effectiveness of freestyle swimming it is essential to examine the different phases of the stroke (in this case, the crawl). This analysis needs to consider the relationship between the biomechanical aspects of the body's movements (which are central to the optimization of technique) and the physiological mechanisms on which depends the efficiency of these movements in energetic terms. This case study uses a non-invasive methodology that does not alter the swimmer's natural movements but which enables us to conduct both a quantitative analysis of the biomechanical and physiological response, as well as a qualitative appraisal of technical behaviour.

The quantitative analysis is based primarily on the relationship between critical swim speed (CSS) and critical stroke rate (CSR), and therefore relates aerobic capacity to the swimmer's technique (Dekerle *et al.* 2002; Wakayoshi *et al.* 1992; Toussaint and Beek 1992; Pelayo *et al.* 2007). The critical swim speed (CSS) is the maximum (theoretical) speed that can be maintained for a long time without exhaustion (Wakayoshi *et al.* 1992) and it is associated with the lactate (or anaerobic) threshold (4 mmol.l^{-1}) (Derkele *et al.* 2002; Toubekis *et al.* 2006). The CSS can be obtained by measuring how long a swimmer takes, at maximum speed, to cover distances ranging from 200 m to 800 m. Specifically, it is based on a regression index which is calculated by dividing the distances covered at maximum intensity by the time taken to do so.

The CSR refers to the number of strokes per minute that can be maintained over a long period of time. It provides a way of monitoring aerobic capacity (Pelayo *et al.* 2007) and is related to two kinematic indicators that assess technical aspects of performance: the stroke length (SL) (Toussaint 1992) and the stroke rate (SR). The latter can also be used to derive another indicator, since the product of SL and the average velocity (V) gives the stroke index (SI), which is considered to be a valid indicator of swimming efficiency.

The qualitative aspect of the present case study examines the specific technical behaviour of swimmers by means of observational methodology and the analysis of temporal patterns (T-patterns). This qualitative analysis considers the different phases of the stroke in relation to established criteria of maximum swim efficiency (Louro *et al.* 2010). Specifically, the procedure examines the similarities and differences in the stroke performance of different swimmers (inter-individual variability) over a given period of time.

Aims and the mixed methods approach: triangulation design

By combining the analysis of both quantitative and qualitative data the study aims to illustrate new ways of understanding swimming performance. Specifically, the mixed methods approach used is that of a *triangulation design* (see Chapter 1,

Figure 1.1). The case study has three main aims: (1) to measure swimming effectiveness in each of the test trials according to the quantitative parameters of stroke rate (SR), stroke length (SL), the stroke index (SI) and velocity (V); (2) to characterize certain patterns in swimming performance according to qualitative observational criteria; and (3) to relate these two sets of data in order to examine variability in performance. Specifically, the quantitative data obtained from an analysis of aerobic capacity over 200 m and 800 m test trials are combined and compared with the qualitative data derived from observation of each swimmer's technical effectiveness. In the terminology of observational methodology the design used was as follows: it was based on the *monitoring* (M) of a sequence of strokes, it was nomothetic (N) because it considered a group of subjects in relation to the same technical objective, and it was multidimensional (M) because several characteristics were studied simultaneously.

Participants

Participants were seven female swimmers who were observed via video recordings of a continuous 800 m test trial that was performed at their CSS and CSR, the analysis being based on seven consecutive crawl strokes (see Table 3.5).

Observation instrument

An ad hoc instrument was developed in order to record through observation the aerial path of the crawl stroke, from the moment the hand of the recovering arm leaves the water until it enters the water again (as this arm becomes the pushing/pulling arm), and so on in the alternating movement of the right and left arms. The technical aspects of performance were identified by means of a category system based on criteria and categories (Campaniço and Anguera 2000; Oliveira *et al.* 2006). These criteria and categories, represented by codes comprising a letter and a number, describe the technical performance of the stroke and refer to the order and frequency of arm recovery behaviours (see Table 3.6). This synchronic and diachronic observation system has been validated according to accepted standards as regards the relevance and internal consistency of its categories.

Table 3.5 Descriptive characteristics of the swimmers studied

	Weight (kg)	BMI (weight/height²)	Height (m)	Exp. (years)	V400 (ms⁻¹)
Mean x̄	43.9	18.0	1.62	3.3	1.199
SD	6.6	1.8	0.1	1.3	0.09
CV	15.0	10.1	4.8	38.2	7.5

Note: weight (kg), body mass index (BMI), height (m), years of competitive experience (Exp) and time over 400 m (V400)

Table 3.6 Observation system in which the crawl stroke is considered in relation to three criteria (ER, FR and EXR) that comprise a total of 46 codes, 22 of which refer to criterion behaviours and 24 to the sub-behaviours associated with these criterion behaviours

Criterion 1: Elevation of the recovering arm (ER)

Criterion behaviour	Codes	Associated sub-behaviours	Codes
Hand position when leaving water:		**Hip position with respect to the water line:**	
• Next to the hip	1M1	• Above	1A1
• Away from the hip	1M2	• Below	1A2
Height of elevation:		**Orientation of the head:**	
• High	1DE1	• Frontal	1C1
• Low	1DE2	• To the side	1C2
Arm alignment:		**Shoulder position with respect to the water line:**	
• Straight	1RA1	• Raised	1O1
• Bent at elbow	1RA2	• Close to the surface	1O2
		Position of opposing arm with respect to the water line:	
		• Close to the surface	1BC1
		• Well below the surface	1BC2

Criterion 2: Fall of the recovering arm (FR)

Criterion behaviour	Codes	Associated sub-behaviours	Codes
Position of the falling arm:		**Hip position with respect to the water line:**	
• Vertical	2CO1	• Above	2A1
• Behind in diagonal	2CO2	• Below	2A2
Orientation of the falling arm:		**Orientation of the head:**	
• Outwards	2CD1	• Frontal	2C1
• Downwards	2CD2	• To the side	2C2
Arm alignment when falling:		**Shoulder position with respect to the water line:**	
• Straight	2RA1	• Raised	2O1
• Bent at elbow	2RA2	• Close to the surface	2O2
Hand position when entering the water:		**Position of opposing arm with respect to the water line:**	
• Raised	2EM1	• Close to the surface	2BC1
• Aligned with the surface	2EM2	• Well below the surface	2BC2
• In dropped position	2EM3		

Criterion 3: Extension of the recovering arm (EXR)

Criterion behaviour	Codes	Associated sub-behaviours	Codes
Entry of the elbow with respect to the hand:		**Hip position with respect to the water line:**	
• Before	3CE1	• Above	3A1
• After	3CE2	• Below	3A2
• Simultaneous	3CE3	**Orientation of the head:**	
Contact between hand and water:		• Frontal	3C1
• Thumb-minimal	3CM1	• To the side	3C2
• Fingers/palm of the hand	3CM2	**Shoulder position with respect to the water line:**	
Forward projection of the arm:		• Raised	3O1
• Extended	2BA1	• Close to the surface	3O2
• Bent at elbow	2BA2	**Position of opposing arm with respect to the water line:**	
	•	Vertical	3BC1
	•	Hand after elbow	3BC2

Recording instruments

The trials took place in a heated 25 m swimming pool and were filmed using a SONY 250P camera (operating at 50 Hz). The resulting images were converted to AVI format using a Toshiba PC (1400 MHz) and the Movie Maker software, before being viewed with the Quintic Player v9.02.

Prior to the test trial all seven swimmers were asked to swim 200 m and 800 m using the crawl technique so as to calculate their CSS, CSR and heart rate (HR). They were each informed of the results prior to performing the actual test. For the test trial each swimmer had to swim (freestyle) the same two distances (200 m and then 800 m), this time while being filmed in the sagittal plane so as to record the arm's movement during the stroke. The video camera was placed at a height of 15 m and perpendicular to the water so as to obtain images that could subsequently be used to categorize the technical performance of each swimmer.

Statistical analysis

The descriptive analysis of quantitative data was performed using Microsoft® Excel (v. 2007), while qualitative data were obtained through the THEME v5.0 software (Magnusson 1996, 2000). As illustrated in other case studies in this book, the THEME software can detect temporal sequences within the behavioural flow and reveals complex relationships between the behaviours of which it is composed. Specifically, THEME searches for sequences of codes that occur at least twice within a critical time interval, with the likelihood of this occurrence being greater than chance.

Control of data quality

The video recordings of the test trial were subjected to a process of systematic observation in order to derive qualitative data. The quality of these observational data was assessed by comparing the results of two independent judges, with the inter-observer reliability being calculated by means of the kappa coefficient (Cohen 1960, 1968). The value obtained (0.95) confirmed the reliability of the data.

Results

Analysis of quantitative results: performance measures

Compared to studies of reference in the field (e.g. Fernandes *et al.* 2003) the results (Table 3.7) are within the expected range and suggest that the swimmers had an intermediate level of performance. Specifically, the values of the stroke rate (SR), stroke length (SL) and stroke index (SI) are below the mean values reported for top-level national swimmers over the same distances. Nevertheless, the values of the standard deviation (SD) and the coefficient of variation (CV) are acceptable for both test distances and confirm that there are similarities in the technical performance of swimmers (Zartsiorski 1989).

The specialist literature shows that non-expert swimmers need a greater stroke rate (SR) to achieve a given velocity (Toussaint 1992), and that both the stroke length (SL) and the stroke index (SI) differ with respect to the performance of experts. In comparison with previous studies the stroke index (SI) obtained here is low, reflecting the fact that the velocity (V) attained by these swimmers depends more on their stroke rate (SR) performance. The values obtained for the CSS and CSR (Wakayoshi *et al.* 1992) are shown in Table 3.8.

Although the CSS and CSR provide a measure of the swimmers' aerobic performance, they do not reflect their technical performance of the crawl stroke. This aspect is addressed in the next section.

Analysis of qualitative results: technical performance

The first step was to describe qualitatively the technique of a swimmer with a mean quantitative performance (CSS = 1.126 ms^{-1}, CSR = 28.25) by interpreting

Table 3.7 Results for both the 200 m and 800 m test trials, showing the corresponding stroke rate (SR), stroke length (SL), stroke index (SI) and velocity (V)

	200 m				800 m			
	SR (strokes/ min)	SL (m/ stroke)	SI (SL × V)	V (ms^{-1})	SR (strokes/ min)	SL (m/ stroke)	SI (SL × V)	V (ms^{-1})
Mean x̄	37.21	1.92	2.28	1.19	33.29	1.96	2.13	1.09
SD	4.20	0.12	0.18	0.09	2.94	0.12	0.31	0.12
CV	11.29	6.30	7.83	7.59	8.84	5.90	14.70	10.91

Table 3.8 Critical swim speed (CSS) and critical stroke rate (CSR) based on 200 m and 800 m trials

	CSS (ms⁻¹)	CSR (strokes/min)
Mean $\bar{x}$	1.058	36.12
SD	0.12	6.13
CV	10.96	17.0

the codes registered in the observation of the 800 m test trial. Figure 3.10 shows the frequency of these codes and their clusters (configurations).

Having done this it was then possible to analyse the temporal patterns (T-pattern) which were detected by the THEME software, and which are presented in the form of tree diagrams in Figure 3.11. These tree diagrams depict the distribution of – and interaction between – the clusters of codes (configurations) shown (Figures 3.10 and 3.11) and which in this case correspond to the performance of the recovering arm.

Let us consider the meaning of these configurations, in chronological order:

(01) e,1m2,1de2,1ra2,1a2,1c2,1o1,1bc1. With the left arm as the recovering arm its exit from the water is performed in a smooth way, with the hand next to the hip, the elbow in line and the arm bent at the elbow, in conjunction with an intake breath to the left and with the opposing (right) arm extended forwards and below the water surface.

(02) e,2a2,2c2,2o2,2bc2,2co1,2cd1,2ra2,2em1. In the most critical phase of the fall of the recovering (left) arm the elbow is raised, with the hand facing downwards and close to the shoulder.

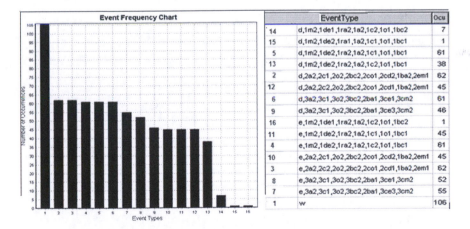

Figure 3.10 On the left (a) a histogram showing the frequencies for the different clusters of codes (configurations) that were obtained using the THEME v5.0 software, and which are shown on the right (b).

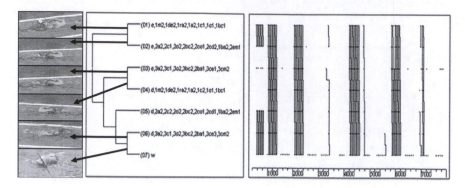

Figure 3.11 The most representative T-pattern for the swimmer studied.

(03) e,3a2,3c1,3o2,3bc2,2ba1,3ce3,3cm2. In the phase in which the left arm is extended forwards it is the palm of the hand that makes contact with the water, with the head in a frontal orientation and the shoulder close to the water surface.

(04) d,1m2,1de2,1ra2,1a2,1c2,1o1,1bc1. With the right arm as the recovering arm it exits the water with the hand rotated next to the hip, in conjunction with the opposing (left) arm being below the surface by the time it reaches its full extension forwards.

(05) d,2a2,2c2,2o2,2bc2,2co1,2cd2,1ba2,2em1. The exit of the recovering right arm coincides with a side turn of the head in order to breathe, this being accompanied by an excessive rotation of the trunk and hip in the longitudinal axis.

(06) d,3a2,3c1,3o2,3bc2,2ba1,3ce3,3cm2. The right arm is not properly extended as the elbow touches the water too soon, at the same time as the hand.

These results show that this swimmer performs the first phase of left-arm recovery in a smooth way, although her performance needs to be perfected. In the second phase her elbow lags behind and is oriented toward the water line, which leads to the recovery stroke being too much to one side. This, combined with the fact that her hip and shoulder are rotated too soon, explains the early propulsive action of the right arm, which affects the overall performance of the stroke, i.e. the left arm enters the water with the palm of the hand facing downwards, and the hand and elbow enter the water simultaneously.

Of course, each individual swimmer will have a specific way of moving which can be detected at each observational point. This is illustrated by the tree diagrams below (Figure 3.12), which correspond to two other swimmers whose stroke

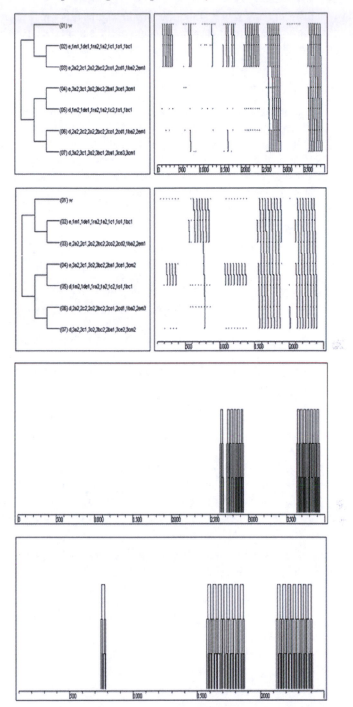

Figure 3.12 Tree diagrams showing the T-patterns derived from two swimmers whose stroke was smoother than that of the swimmer in Figure 3.11.

execution was different and much smoother. In the figure this aspect is reflected by the fact that the stroke patterns towards the end of the observation (on the right) stretch from bottom to top, which means that they were more stable.

Qualitative and quantitative variability in performance

When observing a group of swimmers it is important to take into account their individual differences, which can be observed here through the quantitative parameters that were assessed, as well as in the behaviours represented by the qualitative observational codes. It is therefore of interest to examine the relationship between these two kinds of data. Table 3.9 shows the CSS and CSR for each swimmer in relation to the number of configurations obtained for both their right and left arms.

While acknowledging that the sample size is small (n = 7) we can nonetheless determine the correlation between the values of each swimmer, which reveals the following:

*   A correlation of r = 0.48 between the CSS and the CSR.
*   A correlation of r = 0.58 between the configurations of the two arms and the CSS.
*   A correlation of r = 0.36 between the configurations of the right arm and the CSR.
*   A correlation of r = 0.16 between the configurations of the left arm and the CSR.

There are six configurations of codes which are repeated more than others, and their distribution across the two arms characterizes the level of each swimmer (see Table 3.10).

Accepting that the behaviours are fairly common due to the similar level of the swimmers studied, it can be seen that the first configuration (Table 3.10) appears in 71.4 per cent of the observations and refers to the following movement: the hand exits the water from a position behind the hip (first photo), with the elbow

Table 3.9 Values of critical swim speed (CSS) and critical stroke rate (CSR) in relation to the number of configurations of observational codes that were obtained for each swimmer over a long period of observation

Swimmer	CSS (ms⁻¹)	CSR (strokes /min)	No. of configurations: right arm	No. of configurations: left arm
1	1.126	28.25	4	3
2	1.054	37.44	8	4
3	0.812	27.92	4	4
4	1.019	35.01	5	5
5	1.056	38.50	2	3
6	1.111	39.25	8	8
7	1.220	36.50	13	17

Table 3.10 The six most common configurations of codes and their frequency with respect to the right (R) and left (L) arms (these codes characterize the specific technical performance of each swimmer)

Nadadores	1		2		3		4		5		6		7		
Configurações	D	I	D	I	D	I	D	I	D	I	D	I	D	I	N
1m2,1de2,1ra2,1a2,1c1,1o1,1bc1	57	42	81				5	18		3					71,4
1m2,1de2,1ra2,1a2,1c2,1o2,1bc1	36	57	3	3											28,6
1m2,1de1,1ra2,1a2,1c2,1o2,1bc1	36								9	95	5				42,9
1m2,1de1,1ra2,1a2,1c2,1o2,1bc1			18	14	51	25	48								42,9
1m1,1de1,1ra2,1a2,1c1,1o1,1bc1					43	68	9	60	5	63				15	57,1

insufficiently raised (second and third photos, see Figure 3.13) and the arm bent; there is an intake breath to the side, the opposing arm is extended forwards and the hip/shoulder is raised above the water line.

The mean number of configurations detected among all the observed swimmers was 7.7, which indicates a degree of homogeneity in their performance and is due to the fact that the CSR reflects an adequate technical execution. However, there is variability in the specific technique used by the swimmers observed, and their performance is sometimes less effective than it could be. In this regard, the kind of qualitative analysis used here can serve as a useful complement to the quantitative indices that are commonly used to study technical effectiveness.

Discussion and conclusions

Previous studies within the field of observational methodology as applied to swimming (Oliveira *et al.* 2001; Louro *et al.* 2010) have used qualitative instruments to study butterfly (Oliveira *et al.* 2006), breaststroke (Pereira and Campaniço 2010) and crawl. However, this is one of the first case studies to combine quantitative

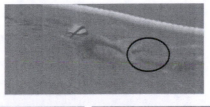

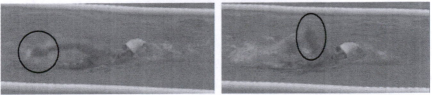

Figure 3.13 Images corresponding to the configuration of observational codes that is most representative of the swimmers' stroke style.

and qualitative data with the aim of examining the relationship between indices of effectiveness and observational criteria of technical efficiency in freestyle swimming.

In line with previous studies (Louro *et al.* 2010; Pereira and Campaniço 2010) the present results show a certain degree of homogeneity and effectiveness in the swimmers' stroke performance. However, the case study is original in two respects: first, it examines the technique of seven swimmers when performing the crawl stroke, not only according to the critical swim speed and critical stroke rate but also in relation to the temporal patterns (T-patterns) that characterize their performance; and second, it reveals the key elements of stroke execution, which is represented here by the configurations of observational codes. This qualitative information serves to complement the quantitative indicators used, thereby enabling greater feedback to be given to swimmers as regards the effectiveness of their performance (Louro *et al.* 2010).

A perfect performance, with no variability, corresponds merely to a theoretical ideal. Indeed, by analysing the variability shown by each individual swimmer, as revealed through the quantitative and qualitative indicators used here, coaches can help swimmers to improve their execution of the stroke and develop a more effective technique.

Acknowledgements

We gratefully acknowledge the support of the Spanish government project *Avances tecnológicos y metodológicos en la automatización de estudios observacionales en deporte* (Dirección General de Investigación, Ministerio de Ciencia e Innovación) [Grant number PSI2008-01179]. We also gratefully acknowledge the support of the Generalitat de Catalunya government project GRUP DE RECERCA E INNOVACIÓ EN DISSENYS (GRID). Tecnología i aplicació multimedia i digital als dissenys observacionals, Departament d'Innovació, Universitats i Empresa, Generalitat de Catalunya [Grant number 2009 SGR 829] and *Sport Sciences Research Group INEFC* Barcelona (Grant number 2009 SGR1054) by Institut Nacional d'Educació Física de Catalunya.

References

Anguera, M.T. (2003). Observational methods (general). In R. Fernández-Ballesteros (ed.), *Encyclopedia of psychological assessment* (pp. 632–637). London: Sage.

Anguera, M.T. (2005). Microanalysis of T-patterns: Analysis of symmetry/assymetry in social interaction. In L. Anolli, S. Duncan, M.S. Magnusson, and G. Riva (eds), *The hidden structure of social interaction: From genomics to culture patterns* (pp. 51–70). Amsterdam: IOS Press.

Anguera, M.T. and Blanco-Villaseñor, A. (2003). Registro y codificación del comportamiento deportivo. En A. Hernández-Mendo: *Psicología del Deporte (Vol. II): Metodología* (pp. 6–34). Buenos Aires: Tulio Guterman.

Anguera, M.T., Blanco-Villaseñor, A., and Losada, J.L. (2001). Diseños observacionales, cuestión clave en el proceso de la metodología observacional. *Metodología de las Ciencias del Comportamiento, 3* (2), 135–161.

Anguera, M.T. and Jonsson, G.K. (2003). Detection of real-time patterns in sport: Interactions in football. *International Journal of Computer Science in Sport (e-Journal), 2* (2), 118–121.

Badets, A., Blandin, Y., Wright, D. L., and Shea, C. H. (2006). Error detection processes during observational learning. *Research Quarterly for Exercise and Sport, 77* (2), 177–184.

Bakeman, R. (1978). Untangling streams of behavior: Sequential analysis of observation data. In G.P. Sackett (ed.), *Observing behavior, vol. 2: Data collection and analysis methods* (pp. 63–78). Baltimore, MD: University of Park Press.

Bakeman, R. and Quera, V. (1992) SDIS: A sequential data interchange standard. *Behavior Research Methods, Instruments and Computers, 24* (4), 554–559.

Bakeman, R. and Quera, V. (2001). Using GSEQ with SPSS. *Metodología de las Ciencias del Comportamiento, 3* (2), 195–214.

Black, C.B., Wright, D.L., Magnuson, C.E., and Brueckner, S. (2005). Learning to detect error in movement timing using physical and observational practice. *Research Quarterly for Exercise and Sport, 76* (1), 28–41.

Bloomfield, J., Jonsson, G.K., Polman, R., Houlahan, K., and O'Donoghue, P. (2005). Temporal patterns analysis and its applicability in soccer. In L. Anolli, S. Duncan, M.S. Magnusson, and G. Riva (eds), *The hidden structure of social interaction: From genomics to culture patterns* (pp. 237–251). Amsterdam: IOS Press.

Borrie, A., Jonsson, G.K., and Magnusson, M.S. (2001). Application of T-pattern detection and analysis in sports research. *Metodología de las Ciencias del Comportamiento, 3* (2), 215–226.

Borrie, A., Jonsson, G.K., and Magnusson, M.S. (2002). Temporal pattern analysis and its applicability in sport: An explanation and exemplar data. *Journal of Sports Sciences, 20*, 845–852.

Brison, T.A., and Alain, C. (1996). Optimal movement pattern characteristics are not required as a reference for knowledge of performance. *Research Quarterly for Exercise and Sport, 67* (4), 458–464.

Bruechert, L., Lai, Q., and Shea, C.H. (2003). Reduced knowledge of results frequency enhances error detection. *Research Quarterly for Exercise and Sport, 74* (4), 467–472.

Campaniço, J., and Anguera, M.T. (2000). Competencia Observacional en Natación: el error versus optimización técnica. In *actas del XXIII Congreso de la Associação Portuguesa de Técnicos de Natação*. Vila Real: Universidade de Trás-os-Montes e Alto Douro.

Carmeni, B. (1989). *Judo per tutti*. Padova, Italy: Edizione GB.

Castellano, J., Perea, A., Alday, L., and Hernández-Mendo, A. (2008). The Measuring and Observation Tool in sports. *Behavior Research Methods, 40* (3), 898–905.

Cohen, J. (1960). A coefficient of agreement for nominal scales. *Educational and Psychological Measurement, 20*, 37–46.

Cohen, J. (1968). Weighted kappa: Nominal scale agreement with provision for scaled disagreement of partial credit. *Psychological Bulletin, 70*, 213–220.

Costill, D.L, Maglischo, E.W., and Richardson, A. (1992). *Handbook of sports medicine and science: Swimming*. Blackwell Scientific Publications.

Creswell, J.W. and Plano Clark, V.L. (2007). *Designing and conducting mixed methods research*. Thousand Oaks, CA: Sage.

Daigo, T. (2005). *Kodokan judo throwing techniques*. Tokyo: Kodansha International.

Dekerle, J., Pelayo, P., Delaporte, B., Gosse, N., Hespel, J.M., Sidney, M. (2002). Validity and reliability of critical speed, critical stroke rate and anaerobic capacity in relation to front crawl swimming performances. *International Journal of Sports and Medicine, 23* (2), 93–98.

Fernandes, R., Billat, V., Cardoso, C., Barbosa, T., Soares, S., Ascensão, A., Colaço, P., Demade, A., and Vilas-Boas, J. (2003). Time limit at VO_2Max and VO_2Max slow component in swimming: A pilot study of university students. In *Proceedings of the IXth Symposium on Biomechanics and Medicine in Swimming* (pp. 331–336). Saint-Etienne.

Fernandes, R., and Vilas-Boas, J. (1998). Critical velocity as a criterion for estimating aerobic training pace in juvenile swimmers. In K.L. Keskinen, P.V. Komi, A.P. Hollander (eds), *Biomechanics and medicine in swimming VIII* (pp. 233–236). Jyväskylä: Gummerus Printing.

Fernández Fonseca, R. (2004). Nueva metodología para la enseñanza de las técnicas de pateos en la práctica del taekwondo (WTF). *Revista Digital* (Buenos Aires), *10* (75). [http://www.efdeportes.com/].

Fernández, J., Camerino, O., Anguera, M.T., and Jonsson, G.K. (2009). Identifying and analyzing the construction and effectiveness of offensive plays in basketball by using systematic observation. *Behavior Research Methods, 41*, 719–730.

FFJDA (1967). *La progression française d'eseignement. Tome I. Techniques de projections Nage Waza.* Paris: FFJDA.

Gasset, A. and Iglesias, X. (2010). *Caracterización de la presión temporal como factor ambiental de la conducta humana en situación de conflicto: El caso de la esgrima de espada.* CD de abstracts del V Congreso Internacional de Educación Física (pp. 131–137). Barcelona: INDE.

Gleeson, G.R. (1977). *Judo para occidentals* [Judo for the West]. Barcelona, Spain: Hispano Europea.

Gutiérrez, A., Prieto, I., Camerino, O. and Anguera, M.T. (2011a). The temporal structure of judo bouts in visually impaired men and women. *Journal of Sports Sciences, 29* (13), 1443–1451.

Gutiérrez, A., Prieto, I., Camerino, O., and Anguera, M.T. (2011b). Identificación y análisis del aprendizaje de los deportes de combate mediante la metodología observacional. *Apunts. Educación Física y Deportes, 104*, 44–53.

Gutiérrez, A., Prieto, I., and Cancela, J.M. (2009). Most frequent errors in judo uki goshi technique and the existing relations betweem them through T-patterns. *Journal of Sports Science and Medicine, 8* (CSSI 3), 36–46.

Heinisch, D. (1997). L'analisi dell'allenamento e della gara nel judo. *Rivista di Cultura Sportiva sds, 37*, 53–62.

Hernández, A., Anguera, M.T., and Bermúdez, M.A. (2000). Software for recording observational files. *Behavior Research Methods, Instruments, and Computers, 32* (3), 436–445.

Iglesias, X. (1997). *Valoració funcional específica en l'esgrima.* Tesi Doctoral. Universitat de Barcelona.

Iglesias, X., González, C., Cortés, A., Tarragó, R., and García, J.J. (2008). Variability of technical actions in épée fencing. In X. Iglesias (ed.), *Fencing, Science and Technology.* Book of abstracts (pp. 117–120). Barcelona: INEFC.

Jonsson, G.K., Anguera, M.T., Blanco-Villaseñor, A., Losada, J.L., Hernández-Mendo, A., Ardá, T., Camerino, O., and Castellano, J. (2006). Hidden patterns of play interaction in soccer using SOF-CODER. *Behavior Research Methods, Instruments and Computers, 38* (3), 372–381.

Kawaishi, M. (1964). *Mi método de Judo* [My judo method]. Barcelona: Bruguera.

Kernodle, M.W. and Carlton, L.G. (1992) Information feedback and the learning of multiple-degree-of-freedom activities. *Journal of Motor Behavior, 24*(2), 187–196.

Kimura, M. (1976). *El judo: Conocimiento práctico y normas* [Judo: Practical knowledge and rules]. Barcelona: Aedos.

Kodokan (no date). *Nage Waza: various techniques and their names [Video].* Tokyo: Kodokan Judo Video Series.

Koizumi, G. (1965). *Mi estudio de Judo* [My study of judo]. México D. F., México: Compañía Editorial Continental.

Kolychkine, A. (1989). *Judo. Nueva didáctica* [Judo: New teaching methods]. Barcelona, Spain: Paidotribo.

Lago, C. and Anguera, M.T. (2003). Utilización del análisis secuencial en el estudio de las interacciones entre jugadores en el fútbol de rendimiento. *Revista Española de Psicología del Deporte, 12* (1), 27–37.

Lai, Q. and Shea, C.H. (1999). Bandwidth knowledge of results enhances generalized motor program learning. *Research Quarterly for Exercise and Sport, 70* (1), 79–83.

Lai, Q., Shea, C.H., Wulf, G., and Wright, D.L. (2000). Optimizing generalized motor program and parameter learning. *Research Quarterly for Exercise and Sport, 71* (1), 10–24.

Lavoie, J.M., Léger, L., Pitre, R., and Marini, J.F. (1985). Compétitions d'escrime. Épée: Analyse des durées et distances de déplacement. *Medicine du Sport, 5* (59), 279–283.

Leitão, J., and Campaniço, J. (2009). Research methods support in observation sports laboratory. *Motricidade – Sport, Health and Human Development, 5* (3), 27–33.

Louro, H., Campaniço, J., Anguera, T., Marinho, D., Oliveira, C., Conceição, A., and Silva, A. (2010). Stability of patterns of behavior in the butterfly technique of the elite swimmers. *Journal of Sport Science and Medicine* 9 (1), 36–50

Magnusson, M.S. (1996). Hidden real-time patterns in intra- and inter-individual behavior. *European Journal of Psychological Assessment, 12* (2), 112–123.

Magnusson, M. (2000). Discovering hidden time patterns in behavior: T-patterns and their detection. *Behavior Research Methods, Instruments and Computers, 32*, 93–110.

Magnusson, M.S. (2005). Understanding social interaction: Discovering hidden structure with models and algorithms. In L. Anolli, S. Duncan, M.S. Magnusson, and G. Riva (eds), *The hidden structure of interaction: From neurons to culture patterns* (pp. 2–21). Amsterdam: IOS Press.

Marini, H.F. (1984). Analyse des assauts d'escrime. Considérations énergetiques: Évaluation de la valeur physique. Dins: *Travaux et Recherches en E.P.S.* París: INSEP.

Mifune, K. (2004). *The canon of judo: Classic teachings on principles and techniques.* Tokyo: Kodansha International.

Miyashita, M. (1975). Arm action in the crawl stroke. In I. Lewillie. and L.P. Clarys, (eds), *Swimming II* (pp. 167–173). Baltimore, MD: University Park Press.

Newell, K.M. and Walter, C.B. (1981). Kinematic and kinetic parameters as information feedback in motor skill acquisition. *Journal of Human Movement Studies, 7*, 235–254.

Ohlenkamp, N. (2006). *Black belt: Judo skills and techniques.* London: New Holland Publishers.

Oliveira, C., Campaniço, J., and Anguera, M.T. (2001). La metodologia observacional en la enseñanza elemental de la natación: el uso de los formatos de campo. *Metodologia de las Ciencias del Comportamiento, 3* (2), 267–282.

Oliveira, C., Santos, J., Campaniço, J., and Jonsson K.G. (2006) Detection of real-time patterns in breaststroke swimming. *Revista Portuguesa Ciências Desporto 6* (Supl.2), 201–282.

Pelayo, P., Alberty, M., Sidney, M., Podevin, F., and Dekerle, J. (2007). Aerobic potential, stroke parameters, and coordination in swimming front-crawl performance. *International Journal of Sports Physiology and Performance*, 2, 347–359.

Pereira, N., and Campaniço, J. (2010). Análise da qualidade do instrumento sistema de observação do comportamento técnico de crol. *XII Congresso de Ciências do Desporto e Educação Física dos Países de Língua Portuguesa*, Porto Alegre, Brasil.

Prudente, J., Garganta, J., and Anguera, M. T. (2004). Desenho e validação de um sistema de observação no Andebol. *Revista Portuguesa de Ciências do Desporto, 4* (3), 49–65.

Salmoni, A. W., Schmidt, R. A., and Walter, CH. B. (1984). Knowledge of results and motor learning: A review and critical reappraisal. *Psychological Bulletin, 95*, 355–386.

Schmidt, R. (1988) *Motor control and learning*. Champaign, IL: Human Kinetics.

Schmidt, R. A. and Lee, T. D. (2005). *Motor control and learning*. Champaign, IL: Human Kinetics.

Swinnen, S. P. (1996). Information feedback for motor skill learning: A review. In H. N. Zelaznik (Ed.), *Advances in motor learning and control* (pp. 37–66). Champaign, IL: Human Kinetics.

Toubekis, A.G., Tsami, A.P., and Tokmakidis, S.P. (2006). Critical velocity and lactate threshold in young swimmers. *International Journal of Sports Medicine*, 27, 117–123.

Toussaint, H. (1992). Performance determining factors in front crawl swimming. In D. Maclaren, T. Reilly and A. Lees (eds), *Swimming science* (vol. VI, pp. 13–32). Cambridge: E & FN Spon.

Toussaint, H. and Beek, P.J. (1992) Biomechanics of competitive front crawl swimming. *Sports Medicine, Auckland*, v.13, 8–24.

Uzawa, T. (1970). *Tratado de Judo* [The judo book]. Madrid: INEF Madrid.

Wakayoshi, K., Ikut, K., Yoshida, T., Udo, M., Moritani, T., Mutoh, Y., Miyashita, M. (1992). Determination and validity of critical velocity as an index of swimming performance in the competitive swimmer. *European Journal Applied Physiology*, 363–366.

Weeks, D.L. and Kordus, R.N. (1998). Relative frequency of knowledge of performance and motor skill learning. *Research Quarterly for Exercise and Sport, 69* (3), 224–230.

Wulf, G. and Shea, C.H. (2002). Principles derived from the study of simple skills do not generalize to complex skill learning. *Psychonomic Bulletin and Review, 9* (2), 185–211.

Zartsiorski, V.M. (1989). *Metrologia Desportiva*. Editorial Pueblo y Educacion. Ciudad de la Habana.

Zubiaur, M. (1998). El conocimiento de la ejecución [Knowledge of performance]. *Motricidad, 4*, 97–111.

Part III

Approaches to kinesics and dance

4   Extending the analysis of motor skills in relation to performance and laterality

---

- Case Study 4.1: How to observe spontaneous motor skills in natural contexts: from children's playgrounds to parkour
  Marta Castañer and Juan Andueza

- Case Study 4.2: The laterality of motor skills: a complex merging of postural support and gestural precision
  Marta Castañer, Juan Andueza, Pedro Sánchez-Algarra and M. Teresa Anguera

---

Although various disciplines have recognized the need to determine the possibilities of human movement, it is important to analyse in greater depth the most effective way of observing, evaluating and analysing the complexity of motor skills. The two case studies described in this chapter combine the use of observation instruments with statistic analysis and interviews or a discussion group.

The first case study uses a specific observational system to analyse the motor skills employed during free movement in two natural contexts, namely children's playgrounds and public urban spaces. In the latter context the activity analysed is *parkour*, also known as free running, in which practitioners seek original and creative ways of moving through urban spaces (Bavinton 2007). The qualitative and subsequently quantitative data derived from the observational analysis is here complemented by qualitative information gained through interviews with experts. In terms of mixed methods this corresponds to an explanatory sequential design.

The second case study examines laterality as a key aspect to be considered when analysing basic and specific motor skills (Castañer and Camerino 2006; Castañer *et al.* 2009). The specific focus is on two factors, *postural support* and *gestural precision*, which act in conjunction when performing any kind of motor skill. An instrument designed to record motor laterality is used to obtain an initial set of quantitative data, which are then complemented with qualitative data obtained through a discussion group involving experts in physical education. The purpose of this was to create a more dynamic version of the recording instrument, with which new quantitative data could then be obtained. In terms of mixed methods this process corresponds to an *embedded design.*

CASE STUDY 4.1: HOW TO OBSERVE SPONTANEOUS MOTOR SKILLS IN NATURAL CONTEXTS: FROM CHILDREN'S PLAYGROUNDS TO PARKOUR

Introduction

Running, jumping, climbing and other similar actions are what we first see when we watch children playing freely in playgrounds. For example, we observe how a child might use a rope for climbing, to make a swing, or for tying to an object that can then be pulled or swung around. This is consistent with how human beings gradually begin to understand the world by learning what its entities and events 'afford' (Johnson 2007). This concept of 'affordance', originally coined by Gibson (1979), refers to the perceived utility of objects and explains how, from childhood, we recognize the utility of elements in the environment around us and, therefore, the action possibilities that they engender, all of which promotes change in the process of development (Savelsbergh *et al.* 2003).

A similar process can also be witnessed in public urban spaces, which are now being used by young people for an activity known as *parkour*. The term derives from the military practice of an obstacle course, known in French as the *parcours du combatant* (Feireiss 2007), and in its contemporary form parkour 'involves moving rapidly and fluidly through the urban environment, reflexively interpreting the objects encountered not as obstacles but as opportunities for movement' (Bavinton 2007: 391). The idea behind parkour was developed by David Belle and Sébastien Foucan in the 1990s, and it is now regarded as a cultural and athletic lifestyle and performance (Atkinson 2009), in which the practitioner interacts with architectural structures or street furniture.

What these two contexts, i.e. children's playgrounds and public urban spaces, have in common is that they both offer opportunities for spontaneous and free interaction with the environment (Saville 2008). Consequently, they are ideal natural contexts in which to identify and observe the multiple motor actions of which human movement is comprised.

Spontaneous motor skills

Human beings have developed both phylogenetically and ontogenetically to be optimally geared to adapt to their multifaceted environments (Johnson 2007). While the roots of fundamental motor skills lie in the phylogenetic contribution, their singular characteristics depend on ontogeny, on the developmental process of each individual, which generates specific motor skills (Rigal 1992; Gallahue 1987). The basic motor skills are locomotion, stability and manipulation (Gallahue and Cleland-Donnelly 2003), which in turn form the basis of a greater number of specific skills and their combinations (Castañer and Camerino 2006; see Table 4.1).

From the earliest stages of development, characterized by exploratory motor behaviour, through to young adulthood, by which time such behaviour will have taken on its own identity, all combinations of motor skills are possible. Yet it is only in adulthood that more specialized skills will appear, and these will depend on the individual's expertise in a given activity, such as parkour. Nevertheless, both children and young adults can manifest imaginative and playful forms of movement in their environment (Saville 2008), and this is also related to decision-making behaviour. Indeed, as Gibbs points out, people 'do not perceive the world statically, but by actively exploring the environment' (Gibbs 2006: 49). Experience does matter, however, and as Davids notes, 'through using information to regulate action, information-movement couplings can be developed to adjust to environmental demands [and in this regard] skilled performers are more sensitive to relevant sources of information to successfully perform a task than novices' (Davids 2010: 11–12).

The need for a clear and meaningful analysis of motor skills

In relation to the above it would clearly be useful to have instruments that enable the exhaustive and mutually exclusive observation of the various chains of motor events that occur in natural contexts of physical activity. This becomes possible if the concept of motor skill is treated as a clearly observable and agreed action in the form of units of behaviour along a behavioural continuum (Castañer *et al.* 2009). With respect to the specific contexts addressed by this case study this means that the motor actions performed by children in playgrounds and young people engaged in parkour can be considered as flows of movement behaviour (Bavinton 2007) that can be observed.

The specific aim here is to offer a view of human movement based on the clear, objective and differentiated identification of actions in the form of motor skills, thereby enabling a more objective approach to the observation of each movement. The observation instrument used for this purpose was the Observational System of Motor Skills (OSMOS; Castañer *et al.* 2009), which was designed to observe the form taken by basic and specific motor skills. Previous research with the OSMOS has shown it to be both easy to use and readily adaptable to various disciplines (Castañer *et al.* 2009; Castañer *et al.* 2011; Torrents *et al.* 2010) and natural study contexts (Anguera 2005).

Aims and the mixed methods approach: exploratory sequential design

This case study has three objectives: first, to illustrate how the OSMOS can provide observational data about distinct forms of motor behaviour; second, to observe how motor skills are spontaneously generated when individuals move freely in natural contexts, such as in children's playgrounds or during an activity such as parkour; and third, to compare the spontaneous motor skills used by children and those employed by parkour experts.

The mixed methods approach used corresponds to an explanatory sequential design: follow-up explanatory model (see Chapter 1, Figure 1.11), since the initial qualitative data (QUAL) come from the OSMOS observation instrument, which provided a register of the chain of motor actions that were produced in the two contexts. Event plots and temporal patterns (T-patterns) could then be obtained from this descriptive analysis generating quantitative data (quan). Subsequently, qualitative data (qual) were gathered through a guided interview with expert parkour practitioners, the focus being on comparing the spontaneous motor skills used by children and those employed by parkour experts.

Instrument 1: The OSMOS observational system

The OSMOS observation instrument (Castañer *et al.* 2009) is well suited to the analysis of motor skills in contexts in which the aim is to observe how such skills are used and relate to one another. The instrument has a multidimensional structure based on a series of behavioural criteria and the categories that give rise to each of them. Although each category is exhaustive and mutually exclusive this does not mean that several categories from different criteria cannot co-occur within the same observation time-unit/frame.

In the present case study we used just four of the OSMOS criteria, and these are shown in Table 4.1. The structure of the criteria consists of:

a)   The first three criteria refer to the type of motor skills, i.e. stability, locomotion and manipulation (Gallahue and Cleland-Donnelly 2003), which can be sub-divided into eleven kinds of specific motor skills (Castañer and Camerino 2006).
b)   The fourth criterion corresponds to space, which is associated with three codes that enable the observation of how motor skills occur in relation to changes in direction and levels in space.

Procedure

In the playground context we observed six children aged 6–8 years, while the parkour observations referred to six young adults aged 19–25 years. In playgrounds, a total of 24 minutes of activity were observed (4 min per child), while for parkour a total of 12 minutes were observed (2 min per practitioner). Participants in the two settings had either sufficient motor ability for their developmental age (children) or sufficient experience (parkour) to enable them to perform all the motor skills on which the observation instrument is based.

In the playground context, recordings were only made after having obtained written informed consent from the children's parents or teachers. As regards the recordings of parkour these were provided voluntarily by the participants themselves. In both cases the quality of the recordings and the number of actions for

Table 4.1 The OSMOS Observation Instrument (adapted from Castañer *et al.* 2009)

Criteria	Categories
Stability	***Support stability* (ss):** motor skills that enable body equilibrium to be maintained over one or several body support points, without producing locomotion (e.g. balancing actions) ***Elevation stability* (es):** motor skills that enable the body to be projected by elevating it in space, without producing locomotion (e.g. jumps) ***Axial stability* (as):** motor skills that enable body axes and planes to be varied from a fixed point, without producing locomotion (e.g. turns) Combination **(cos)** between Es, Ed and Ea
Locomotion	***Propulsion/stop* (lp):** motor skills that occur at the start and finish of a body movement through space ***Sequential locomotion* (sl):** motor skills that enable a space to be moved through via the priority sequence of actions of the segments of the lower limbs (bipedal locomotion) or upper limbs (in inversion) ***Simultaneous coordinated locomotion* (cl):** motor skills that enable a space to be moved through via the combined action of all body segments (e.g. quadrupedal locomotion). Combination **(col)** between pl, sl and cl
Manipulation	***Impact manipulation* (mi):** motor skills in which certain body zones briefly come into contact with objects or other people ***Directing* (md):** motor skills in which certain body segments are in contact with objects or other people (for a given period of time) Combination **(com)** between Mi and Mc
Space	***Change in spatial direction* (d):** variations in the spatial direction of the movement ***Change of spatial level* (l):** change between the different spatial levels (low or floor work, middle or bipedal work, upper or aerial work). ***Combination of variations in spatial level and direction* (ld)**

each of the participants generated a comprehensive database covering different observation sessions.

The observational information obtained with OSMOS was coded by means of the THEME CODER software (Magnusson 2005). Two different observers analysed all the recordings from the observation sessions, and the quality of the data thus obtained was assessed by calculating the kappa coefficient. The resulting value of 0.81 for all sessions provides a satisfactory guarantee of data quality. Finally, the THEME v.5 software (Magnusson 2005) was used to detect and analyse temporal patterns (T-patterns).

Results

The THEME software produces event time plots and can detect T-patterns composed of distinguishable event types, which are coded according to their occurrence time.

Figures 4.1 and 4.2 show event time plots corresponding to motor behaviour observed in the two contexts, children's playgrounds and parkour, respectively.

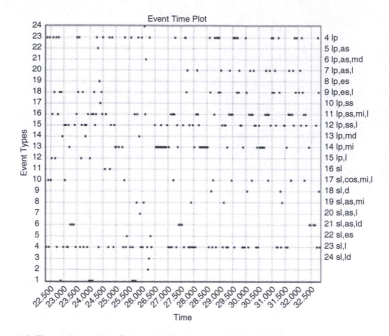

Figure 4.1 Event time plot of motor behaviour in children's playgrounds.

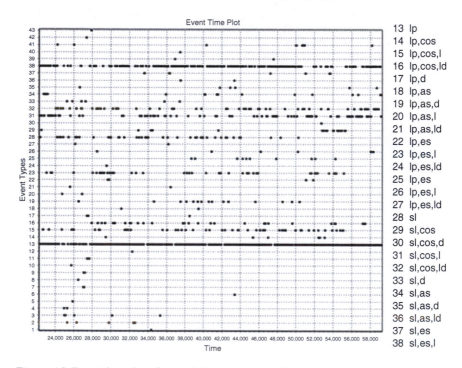

Figure 4.2 Event time plot of motor behaviour observed in parkour.

In the plot for children's playgrounds (Figure 4.1) it can be seen that certain actions are more frequent and show greater continuity. For example, line 4 corresponds to start and stop events (lp), there being a continuous need to start and stop. Line 11 (lp,ss,mi,l) shows how several of these start and stop movements are combined with stability or equilibrium behaviours (ss), together with an impact manipulation (mi) – generally with a physical structure or material – and a change of level in the spatial dimension (l), i.e. up or down. Line 12 shows the same as line 11 but without manipulation (lp,ss,l), while line 14 corresponds to stops and starts with manipulation (lp,mi). This suggests that while impact manipulation (with a physical structure or material) is usually a discrete event, it may at times be accompanied by other motor skills. Finally, line 23 shows that sequential locomotion (generally on two feet) with level changes in the spatial dimension (l) to go up or down is also a frequent and continuous event.

As regards the plot for parkour (Figure 4.2), line 13 shows the frequency and continuity of start and stop movements (lp), which in line 15 (lp,cos,l) are complemented by level changes in the spatial dimension (n) and are combined with stability skills (cos) such as turns with jumps or regaining balance through turns. Line 23 (lp,es,l) shows that these start and stop events (lp) very often appear with stop/jump stability movements (es) when there is a change in spatial level (l) due to the practitioner climbing up or getting down from an architectural structure. As regards sequential locomotion (sl), generally on two feet, line 32 (sl,cos,ld) and especially line 38 (sl,es,l) show that this is usually accompanied by level and direction changes in the spatial dimension (ld), whereas combined stability skills (cos), which are more specific than spatial level changes (l), are used when sequential locomotion is accompanied by stops designed to achieve stability (basically jumps).

Detection of T-patterns

The identification of patterns that are not identifiable through simple observation can be enormously useful when it comes to understanding complex behavioural responses in the form of sequential and concurrent motor skills. In the current data sets the THEME software detected several T-patterns. For each of the two contexts we will consider the T-pattern that best represents the motor behaviour produced therein (see Figures 4.3 and 4.4).

The T-pattern in Figure 4.3 is representative of the motor behaviour shown by children in playgrounds as it illustrates the combination of start and stop movements, as well as sequential locomotion. The children usually begin with a setting-off movement (lp) accompanied by some kind of support or unbalancing action (ss). This is followed by sequential locomotion (sl) in the form of running or walking (generally on two feet), and then an attempt to overcome an obstacle (ramp, steps, slide, etc.) through a level change in the spatial dimension (sl,l). This movement then continues along a given surface (bridge, platform, etc.) without any level change but changing the direction (sl,d). They then return to sequential locomotion (sl), which implies another level change (l) accompanied by a motor

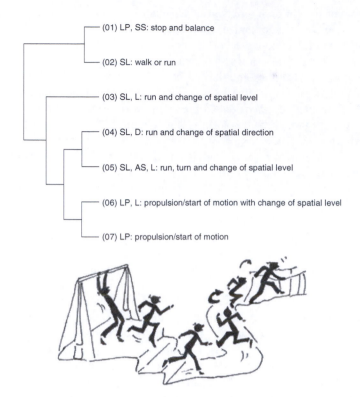

Figure 4.3 T-pattern of motor behaviour in children's playgrounds.

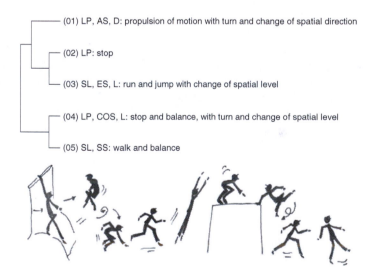

Figure 4.4 T-pattern of motor behaviour in parkour.

skill to enable axial stability, generally, turns on the bars, somersaults or rolling (as). The sequence ends with another stop (lp), which is usually a rest period accompanied by gentle to-and-fro movements of the body.

Figure 4.4 shows the most representative T-pattern detected in parkour. As in the children's playground the sequence begins with a setting-off movement (lp) but here this is accompanied by a slight turn (as) and change of direction (d), which is immediately interrupted (lp) in preparation for the next action. This is followed by sequential locomotion (sl) with a level change in space (l) by means of a jump or sequence of jumps (es) that enables the practitioner to overcome an obstacle (bench, wall, etc.). The next sequence occurs when a difficulty is encountered that cannot be resolved by continuing in this way: the practitioner stops (lp) and changes the spatial level (l), this being performed in conjunction with a stability skill (cos), usually a turn or a swinging movement. Sequential locomotion is then resumed (sl), with another level change, and the level of difficulty increases through the incorporation of support or equilibrium skills (ss).

Instrument 2: Guided interview

Guided interviews were conducted with two experts in parkour, both of whom also had a degree in physical activity and sport. Practitioners such as these are known as *traceurs*, a French term that refers to the act of 'tracing' a trajectory through the environment. There are precedents of conducting open-ended interviews with *traceurs* regarding their experiences with movement (Atkinson 2009; Bavinton 2007). Here the procedure involved showing the two experts the parkour videos so as to gather specific data about the practice.

They were then shown video recordings of the children's playgrounds and asked to compare the motor behaviour produced in the two contexts. Guided interviews with experts such as these are useful in that they provide an opportunity to give greater meaning to behaviours which at the time may have been performed automatically, and this can also shed light on why a given action might have been chosen.

Results

Motor skills specific to parkour

Spatial levels and directions

As regards spatial levels (height) and directions, *traceurs* seem to place greater emphasis on the former, since the objective is to move from one point of the town or city to another. They seek to develop a chain of efficient actions, sometimes of a spectacular nature (Saville 2008), although this does not necessarily mean they perform a greater number of actions.

We try to get from A to B as quickly as possible, and we might look to do something spectacular, which is why we're always looking to change height.

(Expert 1)

The aim is to get from A to B as quickly and as efficiently as possible. That doesn't mean doing more things, but doing it as fast as you can.

(Expert 2)

It's not always a case of seeing whether I go up or down, but rather to look at the most efficient route from where I am.

(Expert 2)

Locomotion skills

With regard to locomotion skills the start and stop movements are important and may involve taking a rest (Brunner 2010) or taking time to decide upon the best strategy for the next action.

You aim to stop as little as possible. When you do it's mainly to rest or to plan a really complex move or to change direction.

(Expert 1)

A really difficult move means you first have to stop and observe, and then stop again afterwards to recover.

(Expert 1)

Stopping is related to performance . . . it enables me to rest or to plan a risky move and work out how I'll do it.

(Expert 2)

Stability skills

Stability skills prove to be a versatile aspect, since jumps, turns, balancing actions and swinging actions serve to redistribute body weight, to play with gravity, or to be ready for or initiate the next move. Moreover, in parkour they are also used to make a move appear more spectacular (Saville 2008).

When you're in a tight spot and you don't have room to move, you can use a swinging action to redistribute your body weight and give yourself the strength needed to overcome the obstacle.

(Expert 1)

With simple movements you can use turns in combination with jumps in order to make it more spectacular, making the move more difficult.

(Expert 1)

Motor skills which are common to parkour and playgrounds

Natural context and movement

The natural context provided by the various playground structures or urban archi-tecture and street furniture is a rich setting in which to explore various motor skills. The results illustrate how the body, through natural movements, interacts (Atkinson 2009) with all these spatial structures.

> All the skills you see in the playground or in parkour are natural movements . . . it's a way of adapting your body to your surroundings.
>
> (Expert 2)

> It's interesting . . . I'd never thought about how much these two activities have in common because of how you're moving between different structures and materials.
>
> (Expert 2)

Technique and efficacy of body movement

The experts also shared their knowledge about the techniques which both they and the children could be seen to be using in order to perform various motor behav-iours (Rigal 1992; Gallahue 1987). Specifically, they referred to the mobilization of body segments and shifting the centre of gravity, for example, shortening cer-tain body segments in order to attain greater centripetal efficiency when turning.

> When you have to jump a long way what you do is shift your centre of gravity so that you can see what's going on, and if you're falling short then you tuck in a little.
>
> (Expert 2)

> That's really interesting . . . if you watch that child you can see how instead of using his hands to turn his body on the bar he does it with his forearms . . . it's a natural way of shifting the centre of gravity closer to the bar and so the turn is faster and better . . . I'm going to try it!
>
> (Expert 1)

Motor challenges, height and direction in space

In both contexts challenges are sought by playing with gravity and height. How-ever, whereas the children often change direction, parkour follows more of a 'lin-ear' direction, which is of course consistent with the origins of the word, which suggest a path. The use of height or level changes in space are more continuous and fluid (Bavinton 2007) in parkour, whereas children tend to make a more iso-lated use of these skills.

Often, when we drop down a level or from a height it's a prelude to looking for a new height to scale . . . it's almost like a kind of bouncing movement that I notice the children don't usually do.

(Expert 1)

Gaining height is about challenging your own body, gravity, or maybe about doing something more spectacular.

(Expert 1)

. . . it seems that we're always going forward, whereas they seem more able to go forward or back, exploring all possible directions.

(Expert 1)

Discussion

On the basis of the quantitative and qualitative results obtained in relation to the observed sequences of motor behaviour the following general conclusions can be drawn:

a) The basic motor skills, i.e. locomotion, stability and manipulation (Gallahue and Cleland-Donnelly 2003), and their combinations (Castañer and Camerino 2006) appear in both the contexts analysed.

b) Both practices (children's outdoor play and parkour) generate creativity and a continuous fluidity of movements. Indeed, the motor behaviour is similar in the two contexts, although some activities are more specific, for example, swinging on swings has a notable presence in the playground setting.

c) In both contexts the motor skills involved in sequential locomotion (sl) are clearly and continuously alternated with start and stop movements (lp).

d) In both settings, stop movements (lp) may have a strategic value or provide the opportunity to rest, the former being more the case in parkour and the latter being more characteristic of children's play. This can be linked to the idea of an oscillation between motion and rest (Brunner 2010), or in the words of Spinoza, 'bodies are distinguished from one another in respect of motion and rest, quickness and slowness' (Spinoza 1992).

e) Most of the observed sequences are accompanied by level changes in the spatial dimension, and it is precisely this aspect that leads the individual to interact with (Daskalaki *et al.* 2008) and adapt to the playground structures or street furniture.

f) The sequences observed in children's playgrounds include hardly any combinations of stability skills, for example, turns with jumps or balancing movements with turns. By contrast, such combinations are common in parkour, whose practitioners often seek to perform a spectacular movement (Saville 2008).

g) Playgrounds are versatile settings in that they encourage the generation and repetition of various motor skills, thereby enabling the children to experience their body's natural way of moving. Indeed, children learn how to regard some kinds of stable regularities in their environment as objects, and other regularities as events (Johnson 2007).

h)   New motor responses are sought as a personal challenge, without the need for a third party to indicate what to do (Torrents *et al.* 2010; Castañer *et al.* 2011).

i)   The qualitative data reveal that parkour tends to be a linear activity based on going from A to B, and practitioners rarely retrace their steps. By contrast, children's activity does not show this spatial linearity as they are constantly changing direction in the playground, this being a form of explanatory motor behaviour.

Conclusion

This case study has enabled us to identify and study a range of singular motor responses produced during free motor activity in two natural contexts (Anguera 2005), namely children's playgrounds and the urban spaces used in parkour. Both these situations encourage experimentation with movement and the findings support the idea that the impressive array of strategies used by humans to negotiate their way around their world is the result of a constant interaction with the environment (Daskalaki *et al.* 2008; Johnson 2007). In line with what some authors have recently argued, the encounter with obstacles in playgrounds or street furniture in parkour 'activates the silent potential for movement located in the relation between bodies and thus reaches beyond material boundaries' (Brunner 2010: 10).

The observational design used here has great potential in terms of interpreting clearly the various configurations of human movement, and can make a significant contribution to a deeper understanding of the tendencies underlying the use of motor skills, whether in sporting or non-sporting contexts. Indeed, the results suggest that there is a very real possibility of discovering new kinds of motor profiles by using detected behavioural patterns in combination with qualitative data. Without such an analysis important information may be overlooked, thereby missing the opportunity to optimize performance or to develop new configurations of motor skills to be used in human movement (Castañer *et al.* 2009; Saville 2008) across the developmental cycle.

CASE STUDY 4.2: THE LATERALITY OF MOTOR SKILLS: A COMPLEX MERGING OF POSTURAL SUPPORT AND GESTURAL PRECISION

Introduction

Although our bodies are anatomically symmetrical this does not have an exact correlate in functional terms, and it is this functional asymmetry that enables our bodies to adapt to a given situation, including those that occur in sport or physical exercise. This laterality is an essential feature of our bodily experience and depends on inherited, socio-cultural and functional factors. It has been suggested, for example, that behavioural lateralization is related to an asymmetry of the cortical areas controlling the cognitive/motor requirements of skilled movements (Daprati and Sirigu 2002; Haaland and Harrington 1996). At all events, this is a complex reality (Provins 1997) which, in our view, requires further study as regards its manifestations in the context of sport and physical activity.

One problem in this regard is that most of the instruments used to assess laterality do not cover the variety of motor skills that human beings are capable of performing. The majority of these tests focus heavily on handedness, and they have not been developed in relation to dynamic situations in natural contexts (Anguera 2005), such as sport or physical education. Similar concerns have been raised in the context of work currently being developed under the constraints-based approach to motor learning (Davids *et al.* 2008; Araújo *et al.* 2004).

Given the above the present case study describes how an instrument for recording laterality can have two versions, one in the traditional format of specific tests and the other a more dynamic version that is adapted to naturalistic educational settings.

Laterality and spatial orientation

Laterality is not merely a question of handedness, foot preference or sensory dominance (visual vs. auditory, etc.), but a process that develops in conjunction with the way in which our body uses and orients itself in space. Thus, the laterality of the body is a key factor in understanding both basic and specific motor skills because it also implies knowing the spatial variables that influence the development of motor behaviour (see upper part of Figure 4.5). Therefore, any assessment of laterality must consider not only which aspects of the body are dominant but also how the body orients itself in relation to space (Cote 2007).

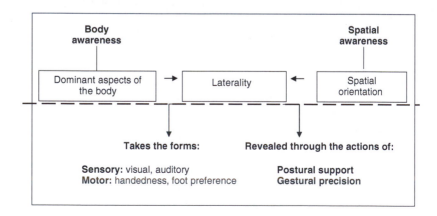

Figure 4.5 Laterality of the body.

Postural support and gestural precision

The performance of any motor skill involves the action of postural support by one body segment in parallel with the action of gestural precision by another segment. Postural support enables stasis and blocks movement, which allows the zone involved in gestural precision to execute the dynamics of the corresponding motor action. By way of an example, think of which leg you use when making a turn, or which leg you use to push off and jump at the same time as throwing a ball with your hand. The most complementary technique is to support the non-dominant segment so as to facilitate the most precise action in the dominant segment, for example, pivot over the left leg so as to shoot with the right foot.

This distinction between dominant and non-dominant body segments is, in our opinion, of key importance in relation to motor learning, and it has also been applied to handedness by Wang and Sainburg (2007), who note that the two arms are differentially specialized for complementary control processes. This aspect is often not taken into account, but it is precisely this which enables us to effectively perform a varied range of motor skills.

At all events, we believe that the various tests used to assess the laterality of different body zones pay insufficient attention to these zones of postural support and gestural precision (Castañer and Andueza 2008; see lower part of Figure 4.5).

Aims and the mixed methods approach: embedded design

In the field of sports science and physical education there is, in our view, a need for more detailed study of laterality in relation to the performance of both basic and specific motor skills. With this in mind the aim of this case study was to determine the lateral distribution of postural support and gestural precision in relation to locomotion, stability and manipulation skills (Gallahue and Cleland-Donnelly 2003). Laterality was first explored using the LATMO (Castañer and Andueza 2008), an instrument designed to record motor laterality. This provided an initial set of quantitative data (QUAN) that was then contrasted with qualitative data (QUAL) obtained from experts in physical education, who gave their opinions in the context of a discussion group. The purpose of this was to create an alternative and more dynamic version of the LATMO, with which new quantitative data could then be obtained. In terms of mixed methods this process corresponds to an *embedded design* (see chapter 1, Figure 1.6).

Instrument 1: Instrument for recording motor laterality (LATMO)

The structure of the recording instrument (Castañer and Andueza 2008) is shown in Table 4.2.

Participants

Forty-seven athletes, all students from the Advanced Institute of Physical Education (INEFC) at the University of Lleida (Spain), took part in the experiment. Of these, 12 were female and 35 were male (mean age 20.1 years, range 18–22 years).

Table 4.2 Structure of the recording instrument LATMO (adapted from Castañer and Andueza 2009)

AGE					
GENDER	Female				
	Male				
STANDARD TESTS	Feet		R	L	A
	Hands		R	L	A
BASIC	STABILITY	Getting up	R	L	A
MOTOR	LOCOMOTION	Pointing	R	L	A
SKILLS	MANIPULATION	Grasping	R	L	A
SPECIFIC	STABILITY	Axial	R	L	A
MOTOR	LOCOMOTION	Support	R	L	A
SKILLS	MANIPULATION	Propulsion	R	L	A
		Regaining balance	R	L	A
		Directing	R	L	A
		Impact	R	L	A

Procedure

We first assessed the handedness of participants using the Edinburgh Handedness Inventory (Oldfield 1971), to which we added three items designed to provide further information about motor laterality (one item for hands: throwing an object at goal; and two items for feet: kicking an object against an obstacle and dribbling a ball over a distance of 5 m (see Tables 4.3 and 4.4). The majority of participants were right-handed (mean laterality quotient = 89) and right-footed (mean laterality quotient = 84). Participants then performed individually each of the tests (tasks) featured in the LATMO. This process was observed by two examiners.

Basic motor skills

A test of basic motor skills was developed for each of the three categories: stability, locomotion and manipulation (Gallahue and Cleland-Donnelly 2003). These were as follows:

- Stability test: action of *getting up*. The observer records the body zone against which the subject leans or supports him/herself when getting up from a seated position on the floor.
- Locomotion test: action of *pointing* with the foot.[1] The observer records the lower extremity which is used to indicate an object towards which the subject then moves.
- Manipulation test: action of *grasping*. The observer records the hand which is used to grasp a ring, the surface of which requires a more specific grasping action than do many other objects.

Specific motor skills

Specific motor skills involve a consolidated and personal execution of the basic skills of locomotion, stability and manipulation, and are adapted here from the observation instrument OSMOS (Castañer *et al.* 2009) that was described in the first case study of this chapter. There were two tests for each of the three skills categories.

Specific stability skills:

> *Axial*: performing a turn by pivoting around one leg. The observer records the direction towards which the body turns and the leg used as support during the turn.

> *Support*: the observer records the foot that acts as the support when the subject has to keep his/her balance on a gym bench.

Specific locomotion skills:

> *Propulsion*: the observer records the side chosen by the subject to go round an obstacle.

> *Regaining balance*: the observer records the leading foot used when jumping over a hurdle.

Specific manipulation skills:

> *Directing*: the observer records the foot used to dribble a ball, and also that used to flip over an inverted cone (mushroom-shaped).

> *Impact*: the observer records the hand used to bounce a ball, and also that used to right an inverted cone (mushroom-shaped) with a single tap.

Results

All the results derived from application of the LATMO were processed using the statistical package PASW Statistics_18. The analysis revealed that in the standard tests of laterality most of the subjects showed a right-sided dominance, with almost no ambidexterity (see Table 4.3).

The two basic types of motor laterality (hands and feet) were significantly correlated with one another (see Table 4.4).

There were also significant correlations between the laterality tests (hands and feet), the test of basic locomotion skills (pointing with the foot) and the two tests of specific manipulation skills (dribbling with the foot and impact with the hand) (see Table 4.5).

Table 4.3 Description of the sample according to laterality

Test	Sample (N)	Right-sided	Left-sided	Ambidexterity
Hands	47	42	5	0
Feet	47	37	9	1

Table 4.4 Significant correlations between the standard laterality tests

Laterality	Sample (N)	Correlation (Pearson)	Two-tailed significance
Hands/feet	47	0.303*	0.038

Note: * Correlation significant at $p<0.05$ (two-tailed).

Table 4.5 Correlations obtained between the laterality tests, the test of basic locomotion skills and the two tests of specific manipulation skills

		Hands	Feet	Pointing	Directing	Impact
Hands	Pearson coefficient	1	.303*	.364*	.261	.553**
	Sig. (two-tailed)		.038	.012	.077	.000
	N	47	47	47	47	47
Feet	Pearson coefficient	.303*	1	.359*	.919**	.536**
	Sig. (two-tailed)	.038		.013	.000	.000
	N	47	47	47	47	47
Pointing	Pearson coefficient	.364*	.359*	1	.290*	.352*
	Sig. (two-tailed)	.012	.013		.048	.015
	N	47	47	47	47	47
Directing	Pearson coefficient	.261	.919**	.290*	1	.576**
	Sig. (two-tailed)	.077	.000	.048		.000
	N	47	47	47	47	47
Impact	Pearson coefficient	.553**	.536**	.352*	.576**	1
	Sig. (two-tailed)	.000	.000	.015	.000	
	N	47	47	47	47	47

Note: * Correlation significant at $p<0.05$ (two-tailed); ** Correlation significant at $p<0.01$ (two-tailed).

Table 4.6 shows the significant correlations for specific stability skills. The analysis revealed that these skills were inversely related to manipulation skills (directing and impact).

Instrument 2: Discussion group

The second instrument used in the embedded design was a discussion group involving experts in physical education. The aim here was to use the experts' opinions regarding each of the tests in the original LATMO to create an alternative version of the instrument, one comprising inter-related and dynamic tests. This second version of the LATMO would then be applied to a different sample to obtain a new set of quantitative data about motor laterality.

Table 4.6 Correlations between the tests of specific stability skills and those of manipulation

		Correlations			
		Axial	*Support*	*Directing*	*Impact*
Axial	Pearson coeff.	1	.386**	−.221	−.424**
	Sig. (2-tailed)		.007	.136	.003
	N	47	47	47	47
Support	Pearson coeff.	.386**	1	−.131	−.189
	Sig. (2-tailed)	.007		.379	.204
	N	47	47	47	47
Directing	Pearson coeff.	−.221	−.131	1	.377**
	Sig. (2-tailed)	.136	.379		.009
	N	47	47	47	47
Impact	Pearson coeff.	−.424**	−.189	.377**	1
	Sig. (2-tailed)	.003	.204	.009	
	N	47	47	47	47

Note: ** Correlation is significant at $p < 0.01$ (two-tailed).

Participants

Two physical education teachers with between 10 and 14 years of professional experience took part in a discussion group chaired by an expert in physical education methods. The two participants were chosen according to the following criteria: (a) having between 10 and 14 years of experience; (b) being employed in state schools; and (c) being representative of the region, since each teacher gave classes in a different area of a medium-sized city (100,000 inhabitants), which was itself considered to be representative.

The aim of the group was to discuss each of the tests included in the original LATMO and to create a new version of the instrument that would comprise dynamic and inter-related (rather than separate) tests of laterality. The idea behind this was to find a way of going beyond 'test' situations in which pupils often sense they are being observed or feel they are performing abstract motor actions that have no real meaning for them. This idea is consistent with Dewey's claim that for the evaluation of human experience one should not consider individual objects, but rather 'situations'.

Procedure

In the first two group sessions the experts achieved the following:

a)   They described different types of motor situations that included three options for each of the three skills categories: locomotion, stability and manipulation.
b)   They drew up a table that included a detailed description of all these situations, along with their advantages and disadvantages.
c)   These situations were then tested in the context of real physical education classes in order to determine which aspects were valid and which could be rejected, thereby generating the definitive list.

A third session was then held in order to select, on the basis of the applicability and coherence of each motor situation, those which were best suited to assessing motor laterality in educational settings.

Results

The outcome of the discussion group was the creation of the Dynamic-LATMO, which became the third instrument to be used in this case study.

Instrument 3: Dynamic-LATMO

The tests included in the Dynamic-LATMO as a result of the discussion group are listed in Table 4.7 and illustrated in Figure 4.6.

Table 4.7 The Dynamic-LATMO, showing the coding of the segments that perform the precision action: (H): hand; (F): foot

Situation	Description	Motor skill	Aspect to be assessed	Left	Right
1	Walking forwards towards the teacher who acts as an obstacle	Sequential locomotion	Foot that takes the first step (F)	☐	☐
2	Dodging the teacher, who immediately follows the pupil	Locomotion: propulsion	Side chosen to go round the obstacle (F)	☐	☐
3	Stepping up onto a gym bench	Stability: support	Foot used to step up onto the bench (F)	☐	☐
4	Standing on one leg on the gym bench	Stability: support	Foot that is lifted (F)	☐	☐
5	With one hand on the bench, swinging both legs together from one side of the bench to the other	Stability: support	Hand used for support (H)	☐	☐
6	Controlled vertical jump in order to touch a hanging ball and make it fall	Manipulation: impact	Hand that touches the ball (H)	☐	☐
7	Picking a ball up off the floor	Manipulation: directing	Hand used to pick up the ball (H)	☐	☐
8	Bouncing a large ball and throwing it	Manipulation: directing	Hand used to bounce the ball (H)	☐	☐
9	Catching a ball and then throwing it	Manipulation: directing	Hand used to throw the ball after catching it (H)	☐	☐
10	Placing a ball on the floor and kicking it against a large obstacle	Manipulation: directing	Foot used for kicking (F)	☐	☐

Figure 4.6 Illustration of the ten actions described in the Dynamic-LATMO.

Participants

In order to test the utility of the Dynamic-LATMO it was applied to 47 schoolchildren (14 girls and 33 boys) aged between six and eight years old, this being the developmental period in which laterality is harmonized (Bala *et al.* 2010).

Procedure

The researcher who originally applied the standard LATMO to the athletes now applied the dynamic version of the instrument to the schoolchildren, in this case during a physical education class. The inter-related and dynamic structure of the various tests acts as a kind of 'motor circuit', and enables the observer to record the laterality of the children's performance for each task.

Results

Correlational analysis

There were significant correlations between the specific motor skills involving the feet, i.e. locomotion (set off, dodge), stability (stand on one leg, step up) and manipulation (kick) (see Table 4.8).

Table 4.9 shows that there were also significant correlations between specific motor skills involving the hands, i.e. stability (support and touch) and manipulation (pick up, bounce and throw) (see Table 4.9).

Cluster analysis

A cluster analysis was then performed. As regards tasks involving the feet the largest cluster (3) indicates the tendency for children to use their right foot when performing these tasks (see Table 4.10).

Table 4.8 Significant correlations between the tests of specific motor skills involving the feet

		Set off	Dodge	Stand on one leg	Step up	Kick
Set off	Pearson coeff.	1	.652**	.370*	.139	.301*
	Sig. (two-tailed)		.000	.010	.350	.039
	N	47	47	47	47	47
Dodge	Pearson coeff.	.652**	1	.265	.319*	.305*
	Sig. (two-tailed)	.000		.072	.029	.037
	N	47	47	47	47	47
Stand on one leg	Pearson coeff.	.370*	.265	1	.151	.357*
	Sig. (two-tailed)	.010	.072		.310	.014
	N	47	47	47	47	47
Step up	Pearson coeff.	.139	.319*	.151	1	.419**
	Sig. (two-tailed)	.350	.029	.310		.003
	N	47	47	47	47	47
Kick	Pearson coeff.	.301*	.305*	.357*	.419**	1
	Sig. (two-tailed)	.039	.037	.014	.003	
	N	47	47	47	47	47

* The correlation is significant at $p < 0.05$ (two-tailed).
** The correlation is significant at $p < 0.01$ (two-tailed).

Table 4.9 Significant correlations between specific motor skills involving the hands

		Pick up	Touch	Support	Bounce	Throw
Pick up	Pearson coeff.	1	.507**	.342*	.398**	.413**
	Sig. (two-tailed)		.000	.019	.006	.004
	N	47	47	47	47	47
Touch	Pearson coeff.	.507**	1	.531**	.376**	.389**
	Sig. (two-tailed)	.000		.000	.009	.007
	N	47	47	47	47	47
Support	Pearson coeff.	.342*	.531**	1	.532**	.422**
	Sig. (two-tailed)	.019	.000		.000	.003
	N	47	47	47	47	47
Bounce	Pearson coeff.	.398**	.376**	.532**	1	.675**
	Sig. (two-tailed)	.006	.009	.000		.000
	N	47	47	47	47	47
Throw	Pearson coeff.	.413**	.389**	.422**	.675**	1
	Sig. (two-tailed)	.004	.007	.003	.000	
	N	47	47	47	47	47

* The correlation is significant at $p < 0.05$ (two-tailed).
** The correlation is significant at $p < 0.01$ (two-tailed).

As regards tasks involving the hands the largest cluster (5) indicates the tendency for children to use their right hand when performing these tasks (see Table 4.11).

Discussion

The teaching of physical activity and sport usually reveals the same pattern of right-sided performance for both basic and specific motor skills. This laterality,

Table 4.10 Final cluster centres

	Cluster				
	1	*2*	*3*	*4*	*5*
Set off	0	1	0	2	0
Dodge	1	2	0	2	1
Stand on one leg	1	1	0	0	0
Step up	2	2	0	0	1
Kick	0	1	0	0	0
N (47)	8	7	21	7	4

Table 4.11 Final cluster centres

	Cluster				
	1	*2*	*3*	*4*	*5*
Pick up	2	2	1	2	0
Jump	0	1	1	2	0
Support	0	1	1	2	0
Bounce	0	1	1	0	0
Throw	0	2	1	0	0
N (47)	7	2	7	1	30

which has always been demonstrated by specialized tests (Oldfield 1971; Rigal 1992), was also observed when applying the LATMO recording instrument (Castañer and Andueza 2008). Indeed, the correlational and cluster analyses showed a predominance of right-sided performance for the motor tasks involving both hands and feet.

Specific stability skills were found to be inversely proportional to those involving manipulation (Table 4.6), which not only confirms the complementary relationship between them but also lends support to our original view of synergistic motor laterality, in which the precision of one body segment is subordinate to the support provided by a contralateral one. This should be interpreted as reflecting the optimum relationship for the performance of motor skills, whether in sport or everyday life. Indeed, problems will arise in the preparatory or performance stages of any motor skill if there is no contralateral combination of gestural precision and postural support.

The instruments applied here revealed a low rate of ambidexterity. At all events, it should be remembered that at certain developmental stages, as in the case of the schoolchildren who were at the stage of laterality harmonization (Bala *et al.* 2010), what appears to be ambidexterity may in fact be an as yet undefined laterality. Therefore, it is advisable to avoid basing any conclusions on recordings of unclear or ambiguous combinations between the gestural precision of one segment and the postural support offered by a contralateral one; rather the focus should be on motor situations that encourage well-defined laterality and a clear combination of support and precision.

The tests that comprise the Dynamic-LATMO were organized according to the body segment to be observed, i.e. hands or feet. The correlational analyses revealed significant correlations between most of the tasks used in each case. For feet: set off, dodge, stand on one leg and step up (Table 4.8); and for hands: pick up, touch, support, bounce and throw (Table 4.9). More importantly, perhaps, the fact that attention is focused on the body segment involved in performing a given action means that fewer observations are required, thereby making the instrument easy to apply in natural contexts.

Conclusions

This case study demonstrates that the performance of basic and specific motor skills requires an optimum contralateral combination between the postural support offered by the non-dominant body segment and the gestural precision of the dominant one. This has been revealed using two versions of the same recording instrument, whose tests can be readily adapted to natural contexts such as those involving schoolchildren. Both versions of the recording instrument confirm that postural support is achieved through stability skills, which favours the emergence of gestural precision by means of locomotion and manipulation skills.

In the context of physical education and sport there is a need for an exhaustive analysis of motor laterality and this should seek to address the following objectives:

- To identify correctly the way in which postural support and gestural precision are combined in the motor laterality of each individual.
- To maintain optimum lateralization when performing each motor skill.
- To achieve the maximum degree of motor efficacy in the dominant segments.
- To encourage the motor training of the non-dominant segments and the adequate combination of postural support and gestural precision.
- To avoid favouring mimetic or stereotypical forms of laterality.
- To promote a degree of ambidexterity that would enable greater autonomy and versatility across the whole range of motor behaviour.

The precision of every movement has its basis in stability (Warren 2006; Araújo *et al.* 2004). Indeed, if the body is not stable then motor behaviour becomes less precise. This is confirmed by the present analysis, which showed that stability skills were significantly correlated with one another, and inversely related to the manipulation skills that require the precise movement of body segments. We further believe, however, that our findings complement also the principles of nonlinear pedagogy and the work currently being carried out under the constraints-based approach to motor learning (Davids *et al.* 2008; Araújo *et al.* 2004) in relation to how children and adults acquire movement skills, and where it is argued that behaviours emerge from a system, 'exemplified by small skips, jumps and regressions in motor learning' (Davids 2010: 3).

At all events, the specific contribution of this case study is to illustrate how precision and support complement one another in order to optimize the laterality of each motor action, the result of this being what could be called a 'lateral synergy' in motor behaviour. This aspect needs to be taken into account and optimized in any process that is designed to teach physical and sporting activities.

Acknowledgements

We gratefully acknowledge the support of the Spanish government project *Avances tecnológicos y metodológicos en la automatización de estudios observacionales en deporte* (Dirección General de Investigación, Ministerio de Ciencia e Innovación) [Grant number PSI2008-01179]. We also gratefully acknowledge the support of the Generalitat de Catalunya government project GRUP DE RECERCA E INNOVACIÓ EN DISSENYS (GRID). Tecnología i aplicació multimedia i digital als dissenys observacionals, Departament d'Innovació, Universitats i Empresa, Generalitat de Catalunya [Grant number 2009 SGR 829]. We are also grateful to the parkour experts for providing the empirical material to be observed and for agreeing to take part in the guided interviews (Case Study 4.1). Thanks are also due to the expert instructors who participated in the theoretical discussion group and the practical transformation of the recording instrument (Case Study 4.2).

Note

1 The action of pointing is a deictic gesture that is usually associated with the upper extremities and is one of the earliest emblematic gestures to have evolved, it being directly linked to the freeing up of the hands in the first hominids. Here it is applied to the lower extremities in order to identify which leg is associated with support and which with precision. If, by contrast, the task for the individual was to walk, then the starting leg could easily vary as the alternating action of walking is highly symmetrical.

References

Anguera, M.T. (2005). Microanalysis of T-patterns: Analysis of symmetry/asymmetry in social interaction. In L. Anolli, S. Duncan, M. Magnusson and G. Riva (eds), *The hidden structure of social interaction. From Genomics to Culture Patterns* (pp. 51–70). Amsterdam: IOS Press.

Araújo, D., Davids, K., Bennett, S., Button, C., and Chapman, G. (2004). Emergence of sport skills under constraints. In A.M. Williams and N.J. Hodges (eds), *Skill acquisition in sport: Research, theory and practice* (pp. 409–434). London: Routledge.

Atkinson, M. (2009). Parkour, anarcho-environmentalism and poiesis. *Journal of Sport and Social Issues*, *33* (2), 169–194.

Bala, G., Golubovic, S., and Katic, R (2010). Relations between handedness and motor abilities in preschool children. *Collegium Antropologicum 34*, 69–75.

Bavinton, N. (2007). From obstacle to opportunity: Parkour, leisure, and the reinterpretation of constraints. *Annals of Leisure Research*, *10*, 3–4.

Brunner, C. (2010). Nice-looking obstacles: Parkour as urban practice of deterritorialization. *AI and Society*, *21*, 1–10.

Castañer, M. and Andueza, J. (2008). Valorar la precisión gestual y la fijación postural en la práctica deportiva mediante un instrumento de observación de la lateralidad motriz LATMO. *Apunts*, *92*, 35–45.

Castañer, M., and Camerino, O. (2006). *Manifestaciones básicas de la motricidad*. Lleida: Publicacions de la Universitat de Lleida.

Castañer, M., Camerino, O., Parés, N. and Landry, P. (2011). Fostering body movement in children through an exertion interface as an educational tool. *Procedia – Social and Behavioral Sciences*, *28* 216–240.

Castañer, M., Torrents, C., Anguera, M.T., Dinušová, M., and Jonsson, G.M. (2009). Identifying and analyzing motor skill responses in body movement and dance. *Behavior Research Methods*, *41* (3), 857–867.

Cote, P. (2007). *Bilateral transfer of motor skills in dance*. Reston, VA: American Alliance for Health, Physical Education and Recreation.

Daprati, E. and Sirigu, A. (2002). Laterality effects on motor awareness *Neuropsychologia*, *40* (8), 1379–1386.

Daskalaki, M., Stara, A. and Imas, M. (2008). The 'Parkour Organisation': inhabitation of corporate spaces. *Culture and Organization*, *14* (1), 49–64.

Davids, K. (2010). The constraints-based approach to motor learning. In I. Renshaw, K. Davids and G.J.P. Savelsbergh. (eds), *Motor learning in practice* (pp. 3–16). London: Routledge.

Davids, K., Button, C. and Bennett, S.J. (2008). Dynamics of skill acquisition: A constraints led approach. Champaign, IL: Human Kinetics.

Feireiss, L. (2007). Urban free flow: the individual as an active performer. In V.F. Borries, S.P Walz and M.Böttiger (eds), *Space time play: Computer games, architecture and urbanism – the next level* (pp. 280–281). Basel: Birkhäuser.

Gallahue, D. (1987). *Development of physical education for today's elementary school children*. New York: Macmillan.

Gallahue, D. and Cleland-Donnelly, F. (2003). *Development of physical education for all children*. Toronto: Human Kinetics.

Gibbs, R. (2006). *Embodiment and cognitive science*. Cambridge, UK: Cambridge University Press.

Gibson, J.J. (1979). *The ecological approach to visual perception*. Boston: Houghton Mifflin.

Haaland, K.Y. and Harrington, D.L. (1996). Clinical implications of ipsilateral motor deficits after unilateral hemispheric damage. In A. Bruno, F. Chollet, B.J. Vellas and J.L. Albarede (eds), *Facts and research in gerontology: Stroke in the elderly* (pp. 101–114). New York: Springer.

Johnson, M. (2007). *The meaning of the body: Aesthetics of human understanding*. Chicago and London: University of Chicago Press.

Magnusson, M.S. (2005). Understanding social interaction: Discovering hidden structure with model and algorithms. In L. Anolli, S. Duncan, M. Magnusson and G. Riva (eds), *The hidden structure of social interaction: From genomics to culture patterns* (pp. 51–70). Amsterdam: IOS Press.

Oldfield, R.C. (1971). The assessment and analysis of handedness: The Edinburgh inventory. *Neuropsychologia*, *9*, 97–113.

Provins, K.A. (1997). The specificity of motor skill and manual asymmetry: A review of the evidence and its implications. *Journal of Motor Behavior, 29* (2), 183–192.

Rigal, R.A. (1992). Which handedness: Preference or performance? *Perceptual and Motor Skills*, *75*, 851–866.

Savelsbergh, G., Davids, K., van der Kamp, J., and Bennett, S. J. (2003). Theoretical perspectives on the development of movement co-ordination in children. In G. Savelsbergh, K. Davids, J. van der Kamp and S. J. Bennett (eds), *Development of movement co-ordination in children: Applications in the fields of ergonomics, health sciences and sport* (pp. 1–14). London: Routledge.

Saville, S.J. (2008). Playing with fear: Parkour and the mobility of emotion. *Social and Cultural Geography, 9* (8), 891–914.

Spinoza, B. (1992). *The ethics.* Indianapolis: Hackett.

Torrents, C., Castañer, M., Dinušová, M., and Anguera, M.T. (2010). Discovering new ways of moving: Observational analysis of motor creativity while dancing contact improvisation and the influence of the partner. *Journal of Creative Behavior, 44*(1), 45–62.

Wang, J.S. and Sainburg, R.L. (2007). The dominant and non-dominant arms are specialized for stabilizing different features of task performance. *Experimental Brain Research, 178* (4), 565–570.

Warren, W. (2006). The dynamics of perception and action. *Psychological Review, 113*, 358–389.

5 Appraising choreographic creativity, aesthetics and the complexity of motor responses in dance

---

- Case Study 5.1: How to analyse dance choreographies: an illustration through contemporary works of Pina Bausch and Maurice Béjart
  Marta Castañer

- Case Study 5.2: A study of motor creativity when dancing contact improvisation
  Carlota Torrents and Marta Castañer

- Case Study 5.3: The aesthetic appraisal of contemporary dance using a motion capture system
  Marta Castañer, Carlota Torrents, Gaspar Morey and Toni Jofre

---

Like the physical and aural materials used by artists and musicians, body gestures and creative movement constitute an expressive language that human beings use to project themselves symbolically through art. Furthermore, when the body is the protagonist its vast range of expression paves the way for a multiplicity of aesthetic resources and creative possibilities.

In contemporary society there is an increasing emphasis on the visual and the idea of spectacle that surrounds not only sporting events but also other activities involving the moving body, such as dance. Unlike sport, however, which is universally understood within the same parameters, dance, as a cultural manifestation, is not a universal language. This cultural specificity of dance derives from the fact that it is both an expression and an emotion; it is not merely an action in the broadest sense.

This chapter presents three examples of research that uses mixed methods in relation to dance. Specific observation systems, semantic differentials, body motion capture and interviews are used in the context of mixed method designs capable of analysing professional choreographic works, contact dance improvisation and contemporary dance.

CASE STUDY 5.1: HOW TO ANALYSE DANCE CHOREOGRAPHIES: AN ILLUSTRATION THROUGH CONTEMPORARY WORKS OF PINA BAUSCH AND MAURICE BÉJART

Introduction

All dance choreography reveals the co-existence of bodies which are inscribed and, at the same time, described in space. As such it is a singular visual experience, like a painting in continuous motion that encapsulates the two dimensions of space and time. Yet any choreographic production can be observed not only from the theatre stalls as something ephemeral, through the successive appearance and disappearance of bodies, but also in a scientific and objective way as a block of text that offers an exhaustive and lasting description of the narrative written by bodies in movement (Castañer 2006). In this regard it is worth recalling that the artistic choreographic projects of Merce Cunningham drew upon the innovations provided by software designed to capture movement.

It is said, however, that the essence of dance is lost if we try to code it in the same way as is done with spoken language. Furthermore, it has been argued that what dance lacks is a discrete unit akin to the syntactic element of generative grammar (Metz 1977). In contrast to this view, the present case study seeks to demonstrate that dance and motor activity in general do contain meaningful discrete units that are referred to by infinitive verbs (to jump, to turn, etc.), and which describe the various actions that the body is capable of performing. However, it is important, especially in the context of dance, to take a more systemic view and consider how these individual units become interwoven with one another.

Observing dance

The body's movement has to be seen as a structure rather than in terms of isolated units, which themselves have no meaning. As in every discourse, meaning is conferred not by indivisible units but, rather, by relationships and reciprocal connections. In the context of dance this idea is exemplified by Labanotation, the system of analysing and recording human movement developed by Rudolf von Laban, or the work of Pavis (1996), who argues that a performance must not be split up in order to study it. More recently, my colleagues and I have sought to develop ad hoc instruments for observing dance and body language, all of which are based on observational methodology and specific software that enables us to conduct sequential and concurrent studies of dance forms (Castañer *et al.* 2009; Torrents *et al.* 2010). As a result we have been able to observe the kinesics of body language in an objective and exhaustive way in naturalistic contexts. This has also allowed us to carry out 'trans-temporal' or asynchronous analyses in relation to the body's morphokinesis (Serre 1984), although more qualitative instruments and studies are needed in order to recreate the context in which this morphokinesis is generated.

Dance as a language

If we consider kinesics as analogous to linguistics then the starting point would be to think that just as speech is generated through the combination of basic units known as morphemes, body movement can also be understood in terms of the combination of basic observable units or *kinemes*. The implication of this is that human gestures can be broken down or atomized by making semantic distinctions between our movements, such that 'shaking hands' or 'folding one's arms' correspond to kinemes, the basic units of our kinesic system that are equivalent to the phonemes of spoken language. This kind of analogy has a precedent in the work of Levi-Strauss, who used the idea of a language triangle to compare the dimensions of language, myth and music (see Figure 5.1):

> In music you have the equivalent to phonemes and the equivalent to sentences, but you don't have the equivalent to words. In myth you have an equivalent to words, an equivalent to sentences, but you have no equivalent to phonemes. So there is, in both cases, one level missing.
>
> (Levi-Strauss 1978: 75)

These ideas can be used to sketch out an understanding of the motor activity that is articulated through body language. Following the analogy the basic unit (in this case, of movement) would be the kineme, while the equivalent to words would be observable motor skills or actions to which meaning is ascribed (Castañer 2001; Castañer *et al.* in press). The truncated point of the triangle is therefore equivalent to sentences (see Figure 5.2). Might kinesic patterns constitute the sentences of body movement?

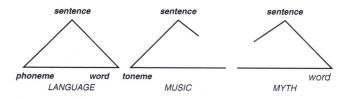

Figure 5.1 Linguistic triangle for comparing the dimensions of language and truncated triangles in relation to music and myth (Levi-Strauss 1978).

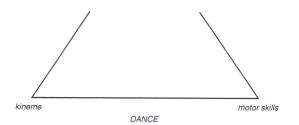

Figure 5.2 Interpretation of the truncated triangle for dance, developed here on the basis of Levi-Strauss' linguistic triangle.

At all events, the fact that the point of the triangle referring to sentences is the one that remains open serves to illustrate that essential aspect of dance which escapes linear and figurative narrative. Thus, rather than sentences in the linguistic sense what one finds in contemporary dance is more akin to a kaleidoscope of movement patterns. This is nowhere better illustrated than in the work of Pina Bausch and Maurice Béjart, and a choreography by each constitutes the material for the present case study.

Aims of the case study and the mixed methods approach: multilevel triangulation

At the beginning of the last century Rudolf von Laban (see Laban and Ullman 1963) developed an exhaustive system for coding movement that was akin to a musical score, although there remains a need for systematic observation and the coding of behaviour. With this in mind the present case study is based on a *multilevel triangulation* design (see Chapter 1, Figure 1.5) in which three instruments are used to move from a quantitative to a qualitative analysis, before obtaining further quantitative data via a specific observational system.

The analysis focuses on two key choreographic works by Pina Bausch and Maurice Béjart: *The Rite of Spring* and *Ravel's Boléro*, respectively. These two works of contemporary dance were chosen as they have several features in common:

- They were created by prestigious, contemporary choreographers of central European origin during the 1970s and 1980s.
- Both are based on classical music compositions and the choreography shares the title of the musical work.
- The two works chosen are among the most important of each choreographer, and they therefore continue to be performed in ways that are faithful to their creator.
- Both involve a similar and large number of dancers.
- Both choreographies use circular spatial formations involving all the dancers.

The aim of the case study is to appraise the specific motor components of each choreographic work and to reveal, therefore, the creative tendencies of the two choreographers.

Instrument 1: Semantic differential

The semantic differential (Osgood *et al.*1957) is a kind of rating scale anchored by bipolar adjectives, i.e. opposites of one another. Its purpose is to enable observers to indicate their appraisal of an event according to each pair of adjectives, which they do by placing a mark along the scale that joins the two (see Table 5.1). The semantic differential used in the present case study (see Table 5.2) is an adapted version of one previously employed to evaluate specific motor components (Castañer *et al.* 2007). As a result it is anchored not by adjectives but by pairs of motor components, the observer's task being to evaluate the extent to which each of these is present.

Table 5.1 General structure of the semantic differential tool

Adjective A	X				Adjective B
Adjective C			X		Adjective D
Adjective E		X			Adjective F
......				X	

Table 5.2 Semantic differential tool for specific motor components

Category	Component	Component
1	Movement from one place to another (locomotion)	Fixed (no locomotion)
2	Support stability	No support stability
3	Axial (turns)	No turns
4	Elevation (jumps)	No jumps
5	Manipulation	No manipulation
6	Anaerobic	Aerobic
7	Strength	Flexibility
8	Muscular potency	Joint slackness
9	Uses whole space	Uses partial space
10	Rhythmic	Arrhythmic

Participants and procedure

Three experts on contemporary dance applied the semantic differential in order to obtain the 'expert appraisal' for each category. The tool was then subsequently applied by twenty students from a degree course on Physical Activity and Sports Science (aged 19 to 22 years), none of whom had any experience of contemporary dance.

The reason for comparing the appraisals of dance experts and students is that the body is the instrument used by both dancers and athletes. Indeed, both dance and sport require a body that has the physical attributes of resistance, strength and potency, etc., and which can perform actions such as locomotion, stability, jumps and turns. However, although both disciplines make use of the athletic body (Shell 1984) this body is not necessarily evaluated or appreciated in the same way.

The task for both experts and students was to observe and appraise the two chosen choreographies: *Ravel's Boléro* by Maurice Béjart and *The Rite of Spring* by Pina Bausch. Obviously, the experts were familiar with these choreographies, whereas the students had never seen them before. Nevertheless, the students did have specific knowledge about the motor components and skills involved in physical activity and sport, and this equipped them for the task at hand.

In order to transform the qualitative appraisals into quantitative data the semantic differential for each pair of adjectives was divided into five cells; the assigned score ranging between +2 and −2 (see Table 5.3). The appraisals could thus be presented in the form of histograms.

Table 5.3 Scores corresponding to each point on the scale

+ Pole	+2	+1	0	−1	−2	− Pole

Results and discussion

The histograms derived from the appraisals of the two choreographic works are shown in Figures 5.3 and 5.4. Let us consider each of these in turn and compare the appraisals of experts and non-experts.

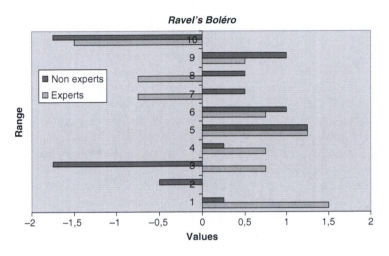

Figure 5.3 Results for *Ravel's Boléro*.

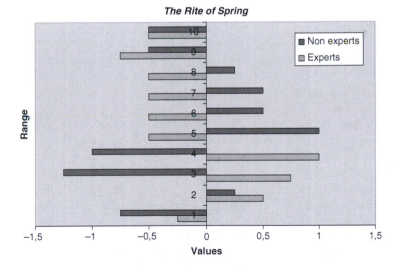

Figure 5.4 Results for *The Rite of Spring*.

Ravel's Boléro

Overall, the results show that the experts tended to agree in relation to all ten ranges of categories, whereas there was some variation among the appraisals of the students (non-experts).

1. As regards specific motor skills there was a notable difference between the appraisals of experts and non-experts. Whereas the former tended to consider that the *Boléro* contained very little locomotion, balancing skills, turns or jumps, the students' appraisals suggested a greater presence of these aspects. This is likely due to the fact that the students were interpreting what they saw in terms of their experience of sport and physical activity, whereas the experts have greater knowledge of what is possible in the world of choreography.
2. Aerobic capacity was appraised similarly by both experts and non-experts. This is consistent with the fact that aerobic capacity is a general physical and motor ability which both dancers and athletes would be able to recognize.
3. Experts were more likely to indicate strength, whereas non-experts tended towards flexibility. The experts would be aware that dancers use flexibility in combination with muscular strength, whereas the students, who are less familiar with dance, would likely be struck by the apparent flexibility required, in contrast to what is seen in sport.
4. As regards the use of space the appraisals of experts and non-experts were similar. This is consistent with the fact that in the choreography of *Ravel's Boléro* the chorus of dancers occupies the whole stage at all times.
5. Both experts and non-experts agreed on the arrhythmic quality of the choreography. Although Ravel's music follows a binary rhythm that builds to a crescendo the fact that some dancers move in a different tempo to others means that their movements appear to have this arrhythmic quality.

The Rite of Spring

Here there was general agreement among the experts, although less so than in the case of *Ravel's Boléro*. As before, the appraisals of non-experts showed some variations. The main results were as follows:

1. As regards specific motor skills the experts' appraisals once again tended towards the negative pole. The exception to this was stability skills, for which the appraisals of both experts and non-experts were slightly more towards the positive pole. This is likely because there are several points in the choreography when the dancers have to pause and remain still. Non-experts awarded a higher score to all the motor skills, a finding which can be interpreted in the same way as was done in relation to *Ravel's Boléro* (see point 1 above).
2. The appraisals differed as regards aerobic capacity. The experts tended to see the choreography as more anaerobic, whereas the students viewed it as being

more aerobic. It may be that the pauses in the choreography made the students think of stopping to get one's breath back, whereas the experts knew that the number and speed of the actions performed by the dancers implied anaerobic capacity.

3.   With respect to the relative presence of muscular strength and flexibility the appraisals differed as in the case of *Ravel's Boléro*, a finding that can be interpreted as previously (see point 3 above).

4.   In terms of the use of space the appraisals of experts and non-experts were similar, and they all agreed that the whole of the stage was used.

5.   The appraisals of rhythm were identical for experts and non-experts. There was a slight trend towards the arrhythmic due to the variations in rhythm used by certain groups of dancers, even though they all danced in unison at several points in the choreography.

Instrument 2: Content analysis of interviews with experts

Procedure

After completing the semantic differential the three experts were asked to give their professional opinion regarding which aspects they believed should be taken into account when appraising the two choreographic works. Their responses were then subjected to a content analysis, the results of which could be compared with those derived from the semantic differential and, as will be seen later, the motor skills patterns derived from the third instrument.

Results

For Ravel's Boléro

As regards the use of space the experts agreed that the emphasis was on a circular area in the centre of the stage, with the rest of the space having a secondary role:

> Despite the large number of dancers the space which is most used is that in the centre, whereas the surrounding space is more decorative, it is like a backdrop.
>
> (Expert 2)

They highlighted the reiterative use of certain motor actions, the absence of locomotion or movement from one place to another, and the specific use of iconic gestures in the form of emblems:

> The actions are very minimalist, they're reiterative, rebounding back and forth, and this gives a certain air of monotony, to which one must add the absence of locomotion.
>
> (Expert 2)

Their movements are very like gestures, almost like emblems, and it seems that what they're seeking is expressivity rather than more extreme dance moves like jumps, turns, regaining balance, etc.

(Expert 1)

The experts also noted that the choreography has a rhythmic quality of crescendo, which is obviously determined by Ravel's music, and this requires aerobic resistance on the part of the dancers:

It seems more aerobic because there's no locomotion, the gestures are very rhythmic, continuous, but without any great explosive quality. On a physical level it's more like running on a treadmill to a binary rhythm, one-two, one-two . . . slowly but building to a crescendo.

(Expert 3)

The Rite of Spring

The experts' impression here was that the dancers used all the stage, although this was contrasted with the use of specific areas at a given point in the choreography:

Here, like in *Ravel's Boléro*, there's a large chorus of dancers, but they use the whole of the stage in different combinations . . . so at times they're in a particular place but the overall impression is that they're using the whole stage.

(Expert 3)

As in the case of *Ravel's Boléro* they considered there to be repetitive actions, but here they highlighted the explosive quality and the presence of locomotion, the latter being almost non-existent in the *Boléro*:

Once again there are very minimalist actions, reiterative ones, rebounding back and forth, but in contrast to the *Boléro* these are combined with very explosive moments and there is a lot of locomotion and manipulation. There are also a small number of jumps and turns, and I think that Pina Bausch is trying to give the impression that there are many dancers using changes of rhythm and continuous movements from one place to another.

(Expert 1)

Unlike the *Boléro* this choreography includes asynchronous rhythms, pauses, canons and many changes of rhythm that surprise the observer:

The changes in rhythm are incredible, although this is encouraged by Stravinsky's music. Pina Bausch uses synchronous and asynchronous rhythms, and her use of the canon in movements gives the sensation of continuous variability.

(Expert 2)

It's very anaerobic, because they never stop . . . well, there are pauses of a few seconds but this is to give greater emphasis, and then it's back to the charge of continuous, explosive almost anarchic actions.

(Expert 3)

Instrument 3: OSMOS-Dance: observational system of motor skills specific to dance

One of the dangers when observing dance choreographies is trying to take into account too many criteria (types of gesture, geometries, movement trajectories, types of rhythm, etc.), as this can merely make the observational process overly complex and produce an unwieldy amount of data that leads to a fragmented choreographic analysis. Given this, and in order to obtain a useful category system for observing choreographic works, the observation instrument used here is an ad hoc version of the OSMOS tool described in Chapter 4 of this book (Castañer *et al.* 2009). This ad hoc version, the OSMOS-Dance, comprises five criteria and nineteen codes (see Table 5.4).

Procedure

The recording instrument used was THEMECODER (PatternVision 2001), an interactive video-coding software package that provides an effective recording of the time of occurrence of behavioural events. This enables the observer to indicate the motor skill category which corresponds to the type of variations seen in the motor actions performed by the participants, as well as the kind of variation that is produced in each situation. Data were collected by a single expert observer. The analysis of intra-observer reliability across the two applications of the OSMOS-Dance (one for each choreographic work) yielded a kappa coefficient of 0.94.

Temporal patterns (T-patterns) in the observational data were then detected and analysed by means of the THEME v.5 software (Magnusson 2005).

Results

The results focus on the most relevant T-pattern detected in each of the two choreographies, the aim being to illustrate their choreographic style and the main differences between them. The most notable finding when comparing the two is that the greater variability of choreographic formations used by Pina Bausch in *The Rite of Spring* (e.g. use of space, motor skills, different tempo, etc.) means that the only repeated patterns which emerge are two chains of events and three event types (see Figure 5.5). By contrast, the repetition of compositions, tempo, space and types of movement which Maurice Béjart resorts to when choreographing *Ravel's Boléro* produces patterns with more chains of events and more sequential event types (see Figure 5.6, which has five levels and six event types).

Table 5.4 THE OSMOS-Dance observation instrument

Criterion	Analytic category	Code	Description
Actor	Solo	Sol	A single dancer
Related to the	Dyad	Dy	Two dancers
number of dancers	Micro group	Mic	Group of dancers composed of more than two dancers but less than half the chorus
	Macro group	Mac	Group of dancers composed of at least
half the chorus	Combination of actors	CAC	Any combination of the categories in this criterion.
Static/pause	Static/pause	Pau	When all the dancers remain paused, without moving
Motor skills			
Broad movement patterns	Locomotion	Loc	Actions in which the body moves through space from one place to another
	Manipulation	Man	Actions involving the handling of objects or other dancers
	Stability	Sta	Actions without any spatial relocation and which include balancing, jumps and turns
	Motor skills combination	CMS	Any combination of the categories in this criterion
Topology			
Use of the stage	Central	Ce	Located in the central area of the stage
	Peripheral	Pe	Located at the periphery of the stage
	Point	Po	Located at a specific point of the stage (corners, central point, etc.)
	Whole	Wh	Use of the whole stage
	Topology combination	CTO	Any combination of the categories in this criterion
Tempo			
How dance movements are adapted to the music	Synchronous	Sy	When the dancers dance in unison in relation to a particular tempo
	Asynchronous	As	When the dancers don't dance in unison in relation to a particular tempo, but neither is it a canon
	Canon	Cn	When the dancers' actions are correlated with or sequential in relation to the tempo
	Tempo combination	CTE CTE	Any combination of the categories in this criterion

Discussion

Despite the above-mentioned commonalities between the two choreographies, the results obtained via the first two instruments reveal both a degree of agreement and a number of differences between the appraisals of expert and non-expert

(01) mic, cms, ce, sy:
group of dancers combine motor skills in synchrony

(02) cac, loc, wh, as:
various formations of dancers move throughout the stage asynchronously

(03) mac, pau, wh:
the whole group is paused while occupying the whole of the stage

Figure 5.5   This T-pattern relates to *The Rite of Spring* and shows that (01) the formation in micro-groups (mic) that perform various motor skills (cms) in a synchronous way (sy) and in the central area of the stage (ce) is followed by (02) various groupings (dyads, micro-groups, solos) which move from one place to another (loc) in an asynchronously way and use the whole of the space. This kind of choreographic arrangement is usually followed by a formation involving the whole group (mac), but paused (pau) and occupying the whole of the space (wh).

(student) observers. In the interviews the experts were able to provide further details regarding these points of convergence and divergence, thereby highlighting the value of the mixed methods approach. The results clearly show that the appraisals of the non-expert observers were closer to the positive pole on all the motor skills. Anaerobic capacity and the use of space were appraised similarly by both experts and non-experts, whereas the scores awarded for the category 'rhythm' differed due to the difficulty of clearly observing temporal and rhythmic features in space.

The third instrument, the OSMOS-Dance observation system, provided a final set of more objective data and further corroborates the use of the multilevel triangulation design.

Overall the results reveal how Béjart gives priority to the simultaneity of the gestural structures of all the dancers' bodies, as if they were one body. By contrast, Bausch only resorts to this at specific moments, when emphasis is required, and instead gives priority to gestural structures in the form of a canon, with which she obtains a harmony of gestures among the bodies of the different dancers. The same aspect can also be seen in the choral parts of other choreographies by both Béjart and Bausch, which always offer the spectator that magical extra, the gregariousness and social synchrony of human beings.

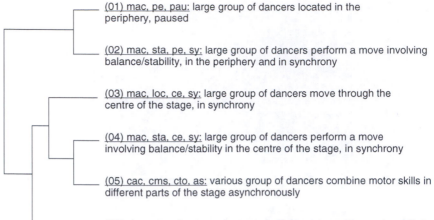

(01) mac, pe, pau: large group of dancers located in the periphery, paused

(02) mac, sta, pe, sy: large group of dancers perform a move involving balance/stability, in the periphery and in synchrony

(03) mac, loc, ce, sy: large group of dancers move through the centre of the stage, in synchrony

(04) mac, sta, ce, sy: large group of dancers perform a move involving balance/stability in the centre of the stage, in synchrony

(05) cac, cms, cto, as: various group of dancers combine motor skills in different parts of the stage asynchronously

(06) cac, cms, cto, sy: various group of dancers combine motor skills in different parts of the stage and in synchrony

Figure 5.6 This T-pattern relates to the large group (but not the soloist) in *Ravel's Boléro* and shows that (01) the formation as a large group (mac) moves (loc) through the periphery (pe) in a synchronous way (sy), and then (02) the dancers perform a stability action (sta) in the periphery (pe) and in synchrony (sy). In (03) and (04) they then repeat (01) and (02), the only difference being that they are now in the central area of the stage (ce). (05) and (06) show how various formations (cac) (micro-groups and dyads) perform different motor skills in various parts of the space, initially asynchronously (as) and then in synchrony (sy).

Conclusion

The results derived from this case study can also be described in a language closer to that which is habitually used in the field of contemporary dance. Maurice Béjart's choreography of *Ravel's Boléro* is made powerful through his use of stage space, and specifically through the centrality and height of the large platform – akin to an altar – upon which a single dancer dances. As the music builds to a crescendo a large chorus is then formed as the remaining dancers progressively appear and perform increasingly accentuated and vigorous movements in a circle around this central platform. I believe that the results obtained are consistent with the interpretations which any spectator might make of this work, and which one of the expert observers described in more metaphorical terms as follows: 'Béjart uses the platform like an altar within a ritual, an altar which attracts ever increasing numbers of dancers who eventually, as the climactic chord of Ravel's music sounds, prostrate themselves before it'.

As for *The Rite of Spring*, Pina Bausch evokes bodies that move vigorously on the stage, obliging the spectator to look in various directions rather than focusing on the central area. Motor actions and gestures are replicated and, at the same time, multiply. This is a composition that offers a new motor discourse, one that is highly dynamic and which, since it was first staged in the 1970s, encourages each generation to reflect and ask new questions. As one of the expert observers said:

> Every time I see this work it is like an accordion that surprises me with its enormous range . . . both its physical extension when opened and the sounds it is capable of producing. Its folds and sounds seem to have no end.

In conclusion, the multilevel mixed methods approach used in this case study demonstrates that it is possible to reveal the defining features of a choreographic work in a more objective way, although this in no way undermines the potential value of other interpretations of these or other dance masterpieces.

CASE STUDY 5.2: A STUDY OF MOTOR CREATIVITY WHEN DANCING CONTACT IMPROVISATION

Introduction

Contact improvisation is a form of contemporary dance that can be defined as a movement form that is improvisational in nature and which involves two bodies in contact (Sidall 1997). For people who are not used to the language of dance this discipline can be surprising, as there is no defined choreography to follow and the aim is to improvise all the time, even when performing before an audience. Contact improvisation was created by Steve Paxton, who defined it as a spontaneous mutual investigation of the energy and inertia paths created when two people engage actively and dance freely, using their sensitivity to guide and safeguard one another (Paxton 1997).

The improvisational characteristics of contact improvisation are such that the generation of movements is not based on fixed and standardized movements or techniques, since this dance form requires a body that responds to the physical exchange of weight and contact (Albright 2003; Novack 1990). As a result, the motor skills that appear during contact improvisation are not foreseeable and are constantly changing, and it is this that provokes the constant use of dancers' motor creativity. The latter can be defined as the combination of perceptions into new motor patterns (Wyrick 1968). However, although the motor skills or movements that emerge when dancing contact improvisation are not pre-defined they can be classified. In a previous study using observational methodology we did just this and investigated whether dancing with a partner could enhance motor creativity compared with dancing alone (Torrents *et al.* 2010). The results showed that during duets, dancers did not repeat any sequence of movements, whereas a number of temporal patterns were detected during their solos.

Aims of the case study and the mixed methods design: triangulation

Although the above-mentioned study enabled us to analyse the different movements produced by the dancers, we could not evaluate the originality of these movements, as this is a more subjective aspect. Indeed, a qualitative tool is needed to study the dancers' own perceptions regarding their creativity. The use of mixed methods, combining observational methodology with interviews, could therefore help to enrich these previous results and enable new conclusions to be drawn. In this case study, therefore, we apply an observational instrument to video recordings of contact improvisation dance, and follow this up with interviews with the dancers involved. The specific design used is triangulation (see Chapter 1, Figure 1.1).

Instrument 1: Observational system

As in the previous case study of this chapter the observational system used here is an adaptation of the Observational System of Motor Skills (OSMOS; Castañer *et al.* 2009; Torrents *et al.* 2010) (see Table 5.5).

Participants and procedure

Three dancers, all with experience in contact improvisation, participated voluntarily in the study. Participant 1 was female, while participants 2 and 3 were male.

The participants warmed up individually and danced alone for five minutes, the instruction being to employ the language of contact improvisation and use only their body and the floor to dance in a limited space measuring 10 m × 10 m. Afterwards each participant had to dance with the other two dancers in duets. As before, each duet had to dance for five minutes in the same limited space. The dancers were allowed a break of at least five minutes between the three dance sessions. None of the participants observed the performance of the others, thus preventing them from being influenced by their style or movements.

The three solos and the three duets were video-recorded and the resulting images were analysed by three observers, all experts in dance, using the adapted OSMOS system. In this observation, the duets were analysed by taking into account the motor skills performed by each of the two dancers, resulting in six duet sessions to analyse. For each of these six duets and the three solos we recorded the number of times each motor skill occurred, as well as the number of occurrences of each category independently of the other categories (see Table 5.6). An analysis of temporal patterns (T-patterns) was also performed for all the sessions and for each dancer, both individually and by grouping the solos and the duets.

Table 5.5 Adaptation of OSMOS for analysing contact improvisation (Torrents *et al.* 2010)

Criteria	Categories
Support stability skills with the floor: Actions of stability or balance using the floor that can be supported by any part of the body	Over arms or hands: Actions of stability or balance supported by the arms or hands Over legs or feet: Actions of stability or balance supported by the legs or feet. For instance, if the dancer is standing on one or two feet Over head or head and upper limbs: Actions of stability or balance supported by the head, head and hands, or head and arms or shoulders. Over torso, back or pelvis: Actions of stability or balance where the dancer is in contact with the floor without using the limbs. The head can also touch the floor when it is accompanied by other parts of the body. Over a combination of parts: Actions of stability or balance supported by a combination of different parts of the body not listed before
Support stability over a partner: Actions of stability or balance supported over a partner	Over arms or hands: Actions of stability or balance supported by the arms or hands over a partner. The dancer will be giving weight to the partner or just touching him/her, but he/she can be at the same time giving weight to the floor. Over legs or feet: Actions of stability or balance supported by the legs or feet over a partner. Over head or head and upper limbs: Actions of stability or balance supported by the head over the partner, with or without the help of arms, hands or shoulders. Over torso, back or pelvis: Actions of stability or balance supported over a partner without using the limbs and not just with the head. Over a combination of parts: Actions of stability or balance supported over a combination of parts not cited before and over a partner.
Axial stability skills: Turns standing	Turning around the longitudinal axis of the body: i.e. when turning while Turning around the horizontal transverse axis of the body: i.e. in a somersault Turning around the transverse anteroposterior axis of the body: i.e. when the body inclines laterally Turning around a combination of axes
Level changing stability skills: Actions that produce a change in the spatial level	Jumping: when the dancer loses contact with the floor while alone. Elevations over a partner: when the dancer loses contact with the floor but helped by the body of the partner. Level changing from down to middle: going up from the floor. Level changing from middle to down: falls. Locomotion on two feet (bipedal): locomotor actions using the lower limbs. Locomotion on all fours (quadrupedal): locomotor actions using
Locomotor skills: displacements	the lower and upper limbs Rolling Sliding
Manipulative skills: Actions that manipulate the partner	Impact or collision with the partner: short impact with the partner and with any body part. Reception of the partner: Taking the partner when he/she is falling off or jumping back onto him/her. Guiding or leading the partner: All actions based on guiding or leading the movement of the partner. Elevation of the partner: Actions involving support to the partner to help him/her jump or to elevate him/her. Sustaining a partner: Actions of sustaining a partner who is elevated or giving weight.

Results

It can be seen in Table 5.6 that when Participant 1 danced alone she performed lots of turning movements around different axes (35 times, compared with 14 for Participant 2 and 19 for Participant 3), her dance having a very spiral and spherical nature. In the duets it was also common for her to turn around a combination of axes while she was elevated, showing a similar type of movement to when she was dancing alone. The action of being elevated while she turned around different axes was the most common action while dancing with Participant 3, and the second most common when dancing with Participant 2.

Participant 2 frequently moved using both feet (bipedal locomotion, 22 times), and he sometimes turned or jumped at the same time. All kinds of spatial level changes were very frequent. The most surprising finding for this dancer was that he jumped 24 times, compared with just a single jump by Participant 1 and 4 by Participant 3 (see Table 5.6). The most relevant T-patterns for Participant 2 showed repeated sequences, especially spatial level changes, such as jumps followed by falling, or jumps preceded by moving from a lower to a middle level (see the example in Figure 5.7). When he danced with his partners he also jumped more than the other two dancers, especially when dancing with Participant 3, which illustrates that dancers tend to maintain the most relevant characteristics of their solos when dancing in duets. Participant 2 often elevated Participant 1, and he was also elevated by her. With Participant 3 he was elevated or he himself elevated his partner while walking and turning. He also jumped while being supported by

Table 5.6 Number of times that each category was performed in solos and in duets, independently of the other categories (P: Participant)

Criteria	Category	P1	P1–P2	P1–P3	P2	P2–P1	P2–P3	P3	P3–P1	P3–P2
Turning	longitudinal	14	10	14	29	15	26	29	26	20
	horizontal	2	6	14	9	4	9	3	0	7
	ante-roposterior axis	4	0	2	3	1	1	1	2	1
	combination	35	15	25	14	7	7	19	8	21
Change spatial level	jumping	1	2	4	24	7	14	4	4	5
	elevation down to	0	21	33	0	15	14	0	12	16
	middle	13	2	1	18	6	8	18	9	7
	falling	13	3	4	29	6	10	18	9	7
Locomotion	bipedal	15	30	26	22	31	30	23	30	37
	quadrupedal	12	0	0	3	1	0	20	2	1
	rolling	5	2	4	7	1	6	11	3	0
	sliding	16	1	2	7	0	1	9	0	0
Manipulation	colliding	0	1	2	0	0	0	0	2	1
	receiving	0	1	1	0	0	3	0	14	5
	guiding	0	28	22	0	22	21	0	4	32
	elevating	0	11	11	0	21	16	0	16	13
	sustaining	0	5	11	0	14	11	0	11	3

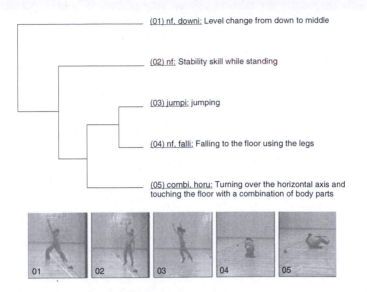

(01) nf, downi: Level change from down to middle

(02) nf: Stability skill while standing

(03) jumpi: jumping

(04) nf, falli: Falling to the floor using the legs

(05) combi, horu: Turning over the horizontal axis and touching the floor with a combination of body parts

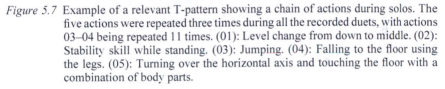

Figure 5.7 Example of a relevant T-pattern showing a chain of actions during solos. The five actions were repeated three times during all the recorded duets, with actions 03–04 being repeated 11 times. (01): Level change from down to middle. (02): Stability skill while standing. (03): Jumping. (04): Falling to the floor using the legs. (05): Turning over the horizontal axis and touching the floor with a combination of body parts.

his partner and guided or led him while walking. The results for the other dancers dancing with him showed that all of them were elevated by him more than by the others, and that they turned in the air. It seems that duets with this participant were more dynamic and aerial, as was the case of his solo.

Participant 3 quite often changed his spatial level and he frequently moved using both feet (bipedal locomotor skills) (see Table 5.6). The T-pattern analysis showed a repetition of bipedal locomotion, either with or without a turn, followed by a falling movement. When dancing with Participant 1 he was often elevated via the centre and guided or led by his partner, whom he also elevated. With Participant 2 he was often elevated, sometimes turning over different axes in the air, and he guided or led his partner while walking and turning. He also walked or ran alone.

Duets analysed separately revealed no relevant T-patterns, which means that there were no movement sequences that were clearly repeated during the five minutes of dance. This suggests that dancing with a partner stimulated a more varied production of motor skills, thereby enhancing motor creativity.

Instrument 2: Analysis of interviews

Following this experiment in CI, all the participants watched video recordings of their own dances and were interviewed about the movements and motor skills they used, as well as about the creative aspects they perceived in their performance. The interview questions are shown in Table 5.7.

A content analysis was then carried out by introducing their responses into the Nvivo-v8 software package and examining them in relation to a category system based on nine criteria: the first six criteria corresponded to the above-mentioned observational instrument, while the remaining three were those proposed by Guilford (1956) for judging creativity, i.e. fluency, flexibility and originality (see Table 5.8).

Table 5.7 The interview questions

Questions for each dance session

1. Do you think you used many different movements?
2. Did you notice whether you repeated any sequence of movements?
3. Do you think you have your own particular dance style?
4. How did you vary this style with this dancer?*
5. Were you surprised by any movements? Did you detect any original movement? Why?

Questions after seeing the three videos

1. What differences do you notice in your dance depending on the partner?
2. As regards any original movements you have noticed, were they in relation to your own dance, to this experiment, or to CI in general?
3. Taking into account the difference between dancing alone and with a partner, when do you think you are more creative? Do you think that dancing with a partner helps you to be more creative?

Note: * This question was not used after observing the solo dance.

Table 5.8 Category system applied to analyse the interviews using Nvivo software

Category system applied when using Nvivo software	
Support stability skills with the floor	
Support stability skills with a partner	
Axial stability skills: turns	
Level changing stability skills	Being elevated
	Falling or going from down to middle
	Jumps
Locomotor skills	
Manipulative skills	
Flexibility	Dancer has his/her own dance style
	The dancer's own style varies depending on other factors, not the partner
	The dancer's own style varies depending on the partner
Fluency	Dancer repeats movements
	There is a high frequency of movements
Originality	There are original movements related to CI
	There are original movements related to this experiment
	There are original movements related to the dancer's own style

Results

The analysis of interviews showed that when Participant 1 talked about her solo, 9.54 per cent of her discourse referred to the use of turns, and she emphasized that spiralling was something she identified with her own style. This is consistent with the findings of the observational analysis. She also remarked on two occasions that she repeated movements during the dance, although she did not identify any particular sequence and said that her dance was very varied. As regards the duets she stated that elevations were very frequent.

The observational analysis had shown that Participant 2 made considerable use of jumps in his solo, and he himself noted this, with such comments accounting for 20.21 per cent and 45.27 per cent of his discourse regarding his solo and his duet with Participant 3, respectively. He also identified his own style with this movement, and on one occasion he considered a specific jump as being the most original movement that he performed.

The observational analysis of Participant 3 had revealed his frequent use of bipedal locomotor skills, and he also commented on this during the interview (accounting for 7.32 per cent of his discourse). Furthermore, he considered that this movement, combined with turning, was characteristic of his own style.

In general, the participants felt that dancing with a partner enhanced their creativity and produced a more varied dance. This is corroborated by the lack of relevant T-patterns identified in the duets, and is also illustrated by a comment made by Participant 3:

> When you are alone you have to find a stimulus, and you can work with images or emotions, but when you dance with someone it's a different world. It's like two worlds that find each other and which bring all their background, all their experiences and emotions.

This is also consistent with the findings of the observational analysis.

The analysis of interviews provided more information about originality than did the observational analysis. The dancers considered that some of their movements were original in relation to their own dance, but all three of them had problems in defining the concept of originality with regard to contact improvisation. In fact, they all agreed that the improvisational nature of this dance means that every movement is original, since it emerges at a given moment and is not 'copied' or 'prepared'. In this context, Participant 1 stated that 'contact improvisation is always original because you don't know what's going to happen', while Participant 2 said that what he liked about contact improvisation was

> the point at which you go into a state that is neither physical nor mental nor emotional, but all three at the same time. Your brain is working all the time, but you flow in the present and you don't think 'I am going to do that', but rather 'I'm doing this because it's happening right now'. This is what makes the dance original.

Another relevant comment about originality was made by Participant 1, who thought that it was not related with the aesthetics of the movement or what observers could appreciate:

> It might not be very interesting from an aesthetic point of view, but the movement may have created something unexpected for me, something surprising. The expectations I might have while dancing don't necessarily have to be observable. This is very common when you're dancing contact improvisation.

Discussion

These results show that observational analysis can indeed be complemented by interviews with participants, especially when the aim is to analyse the subjective characteristics of dance. As Participant 1 suggests, if we regard unexpected or surprising movements as being original, then originality may be unobservable. This aspect would therefore have been overlooked had it not been for the inclusion of qualitative interview data.

The analysis shows that certain individual characteristics of the solos also appear in the duets. This was the case not only of the spherical dance of Participant 1, which was full of turns over different axes when dancing alone and turning while being elevated in the duets, but also of the jumps used by Participant 2 and the bipedal locomotion of Participant 3. The dancers themselves also noted the repetition of these movements, and considered them to be characteristic of their own style.

As regards creativity the results derived from both the observational instrument and the interviews suggest that dancing with a partner encourages dancers to produce more varied motor responses. In a recent study we also found that dancing with a partner can be more pleasant for beginners (Torrents *et al.* 2011). Taken together these results suggest that the use of tasks involving partners can help to stimulate motor creativity when teaching dance. This finding should also be of interest to professional dancers and choreographers in relation to the creative process of any performance.

CASE STUDY 5.3: THE AESTHETIC APPRAISAL OF CONTEMPORARY DANCE USING A MOTION CAPTURE SYSTEM

Introduction

The ephemerality of dance

In dance, each movement, each gesture replaces the one that precedes it, and therefore it is impossible for these individual movements to persist within the observer's visual apparatus. As Castañer points out 'the body is what we see, yet the movement vanishes, and since dance is produced through the body's movement it is an ephemeral art' (Castañer 2006: 42). However, the latest motion capture systems enable what might be called a 'perpetuation' of dance movements, and the kinematic analyses that can be performed using such technology provide new information about the inevitably subjective perceptions and appreciations we make when observing the human body in motion.

Aesthetics and contemporary dance

The internal world of each person is defined by the sum of knowledge acquired through personal experiences. In the case of dancers these experiences lead to a singular and personal aesthetic that is revealed through the kinesics of their performance. As a result, the body language of a performing dancer is like a representation of his or her internal world. Contemporary dance seeks to maximize the potential for such aesthetic expression, although in fact every dance form is subject to aesthetic appraisals based on stimuli, as well as to subjective perception (Daprati *et al.* 2009). However, because dance is dynamic in both space and time it involves fluctuations and perturbations that imply a loss of equilibrium and the constant need for equilibrium to be regained. Of course, this is also the case in everyday body movements such as walking, in which one leg is in the stance phase supporting the body while the other leg is in the flight phase. Where dance differs is that it plays with this aspect so that the spectator comes to expect a chain of movements that form a choreographic pattern. Furthermore, the aim here is not equilibrium in itself, but rather aesthetic expression. For example, a kinematic analysis of centre of gravity might suggest that a dancer is frequently in a position of disequilibrium, yet the dancer may be doing this intentionally in order to generate surprise and a specific aesthetic effect.

Aims and the mixed methods approach: embedded correlational design

This case study made use of three instruments, two quantitative and one qualitative. Quantitative data (QUAN) were obtained by means of motion capture and a semantic differential, and the resulting sets of data were crossed and analysed using multiple factor analysis (MFA) (Escofier and Pagès 1994). In order to complement this with qualitative data (qual) a set of open-ended questions were added to the semantic differential in order to obtain more detailed information regarding the aesthetic appraisals made by observers. The mixed methods approach used was an embedded correlational design (see Chapter 1, Figure 1.7).

Instrument 1: Motion capture

Images corresponding to two different dance skills were captured by means of a 3D motion analysis system using ten cameras (VICON Mx, Oxford Metrics, Oxford, UK). The dance skills were simultaneously filmed by means of a conventional video camera situated in the frontal plane. The reporting tool Polygon

(VICON) was then used to create video clips showing either the conventional video or animated stick figures, the latter shown from the same perspective as the conventional video. The details of the procedure are described below.

Participants and procedure

Four experienced contemporary dancers performed three repetitions of two motor skills used in contemporary dance, in a space measuring $3 \times 4 \times 2.5$ m. This capture volume was previously calibrated for the 3D motion capture system. The two dance skills analysed (see Figure 5.8) were:

- *saut volé en tournant*: a jump combined with a turn that seeks to achieve full body extension in parallel to and facing the floor.
- *arabesque penchée*: a balancing skill, maintained here for a minimum of four seconds.

Retro-reflective markers were attached to the dancers' bodies at defined locations according to the VICON full-body PlugInGait marker set (Figure 5.9). The 3D coordinates of these markers enable the body's motion sequences to be represented in the form of stick figures.

Figure 5.8 Left photo: *saut volé en tournant* (jump with turn). Right photo: *arabesque penchée* (balance skill).

Figure 5.9 From left to right: dancer with retro-reflective markers according to the PlugInGait marker set from VICON; still from a conventional video sequence; and the corresponding stick figure obtained from the 3D analysis.

The skills to be performed were explained to the dancers and they were allowed to practise them until they felt confident about their performance. Each skill was then repeated according to three different movement qualities based on Laban's criterion of muscular tension (strong, moderate and mild). A total of 24 trials were recorded.

The 3D motion capture system provides the position in space and time of each defined body segment: head, arms, forearms, hands, thorax, pelvis, legs, lower legs and feet. As a result, joint motion can be calculated. On the basis of this information a total of 26 parameters (Table 5.9) that were hypothesized to have an influence on aesthetic perception were defined using custom-written MATLAB (The MathWorks Inc.) routines. Some of these parameters referred to more than one skill, while others were specific to a given skill.

Instrument 2: Semantic differential

The semantic differential (Osgood *et al.* 1957) was used to obtain an aesthetic appraisal of the video clips. The scale had a seven-point range and its two poles were 'ugly' and 'beautiful', with higher scores indicating greater perceived beauty (Table 5.11).

Procedure

The observers were 108 students from a degree course in Physical Activity and Sport Sciences (77 male and 31 female, mean age 19.46 ± 1.96 years). None of them had any dance experience. The students observed the 24 clips via the Polygon Viewer software while using the semantic differential to make an aesthetic appraisal of the observed movement. They were first shown the virtual images (stick figures) of dancers obtained via the motion capture system, followed a week

Table 5.9 Motion parameters derived from the 3D data (for nomenclature, see Table 5.10)

Parameter	Skills	Abbrev.
1. Integral of the FFT of the position of the CM (viewing perspective: near-far, right-left, down-up) in the interval from the first value above 0 to 2.5 Hz	*Arabesque*	ITF1CMxyz
2. Integral of the FFT of the position of the CM (viewing perspective: near-far, right-left, down-up) in the interval 2.5–5 Hz	*Arabesque*	ITF2CMxyz
3. Integral of the FFT of the position of the CM (viewing perspective: near-far, right-left, down-up) for frequencies >5 Hz	*Arabesque*	ITF3CMxyz
4. Integral of the FFT of the position of the centre of the pelvis (viewing perspective: near-far, right-left, down-up) in the interval from the first value above 0 to 2.5 Hz	*Arabesque*	ITF1Pxyz
5. Integral of the FFT of the position of the centre of the pelvis (viewing perspective: near-far, right-left, down-up) in the interval 2.5–5 Hz	*Arabesque*	ITF2Pxyz
6. Integral of the FFT of the position of the centre of the pelvis (viewing perspective: near-far, right-left, down-up) for frequencies >5 Hz	*Arabesque*	ITF3Pxyz
7. Duration of the single limb stance	*Arabesque*	TIMEs
8. Right Leg angle relative to the vertical in the plane of view	*Arabesque*	RLAZ
9. Left Leg angle relative to the vertical in the plane of view	*Arabesque*	LLAZ
10. Right arm angle relative to the vertical in the plane of view	*Arabesque*	RAAZ
11. Left arm angle relative to the vertical in the plane of view	*Arabesque*	LAAZ
12. Angle between right leg and right arm in the plane of view	*Arabesque*	AnRLA
13. Angle between left leg and left arm in the plane of view	*Arabesque*	AnLLA
14. Angle of the right arm to the plane of view	*Arabesque*	AnRAZ
15. Angle of the left arm to the plane of view	*Arabesque*	AnLAZ
16. Angle of the right leg to the plane of view	*Arabesque*	AnRLZ
17. Angle of the left leg to the plane of view	*Arabesque*	AnLLZ
18. Area of the polygon joining ankles and wrists, projected on the frontal plane of the pelvis at the instant of take-off (normalized to the square of body height)	*Saut volé*	AREAToff
19. Area of the polygon joining ankles and wrists, projected on the frontal plane of the pelvis at the instant of maximum height of the CM (normalized to the square of body height)	*Saut volé*	AREAMAX
20. Area of the polygon joining ankles and wrists, projected on the frontal plane of the pelvis at the instant of touch down (normalized to the square of body height)	*Saut volé*	AREATdown
21. Vertical amplitude of the CM motion	*Saut volé*	AMPLITUDE
22. Maximum achieved height of the CM	*Saut volé*	HEIGHT

23.	Maximum vertical inclination of the line joining C7 with the right heel at the instant of maximum height of the CM	*Saut volé*	INCLINATION
24.	RMS of the angle between thorax and pelvis during flight (Euler rotations, pelvis around thorax in the sequence mediolateral, anteroposterior,, vertical)	*Saut volé*	RMSTP
25.	RMS of the angle between pelvis and right leg during flight (Euler rotations, leg around pelvis in the sequence mediolateral, anteroposterior, vertical)	*Saut volé*	RMSPRL
26.	RMS of the angle between pelvis and left leg during flight (Euler rotations, leg around pelvis in the sequence mediolateral, anteroposterior, vertical)	*Saut volé*	RMSPLL

Table 5.10 Nomenclature for Table 5.9

Abbreviation	Meaning
RCS	Room coordinate system
FFT	Fast Fourier Transform
X, Y, Z	Forward oriented axis, Transverse axis, Vertical axis
CM	Centre of mass
RMS	Root mean square
C7	7th cervical vertebra

Table 5.11 Structure of the semantic differential used to obtain the aesthetic appraisals

Ugly	*Beautiful*

later by the original filmed images. All the video clips corresponding to each skill were shown together, but clips were presented in a random order as regards the dancer or the quality of the movement. Each animation or video was shown three times, after which a black screen was presented for five seconds.

Results

The first, quantitative stage of the embedded correlational design involved correlating the kinematic data obtained from the motion capture system with the data obtained from the semantic differential. These data were subjected to multiple factor analysis (MFA). MFA (Escofier and Pagès 1994) is a generalization of principal components analysis (PCA) that enables the simultaneous analysis of tables in which the same set of individuals is described by several groups of variables. These groups of variables may derive from the combined use of different kinds of data (e.g. quantitative and qualitative) or from the same set of variables measured at different points in time, etc. In the present case study each dancer was described by three sets of variables: biomechanical variables 1, biomechanical variables 2, and the aesthetic appraisal score for the two skills.

For both skills, the *saut volé en tournant* (jump with turn) and the *arabesque penchée* (balance), Table 5.9 shows the motion parameters derived from the 3D data, while Figures 5.10 and 5.11 illustrate the output of the MFA analyses. The results for the *saut volé en tournant* (jump with turn) showed that when viewing the stick figures the highest appraisal scores (6–7) were clearly associated with the amplitude of movement and inclination of the body with respect to the floor (44.33 per cent of the total variability; principal component 1). Similar results were obtained when viewing the original filmed images, where the highest scores were once again associated with the amplitude of movement and inclination of the body with respect to the floor (39.63 per cent of the total variability; principal component 1, referred to as Dimension (Dim) 1 in Figure 5.10). However, the height of the jump was also related to high scores here.

For the *arabesque penchée* (balance skill) the results of the MFA depicted in Figure 5.11 show that the highest appraisal scores (5–7) were associated with the following kinematic variables: the perpendicular of the left leg, the time during which balance was maintained, the angles in the sagittal plane of the left arm and the right leg, and the parallelism between the left arm and left leg (24.71 per cent of the total variability; principal component 1). Similar results were obtained when viewing the original filmed images (where principal component 1 explained 24.29 per cent of the total variability). In both cases (real images and stick figures), fluctuations of the body in all planes at the lowest frequencies (between 0 and 2.5 Hz) were associated with the lowest scores in terms of the aesthetic appraisal.

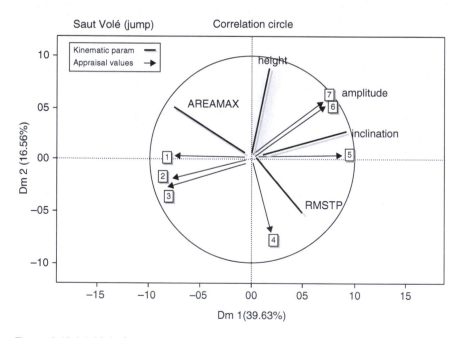

Figure 5.10 Multiple factor analysis of the *saut volé en tournant* (jump with turn).

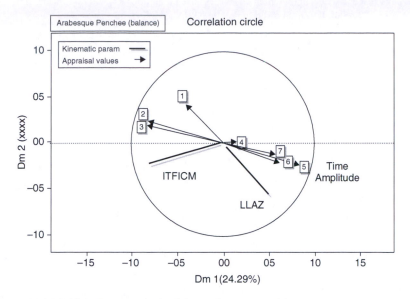

Figure 5.11 Multiple factor analysis of the *arabesque penchée*.

Instrument 3: Open-ended questions

Several open-ended questions were also added to the semantic differential in order to obtain more detailed information regarding the features on which the observers based their aesthetic appraisals of jumps and balance skills, both in general (in sport and physical activity) and in relation to the two specific dance skills. The material obtained was subjected to a content analysis. In the context of the embedded correlational design these qualitative data add greater detail to the quantitative findings.

Procedure

After viewing the animations, 20 of the previous 108 students were asked to answer four questions regarding the aesthetic features of what they had observed. These questions were: (a) Which aspects of this jump/balance skill do you regard as being the most attractive?; (b) Which aspects of this jump/balance skill do you regard as being the most unattractive?; (c) Which aspects of jumps/balance skills in general (in sport and physical activity) do you regard as having the greatest aesthetic value?; and (d) Which aspects of jumps/balance skills in general (in sport and physical activity) do you regard as having the least aesthetic value?

Results

The characteristics which the student observers felt were most relevant as regards the aesthetics of the two skills are shown in Table 5.12.

Table 5.12 Key aspects upon which observers based their appraisals of beauty and ugliness in relation to jumps and balancing skills

Aspect	Beauty in the saut volé	Beauty in jumps in general	Ugliness in the saut volé	Ugliness in jumps in general
Marked definition of body segment lines	25%	15%		
High elevation in the flight phase	25%	35%		
Maintaining the figure in the air and inclination.	20%	20%		
Low elevation in the flight phase			25%	35%
Fall is unbalanced or lacks control			15%	15%

	Beauty in the arabesque penchée	Beauty in stability actions in general	Ugliness in the arabesque penchée	Ugliness in stability actions in general
Marked definition of body segment lines	45%	45%		
Maximum extension of segments	20%	5%		
Body is controlled when maintaining balance	40%	45%		
Segment lines are poorly defined			25%	10%
Trembles when maintaining balance			45%	25%

In both the *saut volé en tournant*, specifically, and in jumps in general (in sport and physical activity) clearly defined body segment lines and a high elevation during the flight phase were considered to be aspects that made the action more beautiful to watch. By contrast, minimal elevation in the flight phase and a lack of balance when falling back to the floor were regarded as having little aesthetic value.

With respect to the *arabesque penchée* and to balancing skills in general (in sport and physical activity) good body control while maintaining balance and, once again, clearly defined body segments were considered to be features that made the action more aesthetically pleasing. By contrast, poorly defined segment lines and trembling while trying to maintain balance were regarded as spoiling the potential beauty of the action.

Discussion

In the context of the embedded correlational design the data derived from the third instrument served to corroborate some of the quantitative results obtained through the multiple factor analysis. In relation to the *saut volé en tournant* the two sets of data (QUAN and qual) clearly coincide regarding the importance of high elevation during the flight phase of the jump, as well as the ability to maintain the figure in the air and the body's inclination with respect to the floor.

As regards the *arabesque penchée* the maximum extension of body segments and the clear definition of segment lines were considered to be key aspects that heightened the aesthetic value of the action. This corroborates the quantitative findings regarding the angle between body segments. Another factor for which there was clear agreement concerned the dancer's ability to maintain her balance for a period of time. In this context, brusque movements or trembling while attempting to perform and maintain the figure were regarded as undermining the aesthetic value of this type of motor skill.

Conclusions

This case study has presented an in-depth analysis of two motor skills used in contemporary dance, namely balance and jumps. The features that were adjudged to be the most attractive or unappealing give some idea of the aspects on which observers or spectators base their aesthetic appraisals of these two actions, both of which are central to any choreographic work. The results derived from this investigation into the aesthetic appreciation of the dancing body support Johnson's (2007) contention that humans' appreciation of art is entirely rooted in the body.

Acknowledgements

We gratefully acknowledge the support of the Spanish government project *Avances tecnológicos y metodológicos en la automatización de estudios observacionales en deporte* (Dirección General de Investigación, Ministerio de Ciencia e Innovación) [Grant number PSI2008-01179]. We also gratefully acknowledge the support of the Generalitat de Catalunya government project GRUP DE RECERCA E INNO-VACIÓ EN DISSENYS (GRID). Tecnología i aplicació multimedia i digital als dissenys observacionals, Departament d'Innovació, Universitats i Empresa, Generalitat de Catalunya [Grant number 2009 SGR 829]. We would also like to thank the volunteer dancers and observers who participated in this study.

References

Albright, A.C. (2003). Contact improvisation at twenty-five. In B.C. Albright and D. Gere (eds), *Taken by surprise. A dance improvisation reader.* Middletown, CT: Wesleyan University Press.

Castañer, M. (2001). El cuerpo: gesto y mensaje no-verbal. *Tándem 3*, 39–49.

Castañer, M. (2006). *La dansa contemporània és . . .* Lleida: INEFC Publicacions de la Universitat de Lleida.

Castañer, M. and Camerino, O. (2006). *Manifestaciones básicas de la Motricidad.* Lleida: INEFC Publicacions de la Universitat de Lleida.

Castañer, M., Camerino, O., Anguera, M.T. and Jonsson, G.K. (in press). Kinesics and proxemics communication of expert and novice PE teachers. *Quality and Quantity.*

Castañer, M., Torrents, C., Anguera, M.T., Dinusôva, M., and Jonsson, G. (2009). Identifying and analyzing motor skill responses in body movement and dance. *Behavior Research Methods* 41 (3), 857–867.

Castañer, M., Torrents, C. and Dinušová, M. (2007, September) Specific motor components of contemporary dance productions: A semantic differential tool. *21st World Congress on Dance Research*, Athens, Greece.

Daprati, E., Iosa, M., and Haggard, P. (2009). A dance to the music of time: Aesthetically-relevant changes in body posture in performing art. *PLoS ONE* 4 (3): e5023.

Escofier, B. and Pagès, J. (1994). Multiple factor analysis (AFMULT package). *Computational Statistics and Data Analysis*, 18, 121–140.

Guilford, J.P. (1956). The structure of intellect, *Psychological Bulletin*, *53*, 267–293.

Johnson, M. (2007). *The meaning of the body: Aesthetics of human understanding*. Chicago and London: University of Chicago Press.

Laban, R. and Ullman, L. (1963). *Modern educational dance*. London: Macdonald & Evans.

Lepecki, A . (2006). *Exhausting dance*. New York: Routledge.

Levi-Strauss, C. (1978). *Myth and meaning*. London: Routledge.

Magnusson, M.S. (2005). Understanding social interaction: Discovering hidden structure with model and algorithms. In L. Anolli, S. Duncan, M. Magnusson and G. Riva (eds), *The hidden structure of social interaction: From genomics to culture patterns* (pp. 51–70). Amsterdam: IOS Press.

Metz, C. (1977). *Le significant imaginaire*. Paris: Collection Psychoanalyse et cinéma.

Novack, C. (1990). *Sharing the dance: Contact improvisation and American culture*. Madison: University of Wisconsin Press.

Osgood, Ch. E., Suci, J., and Tannembaum, P.H. (1957). *The measurement of meaning*. Urbana-Champaign, IL: University of Illinois Press.

Pattern Vision (2001). *THEME Coder* (software), Retrieved January 15, 2002, from http://www.patternvision.com.

Pavis, P. (ed.) (1996). *The intercultural performance reader*. London: New York: Routledge.

Paxton, S. (1997). Contact improvisation views: Round up. In L. Nelson and N. Stark Smith. (eds), *Contact Quarterly's contact improvisation sourcebook* (p. 79). Florence, MA: Contact Editions.

Serre, J.C. (1984). La danse parmi les autres formes de la motricité. *La Recherche en Danse, 3*, 135–156.

Shell, C.G. (1984). The dancer as athlete. *Olympic Scientific Congress Proceedings*. Vol. 8.

Sidall, C. (1997). Round up: To definition. Volume 5, 1979–80. In L. Nelson and N. Stark Smith (eds), *Contact Quarterly's contact improvisation sourcebook* (p. 54). Florence, MA: Contact Editions.

Torrents, C., Castañer, M., Dinušová, M., and Anguera, M.T. (2010). Discovering new ways of moving: Observational analysis of motor creativity while dancing contact improvisation and the influence of the partner. *Journal of Creative Behavior, 44* (1), 45–61.

Torrents, C., Mateu, M., Planas, A., and i Dinušová, M. (2011). Posibilidades de las tareas de expresión corporal para suscitar emociones en el alumnado. *Revista de Psicología del deporte, 20* (2), 401–412.

Wyrick, W. (1968). The development of a test of motor creativity. *Research Quarterly, 39*, 756–765.

Part IV

Assessing coaches, teachers and instructors

6 Optimizing verbal and nonverbal communication in physical education teachers, fitness instructors and sport coaches

- **Case Study 6.1: Identifying and optimizing nonverbal communicative styles in physical education teachers**
  Marta Castañer

- **Case Study 6.2: Coaches' communication in competitive match situations**
  Catarina Miguel and Marta Castañer

- **Case Study 6.3: The behaviour of fitness instructors and the preferences and satisfaction levels of users**
  Susana Franco, Jose Rodrigues and Marta Castañer

The case studies described in this chapter refer to research into the communication of teachers, coaches and instructors in the context of physical education and sport. The aim is to illustrate the versatility of verbal and nonverbal communication in these professionals and to examine its importance as regards the teaching or training process, in the way that Guardiola comments in an interview:

> I take note of what coaches do in other sports, such as basketball, Formula 1 or boxing, so as to gather ideas and open my mind to different ways of doing things, and this enriches my own professional work as a coach.
> (Josep Guardiola, Coach of FC Barcelona)

What the studies described have in common is that they all made use of observational methodology. This approach was chosen due to the habitual nature of the behaviour being observed and the fact that the context is a naturalistic one. Furthermore, the flexibility and rigour of this methodology makes it fully consistent with the characteristics of this kind of research and it has become a standard approach to observational enquiry (Anguera 2003).

The results derived from the observations of physical education teachers, fitness instructors and coaches were combined with those obtained via questionnaires and interviews conducted with them. This enabled us to obtain and combine both QUAN and QUAL data, the aim being to identify and, subsequently, to optimize the communication of these professionals.

CASE STUDY 6.1: IDENTIFYING AND OPTIMIZING NONVERBAL COMMUNICATIVE STYLES IN PHYSICAL EDUCATION TEACHERS

Introduction

One of the keys to optimizing teaching tasks lies in paying close attention to the communication and teaching style that each teacher may develop and rework over time. Although each individual has a characteristic style of communicative fluency, it is also possible to identify certain nonverbal and immediacy behaviours (Mehrabian 1969; Baringer and McCroskey 2000) which are of considerable relevance to the process of teaching in the academic context. Specifically, the uses made by teachers of kinesics and proxemics influences every process of teaching and learning, and the aim of the research described in this chapter is to analyse these aspects.

Almost three decades ago Weinmann and Backlund (1980) noted that specific references to actual communicative behaviour are required in order to develop a model of communicative competency. However, there remains a need for further educational research into the specific role of nonverbal behaviours in teaching and learning (Cristophel 1990; Crowder and Newman 1993; Lemke 1999; Roth 2001, 2002). For example, an intrinsic part of all teaching activity is a constant communicational flow, in which the spontaneous nature of communication is considered to be a habitual feature. Buck and VanLear (2002) defined this as non-intentional communication. In terms of promoting teaching quality it is essential to be aware of the uses made of such nonverbal communication, as only thus will it be possible to maximize its potential and efficacy and attain optimum levels of classroom communication.

The singular nature of nonverbal communication

Nonverbal communication refers to a type of behaviour that despite being totally perceivable, tends to be largely overlooked due to the socio-cultural value that has traditionally been ascribed to it. Indeed, the communicative reality in which humans live tends to be considered in terms of the linear and sequential nature of verbal language, which is produced by a single phonatory organ that is unable to emit simultaneous sounds; in other words, we can't say *a* and *b* at the same time. However, all discourse which is not strictly verbal is characterized by simultaneity. As a result, the diverse and bilateral structure of our corporeity enables us to generate bodily postures (dynamism), gestures (dynamism) and attitudes (meanings or expressive movement) in a simultaneous way (Castañer and Camerino 2006; Castañer *et al.* in press). In this context, nonverbal teaching style refers to the ways in which teachers convey their educational discourse, and this is why it is sometimes associated with the idea of expressive movement (Gallaher 1992). De Vries *et al.* (2009) also define communicative style as the characteristic way a person sends verbal and nonverbal signals in social interactions.

The nonverbal structure of communication has traditionally been addressed according to four dimensions: kinesics, proxemics, chronemics and paralanguage (Ekman and Friesen 1969; Hall 1968; Poyatos 1983). In relation to teachers' discourse these dimensions can be defined as follows:

> *Kinesics:* the study of patterns in gesture and posture that are used by the teacher with or without communicative meaning.
>
> *Proxemics:* the study of how the teacher uses the space in which teaching takes place.
>
> *Chronemics:* the study of how the teacher uses the temporal factors that influence the teaching setting.
>
> *Paralanguage:* the study of all those vocal emissions that do not form part of arbitrary verbal language but which do accompany it.

These dimensions are therefore associated with the study of body gestures, the use of space, the use of time, and voice-related paralanguage. They may appear simultaneously or concurrently, functioning in an integrated and systemic way. If communication is to be effective, however, it is necessary to ensure that all the nonverbal dimensions are congruent, i.e. that they seek to transmit the same message, strengthening, confirming and heightening it in accordance with the educational circumstances (Jones and LeBaron 2002).

The present case study is focused on the first two of these dimensions, proxemics and kinesics, and the next section provides a more detailed conceptual description of these.

From kine to gesture

Let us begin with some definitions. The term *kine* refers to the basic unit of movement, comparable to the phoneme of verbal language (see Figures 5.1 and 5.2 in Chapter 5). *Body posture* refers to the static nature of the body in relation to the position of its various osteoarticular and muscular parts, whereas *body gesture* refers to the dynamic nature of the body, without forgetting that each gesture is comprised of multiple micro-postures. *Body attitude* refers to the meaning that each social group gives to the emotional and expressive ways of using postures and gestures.

On the basis of this initial clarification, gesture can be regarded as the basic unit of meaning for constructing the nonverbal kinesic observational system (Figure 6.1).

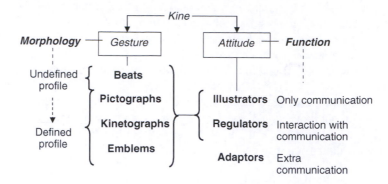

Figure 6.1 Morphology and functions of human kinesic nonverbal communication.

As regards the morphology of the categories, they range from gestures that offer a highly-defined profile and which are clearly observable by the receiver, to gestures with a less well-defined and weaker profile. What are usually referred to as *emblems* are a clear example of kines that have their own meaning, and which offer a highly-defined gesture profile (Ekman 1985). With respect to the functionality of the categories the continuum encompasses gestures with a purely communicative purpose, gestures whose purpose is communication with interaction, and extra-communicative gestures, i.e. those without any explicit interactive or communicative purpose.

It should be stressed at this point that the structure presented here is suitable for carrying out empirical research of the kind described in this chapter. Indeed, it is the basis of the criteria on which the SOCIN and SOPROX systems used in this case study are based (Tables 6.1 and 6.2) (Castañer 2009; Castañer *et al.* 2010; Castañer *et al.* in press).

Aims of the case study and the mixed methods approach: an explanatory sequential design

In light of the above, the present case study focuses on how to analyse and optimize the nonverbal communicative fluency of teaching styles using the observational instruments SOCIN and SOPROX (Tables 6.1 and 6.2). These enable a clear analysis of the use of kinesics and proxemics in teaching, and are well suited to the analysis of temporal patterns. However, the quantitative observational data (QUAN) are complemented here by information gathered through a discussion group with university experts in teaching, who gave their opinion (QUAL) about the communicative actions of the observed teachers. In terms of mixed methods this combination corresponds to a variant of the explanatory sequential design, i.e. the follow-up explanatory model with an emphasis on QUAN (see Chapter 1, Figure 1.13).

In sum, the present case study seeks to answer the following questions:

1. Which kinesic and proxemic behaviours are used when teaching physical education?
2. Can behavioural patterns be derived from teachers' communicative competencies that reveal both kinesic and proxemic aspects at the same time?
3. Can nonverbal communication be adequately detected by the SOCIN and SOPROX instruments?

Instrument 1: SOCIN and SOPROX observational systems

SOCOP is an observational system for nonverbal communication (Castañer *et al.* 2010; Castañer *et al.* in press) and corresponds to the general communicative structure found in all classroom-based teaching discourse. It comprises five changing criteria: demonstrate, help, participate, observe, and provide material. SOCOP includes two sub-systems, SOCIN and SOPROX, which are used here to enable the exhaustive and mutually-exclusive observation of the chain of kinesic and proxemic actions that are produced during the teaching process. The instrument is structured around broad categories, which makes it easy to use and readily adaptable to various naturalistic communicative contexts (Castañer *et al.* 2009), as will be seen in the second case study involving coaches. Each of the dimensions, categories and codes that form part of the SOCIN (Table 6.1) and SOPROX (Table 6.2) systems are defined below.

Table 6.1 SOCIN: System to Observe Kinesic Communication (Castañer *et al.* 2010)

Dimension	Analytical categorization	Code	Description
Function Dimension that refers to the intention of the spoken discourse that the gesture accompanies.	Regulatory	RE	Action by the teacher whose objective is to obtain an immediate response from receivers. It comprises imperative, interrogative, and instructive phrases with the aim of exemplifying, giving orders or formulating questions and answers.
	Illustrative	IL	Action that does not aim to obtain an immediate response from the receiver (although possibly at some future point). It comprises narrative, descriptive and expository phrases with the aim of getting receivers to listen.
Morphology Dimension that refers to the iconic and biomechanical form of gestures.	Emblem	EMB	Gesture with its own pre-established iconic meaning.
	Deictic	DEI	Gesture that indicates or points at people, places or objects.
	Pictographic	PIC	Gesture that draws figures or forms in space.
	Kinetographic	KIN	Gesture that draws actions or movements in space.

Table 6.1 Continued

Dimension	Analytical categorization	Code	Description
	Beats	BEA	Iconically undefined gesture used exclusively by the sender and which usually only accompanies the logic of spoken discourse.
Situational Dimension that refers to a wide range of bodily actions which usually coincide with parts of the teaching process that cover a certain period of time.	Demonstrate	DE	When the teacher performs in gestures that which he or she wishes the students to do.
	Help	HE	When the teacher performs actions with the intention of supporting or improving the contributions of students.
	Participate	PA	When the teacher participates alongside students.
	Observe	OB	Period of time during which the teacher shows an interest in what is happening in the classroom with the students.
	Provide material	PM	When the teacher handles, distributes or uses teaching material in accordance with the educational setting.
	Show of affect	AF	When the teacher uses an emotionally-charged gesture with respect to the students.
	Object adaptor	OB	When the teacher maintains contact with objects but without any communicative purpose.
Adaptation Dimension that refers to gestures without communicative intentionality in which the teacher makes contact with different parts of his/her body, or with objects or other people.	Self-adaptor	SA	When the teacher maintains contact with other parts of his/her body but without any communicative purpose.
	Hetero-adaptor	HA	When the teacher maintains bodily contact with other people but without any communicative purpose.
	Multi-adaptor	MUL	When several of these adaptor gestures are combined.

Participants and procedure

Participants were four experienced, secondary-level, physical education (PE) teachers. One complete class per teacher was video-recorded and coded using the SOCIN and SOPROX systems. Although this approach yielded data regarding the communicative style of each individual teacher, we are only interested here in identifying teachers' communicative style as a whole. Therefore, the study material corresponds to four teaching sessions with a mean duration of 50 minutes.

Table 6.2 SOPROX: System of Observation for Proxemic Communication (Castañer *et al.* 2010)

Dimension	Analytical categorization	Code	Description
Group Dimension that refers to the number of students to whom the teacher speaks.	Macro-group	MAC	When the teacher speaks to the whole class/group.
	Micro-group	MIC	When the teacher speaks to a specific sub-group of students.
	Dyad	DYA	When the teacher speaks to a single student.
Topology Dimension that refers to the spatial location of the teacher in the classroom.	Central	C	The teacher is situated in the central area of the classroom.
	At a distance	DIS	Bodily attitude that reveals the teacher to be absent from what is happening in the classroom, or which indicates a separation, whether physical or in terms of gaze or attitude, with respect to the students.
Interaction Dimension that refers to the bodily attitude which indicates the teacher's degree of involvement with the students.	Integrated	INT	Bodily attitude that reveals the teacher to be highly involved in what is happening in the classroom, and in a relation of complicity with the students.
	Tactile contact	TC	When the teacher makes bodily contact with a student.
	Facing:	FAC	The teacher is located facing the students, in line with their field of view.
	Behind:	BEH	The teacher is located behind the students, outside their field of view.
Orientation Dimension that refers to the spatial location of the teacher with respect to the students.	Among:	AMO	The teacher is located inside the space occupied by the students.
	To the right	RIG	The teacher is located in an area to the right of the classroom and of the students, with respect to what is considered to be the facing orientation of the teaching space.
	To the left	LEF	The teacher is located in an area to the left of the classroom and of the students, with respect to what is considered to be the facing orientation of the teaching space.
	Fixed standing posture	FB	The teacher remains standing without moving.
	Fixed seated posture	FS	The teacher remains in a seated position.
	Locomotion	LOC	The teacher moves around the classroom.
Transitions Dimension that refers to the body posture adopted by the teacher in space.	Support	SU	The teacher maintains a support posture by leaning against or on a structure, material or person.

Two different trained observers analysed all the recordings from the observation sessions. Data quality, in terms of inter-observer reliability, was controlled by calculating the kappa coefficient, which in this case was 0.82. Sessions were digitized to make them available for frame-to-frame analysis and to enable them to be coded in the THEME CODER software (Magnusson 2005). The resulting data file was then exported (in csv format) so that the THEME software could process the data in terms of frequency of occurrences and temporal patterns (T-patterns). The latter can be obtained in the form of tree diagrams, as shown in the results section.

Results

Obviously, each teacher has his or her own nonverbal communicative style. However, the objective of this case study is not to compare styles but, rather, to reveal the trends in this dimension of communication among teachers working in a similar naturalistic context. As noted above, the THEME software grouped all the recordings of each PE teacher and derived temporal patterns (T-patterns) that reveal the trends in kinesic and proxemic nonverbal communication from an ideographic perspective. In fact, the THEME software detected a number of such patterns of relevance. By way of an example, let us consider the T-pattern shown in Figure 6.2, which is of interest as regards the generation of nonverbal communicative responses related mainly to regulatory and illustrative functions.

In the figure we have used circles to indicate how the regulatory function (re) directed at the group (mac) is associated with well-defined and deictic (dei) gestures, with the teacher pointing at something while in a fixed standing position so as to focus the students' gaze. By contrast, the illustrative function (il) is usually performed with undefined gestures (bea) as the teacher moves around (loc), or with more defined pictographic gestures (pic) in the context of a demonstration (de).

Instrument 2: Group discussion

The group discussion with the teaching experts was structured around the criteria of the category system used in the observational instruments.

Participants and procedure

Three expert PE lecturers with more than 12 years teaching experience, and who had attended continuing education programmes, were brought together to watch the video recordings of the secondary-level PE teachers. They observed periods lasting 4–6 minutes from each part of the PE classes given. After each session they were asked to give their opinion about the types of gestures used and the use of space made by the observed teachers as a whole. In other words, they were asked to comment not only on each observed teacher's way of communicating but also on the general trends shown by them all, the aim being to compare their con-

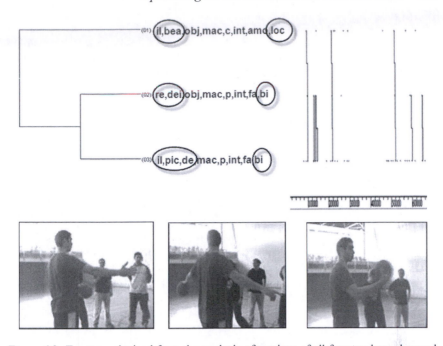

Figure 6.2   T-pattern obtained from the analysis of sessions of all four teachers observed. It consists of three levels and a sequence of three events, each one of which comprises a complex combination of codes (combinations of eight codes), occurring on three occasions during the observation period with the same sequence of events and significantly similar time intervals between each event occurrence. This T-pattern shows the alternation between the use of illustration (IL) and regulation (RE). As can be seen in (01), most illustrative (IL) situations involve expository, narrative and descriptive phrases that are usually accompanied by gestures whose morphology takes the form of beats (BEA), and also accompanied by locomotion (LOC) or movement by the teacher around the classroom or among the students (AMO) and in the centre of the space (C). As can be seen in (02), situations of regulation (RE), in which the teacher uses imperative, interrogative or instructive phrases, are usually accompanied by deictic (DEI) gestures made from a peripheral (P) area of the classroom. In (03) one can see another trend in the illustrative function (IL), accompanied by more defined gestures, in this case pictographs (PIC), which are usually used when the teacher has a fixed standing (BI) posture. The object adaptor (OBJ) appears frequently, except when the teacher begins to demonstrate (DE) with material of some kind (a ball, etc.) in his/her hand (OBJ) but then begins to use it (DE) or puts it down so as to demonstrate something more clearly with his/her hands.

clusions with the T-pattern corresponding to the teachers as a whole. They were offered guidance in relation to aspects such as the quantity, quality and definition of gestures, and the point at which they were made, etc. They were also asked about elements such as topology, location and the groupings created in the use of space. The discussion session was recorded, transcribed verbatim and analysed by means of NVIVO 8.0 software.

Results

The content analysis of the transcript reinforced several aspects of the quantitative data obtained. In what follows we present extracts from the discussion group based on the categories established for the content analysis, and which support the quantitative data obtained via the observation systems. The teacher making the comment is indicated by means of a number in brackets at the end of the extract (for example, T3 refers to teacher 3).

Gesture frequencies

As regards the frequency of the use of gestures when communicating, the experts stated that it was important to make a balanced use of gestures, since an excess or underuse of gestures could undermine the quality of the teacher's communication.

> . . . and looking at these teachers I think it's important to get the balance right . . . making no gestures is no good, but neither do you want to make too many.
>
> (T3)

This observation is consistent with what has been argued by authors such as Berends and Van Lieshout (2009), who state that while the illustrative function of gestures is interesting in terms of fostering students' learning, too much illustration can have a negative effect.

Iconically defined gestures

The gestures we use when communicating can take many different forms. Some gestures speak for themselves and are clearly drawn in space, such as in the case of emblems, while others are undefined and tend to be highly repetitive, as in the case of beats or ideographs.

> It does make a big difference if the gesture the teacher uses when speaking is clearly defined and expressive, because lots of teachers use gestures but they're not very well defined . . . it's usually the same type of gesture repeated over and over.
>
> (T2)

> It does seem that there are gestures which are more defined, that can almost be understood in themselves, and some of the teachers make use of them quite a lot.
>
> (T2)

> In fact, in physical education you make a lot of gestures that are almost demonstrations. Sometimes they demonstrate things with their whole body, but

often their hand gestures speak for themselves and reinforce what the teacher is saying.

(T1)

The regulatory function

The regulatory function is a key aspect of teaching, and takes the form of giving orders, instructions or asking questions, etc. Teachers continually use such actions in the classroom and this function is often accompanied by gestures that are specific to the individual teacher, and which reinforce the regulatory aspect.

> In physical education we use a lot of gestures with a regulatory function . . . it's as if we were continually saying things of an imperative nature.
>
> (T2)

> When the function of the message is regulatory the gestures are clearer, perhaps more exaggerated . . . they're not as ambiguous as when you're explaining to the students what they have to do . . . sometimes you don't control these gestures so much.
>
> (T3)

These comments are consistent with the idea that the regulatory function makes use of clearly-defined kinesic gestures such as emblems and kinetographs, as opposed to the illustrative function, which is accompanied by largely undefined kinesic gestures such as beats.

Emblem gestures

Gestures which are arbitrarily agreed upon and recognized by a social group are known as emblems. Their nature varies and may be social, cultural, technical or utilitarian, etc. Many of them appear as icons on signs, such as the emblem indicating silence, in which an index finger is placed perpendicularly across the lips. Some sports, such as diving or basketball, have an established code of gestures, which are sometimes applied to other situations such as PE classes.

> They're really interesting to use in class, these gestures that say it all, what you're calling emblems . . . they're direct and help you to give orders and organize things . . . They should be used more because often the students don't hear you, or you're a long way away . . . this makes me think that I'm going to try to use them more.
>
> (T1)

> Some sports have their established codes of gestures (emblems), and I noticed here that the teacher in the red T-shirt used some from basketball.
>
> (T2)

Proxemic behaviours

In addition to body gestures associated with communication the other dimension being analysed here is the use of space, which is also regarded as a key aspect when it comes to optimizing classroom communication. Just as all teachers have their own style of gestures, they likewise have a particular way of locating themselves in space and of using it to facilitate the educational communication with their students.

> Each teacher has his own way of situating himself in space . . . some stand back from the group while others are more involved, although in general all the teachers move closer when they have to explain something.
>
> (T3)

> I think that all teachers should do what this one in the blue tracksuit does . . . he keeps to the outside of the space so that the students can see him easily . . . whereas if you do what the first teacher we saw does, well, the students never know where he is and they lose this reference point.
>
> (T2)

Relationship between kinesic and proxemic behaviours

In line with what the observational systems showed to be a relevant aspect, the experts also noted that the regulatory function is combined with a static posture, whereas the illustrative form accompanies locomotion. This is consistent with the findings of recent research by our group (Castañer *et al.* 2010; Castañer *et al.* in press).

> It's interesting that, in general, they tend to gesticulate a lot when they're giving information, or to redirect the situation or when giving feedback, etc.
>
> (T1)

> When the teachers are explaining something they often move around and make gestures that aren't necessary . . . Maybe this is like a crutch to lean on or a way of feeling more secure in themselves.
>
> (T2)

> The important thing is to identify what is effective in terms of gestures and proxemics according to each teacher's way of communicating . . . Here, for example, we saw that each teacher has a particular way of combining gestures with their location in the classroom.
>
> (T1)

Discussion

The data obtained from the sequential analysis (T-patterns) revealed certain trends in the nonverbal communication of PE teachers, and illustrated some of the ways in which they tend to use such communication from both a kinesic and proxemic perspective. The information obtained from the subsequent discussion group corroborated these quantitative findings and offers a broader interpretation of the communicative behaviour of these teachers. Specifically, the results reveal two main tendencies:

1. The power of gestures that have an illustrative and regulatory function and which are associated with various forms or morphologies, as well as with key aspects of how the teacher moves in space. Thus, when teachers perform a regulatory function (giving orders, etc.) they stand or sit still in order to give greater emphasis, whereas when the function is solely illustrative (explaining or giving information) they move around. Specifically:

    *   Regulatory gestures (RE), i.e. giving instructions, asking questions, giving orders, etc., are usually made while the teacher is in a static position (especially standing (BI), although also seated (FS)).
    *   However, pictographic (PIC) and kinetographic (KIN) gestures that accompany an illustration or explanation, and which are as if the teacher is drawing objects or ideas in space, are generally used during periods of locomotion (LOC).
    *   When teachers move around (LOC) they tend to use, above all, illustrative beats (IL).

2. Regulatory gestures (RE) are shown to be morphologically coded predominantly by means of emblems (EMB) and deictic forms (DEI), i.e. they are well-defined gestures, whereas illustrative gestures (IL) are coded by both undefined gestures such as beats (BEA) and well-defined gestures such as pictographs (PIC) and kinetographs (KIN). Specifically:

    *   As beats (BEA) do not have their own meaning they can be employed when the attention of others is focused not on the meaning of the gesture but, rather, on the meaning of what is being said.
    *   Emblems (EMB), deictic forms (DEI), are generally used with a regulatory function.
    *   When a teacher demonstrates (DE), he or she tends to use illustrative gestures (IL) that may be morphologically coded as pictographs (PIC) or kinetographs (KIN), and to a lesser extent as beats (BEA).

Conclusion

The use of gestures and space by PE teachers

The sequential analysis shows that the gestures used by teachers have a variety of functions and morphology. The experts in the discussion group stated that it was useful to distinguish between these different forms, and also highlighted the importance of a balanced use of gestures if communication is to be effective. The relationship between the criterion Orientation and Topology or Transitions enables us to investigate whether there is a significant relationship between the way in which teachers move around, the spatial orientation chosen, and the topology used with respect to the group and the space in which teaching takes place.

How is the function of gestures combined with the use of space?

The analysis revealed that most illustrative (IL) situations involve expository, narrative and descriptive phrases that are usually accompanied by gestures whose morphology is poorly defined, such as beats (BEA), and which are also accompanied by locomotion (LOC) or movement by the teacher. This aspect was also commented on in the discussion group, with the experts noting that some gestures and movements were not really necessary, and perhaps served merely to make the teacher feel more secure.

Regulatory actions (RE), in which the teacher uses imperative, interrogative or instructive phrases, are usually accompanied by deictic (DEI) gestures, emblems (EMB) or pictographs (PIC), which are usually used when the teacher has a fixed standing (BI) posture. The experts also detected this aspect, stating that the intention to regulate required greater attention. In this regard, it seems that maintaining a fixed posture helps to achieve the concentration required to make highly-defined gestures such as kinetographs or pictographs.

Clear and manageable observational systems

The observation instruments have been shown to be effective tools for recording in an exhaustive, clear and manageable way all the possible forms of nonverbal communication used by teachers, whether this be kinesic (by means of SOCIN) or proxemic (via SOPROX). As pointed out in the results section (for both the observational systems and the group discussion), it was possible to identify trends in relation to each criterion of both SOCIN and SOPROX, as well as combinations of the two. Although we have seen how kinesic gestures are associated with specific proxemic behaviours, their power resides in their being effectively combined with verbal expression. Therefore, despite the concrete and unique nature of each human body it is possible to identify certain kinesic and proxemic functions and morphologies that are sufficiently generalized, and which are of considerable interest with respect to teaching, immediacy behaviours (Mehrabian 1969; McCroskey *et al.* 1996), and both affective and cognitive learning (Cristophel 1990; Rodríguez *et al.* 1996).

This case study illustrates that the use of mixed methods provides different points of reference and indicators that may help newly-qualified professionals to understand, modulate and adjust the development of their self-perception and behaviour. With regard to teachers, having an optimum nonverbal communicative style (both kinesic and proxemic) in combination with effective verbal communication is important in terms of the efficacy of instruction. We firmly believe that the optimization of these communicative styles would have a direct positive effect on students' learning.

CASE STUDY 6.2: COACHES' COMMUNICATION IN COMPETITIVE MATCH SITUATIONS

Introduction

Coaches' behaviour in competitive situations has been widely studied, although at the level of communicative competences there is a need for further and better quality research (Jonsson *et al.* 2006; Camerino *et al.* in press). This is important because the communication between a coach and his or her team enables the former to show leadership in both training and competitive contexts, and this can have a direct effect on the team in terms of motivation, self-confidence and self-esteem, thereby fostering improved performance.

However, the field of human communication is so complex and exhaustive that its study must take into account not only verbal speech but also several areas of nonverbal expression. To this end we will make use of the nonverbal structure described in the first case study, which comprised two dimensions: *kinesics*, which concerns the study of standard bodily gestures that are used with or without communicative meaning; and *proxemics*, which involves studying the use of space in a given communicative context. The specific aim is to provide information that may help coaches to develop more efficient communicative styles with their teams in both training and competitive settings.

The contact between coaches and players is developed fundamentally through verbal and nonverbal communication, although the former is clearly more widely used in the context of team performance (Castañer *et al.* 2009). Cook (2001) noted that during both training and competition, coaches spend most of their time giving orders, instructions or information to athletes, and it is therefore essential that they are able to communicate efficiently. Indeed, the more efficient the transmission of information regarding what is required in terms of technical/tactical performance, the quicker will be the athletes' learning process. If we acknowledge, therefore, that those coaches who are good communicators are more likely to achieve their goals then it is necessary to be able to identify those aspects of a coach's communicative competences that require further development.

Aims and the mixed methods approach: a triangulation validating quantitative data design

The aim of this case study was to examine how coaches convey the whole range of verbal feedback and nonverbal communication during the course of competitive matches, comparing their performance in home, away and cup matches. The context analysed was that of a professional women's futsal team during the 2008–09 season. The mixed methods design used was validation of quantitative data, since data about the same phenomenon were obtained in parallel from two sources (i.e. quantitative and qualitative), there being a predominance of quantitative data (QUAN) over the more secondary qualitative data (qual) (see Chapter 1, Figure 1.4). Specifically, data were gathered simultaneously through systematic observation and the application of an open-ended survey regarding the verbal and nonverbal behaviour of the coach. This survey was administered to an assistant coach, to the team captain, to the 'star' player and to two other players.

The study was consistent with the basic tenets of observational methodology in that the coaches' behaviour was analysed without influencing it (spontaneity of the behaviour), it was studied in a competitive situation (naturalistic context), and the design was idiographic and multidimensional. Idiographic because it was centred on the analysis of different subjects and multidimensional because the ad hoc system of codes consisted of seven criteria and 23 codes. The data were derived from the study of two coaches and three competitive situations (home, away and cup matches), giving a total of 480 minutes of empirical material.

Instrument 1: SOCOP-Coach observational system

The SOCOP system for observing nonverbal communication (Castañer *et al.* 2010; Castañer *et al.* in press) was adapted to communicative situations

Table 6.3a Structure of SOCOP-Coach: verbal observational system

Criteria	Categories	Code	Description
Typology: The information concerns the sort of action to be performed by the athlete.	Instruction	I	The information is given with the aim of encouraging future actions.
	Feedback	F	The reciprocal action takes the form of a value judgement based on the athlete's performance.
Verbal Communication of Function: The information given by the coach plays a mediating role with respect to the athlete's performance.	Positive evaluation	EP	The coach makes a favourable judgement of the athlete's performance.
	Negative evaluation	NE	The coach makes an unfavourable judgement of the athlete's performance.
	Description	D	The coach describes the way in which the athlete performs or performed.
	Prescription	P	The coach communicates with and directs an athlete as to how he/she must carry out future actions.
Verbal Communication of Morphology: The information given by the coach is of a given form designed for the athlete.	Interrogative	IRG	The coach questions the athlete as to his/her performance with the aim of raising his/her awareness of the mistakes made or the correct way to perform the action.
	Imperative	IMP	The coach tells the athlete firmly what to do or what should have been done in order to draw his/her attention to this aspect.
	Exclamatory	EXC	The coach expresses a strong emotion in response to the athlete's performance.

Table 6.3b Structure of SOCOP-Coach: nonverbal observational system

Criteria	Categories	Code	Description
Nonverbal Communication of Function	Regulator	RE	The information is given via kinesic gestures that control and link together the moments of interaction between people. It requires an immediate response from the athlete.
	Illustrator	IL	The information is supplied via kinesic gestures with the aim of reinforcing the verbal language that is used by the coach, and does not require an immediate response from the athlete.
	Observation	VB	The coach watches without working or illustrating the result of the competition.
Nonverbal Communication of Morphology	Emblem	EMB	The information is supplied via kinesic gestures which are iconically defined and agreed upon, where verbal language is not necessary.
	Deictic	DEI	The information is supplied via kinesic gestures that indicate the location of people and/or objects.
	Kinetographic	KIN	Gesture that draws actions or movements in space.
	Beats	BEA	The information is supplied via kinesic gestures that are iconically defined, in accordance with the communicative style of the coach.
Nonverbal Communication of Posture	Standing	BI	The coach remains standing but without moving around.
	Sitting	SEA	The coach is seated.
	Locomotion	LOC	The coach moves to the technical area.
	Alteration of level	ALT	The coach alters his/her posture with respect to the height of his/her body.
Communication of Adaptation	Self-adaptor	SE	The coach maintains contact with other parts of his/her body but without any communicative purpose.
	Hetero-adaptor	HE	The coach maintains bodily contact with other people but without any communicative purpose.
	Multi-adaptor	MUL	When several of these adaptor gestures are combined.

involving coaches, thereby yielding the SOCOP-Coach (Castañer *et al.* 2009, 2011), an observational instrument that can be applied to any type of intervention by coaches. The SOCOP-Coach draws upon the most relevant criteria of the SOCIN sub-system used in the previous case study (see Table 6.1), but also includes three criteria relating to verbal communication (see Tables 6.3a and 6.3b).

Procedure

Coding was carried out using THEME Coder, while data were analysed using THEME v.5 software. Data quality was evaluated using a sample of 150 minutes of observational material relating to more than one coach in different kinds of competitive situation. This material corresponded to a single observer, who was an expert in futsal. The kappa coefficient of intra-observer reliability was 0.94. In order to obtain temporal patterns (T-patterns) a total of 480 minutes of empirical material were analysed (160 minutes for each competitive situation: home, away and cup matches).

Results

Figures 6.3, 6.4 and 6.5 present the T-patterns that best illustrate the verbal and nonverbal behaviour of the coaches in the three competitive situations analysed

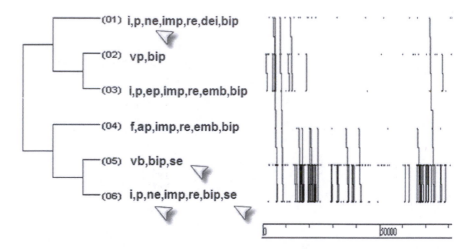

Figure 6.3 T-pattern corresponding to coach communication in the 'away match' situation. This T-pattern is the most complex of those obtained. It comprises five levels and a sequence of six events, each one of which is composed of a complex combination of codes (combinations of between two and six codes). The six steps of this sequence can be interpreted as follows: (1) The coach gives a prescriptive (negative evaluation) and imperative instruction with a regulatory function. The coach continues to use a deictic gesture and this whole sequence is carried out in the standing position. (2) The coach then remains silent while observing, still in the standing position. (3) After this silent observation the coach gives a prescriptive and imperative instruction with a regulatory function. All this sequence is carried out in the standing position. (4) The coach then gives some positive feedback, which is imperative and regulatory, and makes use of an emblem gesture to consolidate this information. (5) This is followed by another period of silent observation in the standing position and with a self-adaptor. (6) The coach gives another prescriptive (negative evaluation) and imperative instruction with a regulatory function, again in the standing position and with a self-adaptor. The arrow heads point to the negative evaluation and self-adapter gestures that characterize this behavioural pattern.

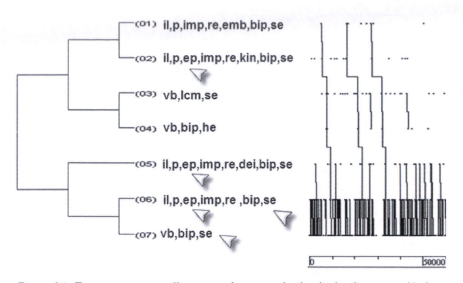

Figure 6.4 T-pattern corresponding to coach communication in the 'home match' situation. This T-pattern comprises six levels and a sequence of seven events. (1) The coach issues an instruction of a prescriptive and imperative nature (using a regulator) because he wants an immediate response from the players; the coach uses an emblem in order to consolidate the interaction, and this whole sequence is conducted from a standing position and accompanied by a self-adapter gesture. (2) The coach communicates in a prescriptive (positive evaluation) and regulatory way because he wants an immediate response from the players; he uses deictic gestures when pointing from a standing position, and also uses self-adaptor gestures. (3) The coach then remains silent while observing and in locomotion, making use of self-adaptor gestures. (4) He maintains this situation but now with hetero-adapter gestures. (5) The coach again makes a prescriptive (positive evaluation) and imperative statement, with a regulatory function, in order to get a quick response from the players; he uses a deictic gesture, which is designed to locate the opposing players, and this entire behavioural sequence is conducted from a standing position accompanied by self-adapter gestures. (6) He then makes another prescriptive (positive evaluation) and imperative statement, implying a regulatory standing position with self-adapter gestures. (7) The coach remains silent while observing in a standing position and with self-adaptor gestures. The arrow heads point to the positive evaluation and self-adapter gestures that characterize this behavioural pattern.

(home, away and cup matches). These T-patterns will be analysed according to each of these three situations.

Observation of home games showed that coaches initially adopt a posture whose main aim is instruction, predominantly of a prescriptive and mandatory kind. This is followed by a period of silent observation, after which they give positive feedback. With respect to away games, the coaches' communicative behaviour was again centred around instruction, although this also had a regulatory function in addition to its prescriptive qualities. The purpose here was to indicate to players the positions they should take up, and where they should seek to direct their opponents.

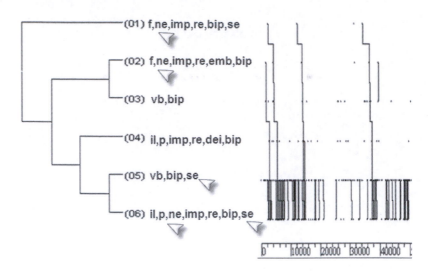

Figure 6.5   T-pattern corresponding to coach communication in the 'cup match' situation. This T-pattern comprises five levels and a sequence of six events, where each is composed of a complex combination of codes (combinations of between two and six codes). The six steps of this sequence can be interpreted as follows: (01) The coach gives negative feedback (regulatory and imperative) in the standing position and using a self-adapter. (2) The coach gives more negative feedback (regulatory and imperative), accompanied by the use of an emblem in the standing position. (3) The coach observes in silence, still in the standing position. (4) After this period of observation, the coach makes another prescriptive regulatory statement, using a deictic gesture and in the standing position. (5) The coach, still in the standing position, observes again in silence and use a self-adapter. (6) After this period of silent observation the coach makes another prescriptive (negative evaluation), imperative and regulatory statement, in the standing position and using a self-adapter. The arrow heads point to the negative evaluation and self-adapter gestures that characterize this behavioural pattern.

As regards cup matches, their knock-out format makes them more intense and this leads to greater anxiety among coaches, an aspect that is reflected in the increased use of self-adapter gestures. These are matches in which the coach uses more negative feedback, and where regulatory gestures mainly have the function of indicating and adjusting the position of players. Subsequently, they resort to silent observation and then give new instructions and prescriptions, which highlight the positions that players need to take up. It is noteworthy that despite differences between these match situations, coaches tend to adopt a standing position and often use self- and hetero-adapters.

Instrument 2: Open-ended survey

The survey comprised 17 open-ended questions and focuses on the main aspects of coaches' communication skills in competitive situations, corresponding to the verbal and nonverbal categories described in Tables 6.3a and 6.3b.

Participants and procedure

The survey instrument was based on the criteria and codes of the SOCOP-Coach observation system. The initial version was piloted with several experts in futsal and qualitative research in order to validate it, with any problems or discrepancies being resolved by consensus among experts. The survey was then administered to the above-mentioned members of the women's futsal team, i.e. the assistant coach, the team captain, the 'star' player and two other players.

Results

The information provided by the open-ended survey was consistent with the quantitative data obtained via the ad hoc observation instrument.

Regarding the criteria of verbal communication

As regards the coaches' verbal behaviour, the survey information showed that this served to encourage the players' performance:

> . . . both the tactical play needed to meet the team's objectives, and how to play, the technical performance of each player and how to approach the game . . . like the best way to pass or shoot.
>
> (Player)

The verbal feedback given by the coach appears to be matched to the players' performance levels:

> The instructions are given according to the physical, technical and tactical ability of the player.
>
> (Assistant coach)

Thus, when coaches announce a future move, they do so by identifying the key issues:

> . . . he identifies the basis of what he wants the team to do, the basic tactical aspects, assuming that we already know more or less what these are. But you can approach him when you need to know what the best thing to do is.
>
> (Player)

Coaches often give feedback, and in fact this is one of their main ways of being constantly involved in the game:

> . . . positive or negative feedback, depending on the situation.
>
> (Player)

During the match the coach shows a lot of emotion and this seems to help the players:

... yes, a lot (referring to coach showing emotion), mainly during the match, when a pass goes wrong or a shot's off target or there's one error after another ... but also when we score a goal or develop a good move, or the goalkeeper makes a good save.

(Player)

Regarding the criteria of nonverbal communication

The nonverbal behaviour of coaches serves to improve the outcome of communication:

... because then it's easier for players to understand what the coach wants.

(Player)

Coaches use gestures and signals when they want to illustrate what players should do:

... especially when we have a free-kick or corner.

(Player)

However, coaches spend much less time in silent observation:

They're constantly giving directions to those of us on the pitch.

(Player)

At all events, they always seek to motivate players:

... clapping and shouting words of encouragement.

(Assistant coach)

The coach uses gestures to indicate where the other team's players are, to highlight the position of a direct opponent:

... in some situations the coach uses gestures to show the players where the other team's players are, although he often does this verbally.

(Assistant coach)

With regard to adapters, it was noted that the coach:

... has a tic in his nose ... [and during the match] he's almost always standing up, watching how the players perform, trying to correct mistakes and giving instructions

(Player)

While transmitting information, coaches do not cross their arms and legs:

... no, they only adopt this posture when you're watching.

(Player)

However, when transmitting information coaches do make use of specific and individual gestures:

> When the coach gives instruction to a player, for example, to one who's about to come on as a substitute, then he uses his own characteristic gestures.
>
> (Assistant coach)

Discussion

The observational analysis of coaches' behaviour in the different match situations, and specifically the T-patterns obtained, revealed a number of logical sequences in their behaviour over time. In addition, the mixed methods design enabled these quantitative data to be corroborated by the qualitative information derived from the survey. The results indicate that the players feel considerable 'affinity' (McCroskey *et al.* 1996) with what the coaches communicate during match situations. Furthermore, the communicative behaviour of coaches corresponds to each of the criteria analysed by the SOCOP-Coach observation system (Castañer *et al.* 2009, 2011) (see Tables 6.3a and 6.3b).

In this case study, three competitive situations (home, away and cup matches) were analysed with the same team, and the results reveal notable differences in the coaches' communicative style across the three contexts:

- When playing before a home crowd in a familiar setting the coaches showed more confidence in the natural context (Anguera 2005), and their communicative behaviour differed from that in the other two competitive situations. During home matches they mainly used prescriptive instruction and gave positive feedback, and also spent a considerable amount of time in silent observation.
- When playing away in a non-habitual context the coaches' communication was again based on prescriptive instruction, but it was focused more on indicating to their team where the opposing players were, thereby giving additional information and support to their players. As in home matches they made use of silent observation, but this was normally accompanied by self-adapter gestures, which indicate greater levels of tension or nervousness.
- In cup matches, in which one of the teams will be knocked out, the coaches' communicative behaviour was again based on prescriptive instruction but was now accompanied by more negative feedback, as well as silent observation with a considerable number of self-adapters.

In addition to the different communicative styles that appear in these three match situations the results also show that communicative style was influenced by the relative importance of the match. In league matches played at home the coaches appeared less 'anxious' than they were during cup matches or those played away.

Conclusion

Given the lack of research to date on the specific aspects addressed by this case study we believe it is essential to examine in greater depth the verbal and nonverbal communication of coaches in competitive situations. When people compete, whether in everyday life or sport, there is a need for immediacy behaviours that 'enhance closeness to and nonverbal interaction with another' (Mehrabian 1969: 302). Immediacy is a potential tool to increase 'affinity' (McCroskey *et al.* 1996), which is a key aspect in relation to the dynamics of team sports.

While the aim of all competitive sport is clearly to win, the wide range of competitive situations means that the communicative behaviour of those involved is also varied. Moreover, competitive encounters need to be regarded as processes that are intrinsically linked to what is at stake; hence the differences observed between league and cup matches. The success of these processes requires not only communicative affinity between coaches and players, but also the optimal use by coaches throughout of the verbal and nonverbal registers. The quality of communication looks set to become a key aspect in terms of developing the effectiveness of team and competitive sports.

CASE STUDY 6.3: THE BEHAVIOUR OF FITNESS INSTRUCTORS AND THE PREFERENCES AND SATISFACTION LEVELS OF USERS

Introduction

Despite the existence of numerous technical books regarding how fitness instructors should approach the various activities in this field, there are very few studies about their actual pedagogical behaviour. Although some authors have sought to characterize this (Simões and Franco 2006; Simões *et al.* 2009), little is known about what types of pedagogical behaviour might influence user satisfaction and contribute to exercise adherence (Lippke *et al.* 2003; Loughead and Carron 2004). Nevertheless, a number of studies (Allen and Howe 1998; Loughead and Carron 2004; Nicaise *et al.* 2006; Papadimitriou and Karteroliotis 2000; Theodorakis *et al.* 2004; Wininger 2002) have suggested certain pedagogical behaviours that are believed to increase user satisfaction: information, positive evaluation, correction, encouragement, conversation and positive affectivity, coupled with a minimum of negative feedback.

In this context, it is important that researchers use systematic observation instruments to study the behaviour of fitness instructors and establish a representative database covering a variety of settings, as has already been done in relation to many sports and physical education (Lacy and Goldston 1990). Furthermore, a fuller understanding of the instruction process requires not only a systematic description of instructors' behaviour in a given context, but also the triangulation of this information so as to elucidate why instructors behave in a certain way, to determine the impact of their behaviour on users, and to examine both how users perceive their instructor's behaviour and the effects which instructors themselves believe their behaviour has on users. The use of such a multilevel mixed methods approach, with triangulation of information, has been described by several authors (Bericat 1998; Hackfort and Birkner 2003; Potrac *et al.* 2000).

Aims and the mixed methods approach: a multilevel triangulation design

This case study focuses on the pedagogical behaviour of fitness instructors in the context of group-based resistance training. In line with what was noted in the previous section the study is conducted from four different perspectives: observation of instructors' behaviour; instructors' behaviour as perceived by users; users' preferences regarding instructors' behaviour; and users' satisfaction with instructors' behaviour. In order to assess the degree of congruence between these perspectives we examined the following aspects: the relationship between users' perceptions of instructors' behaviour and the observational data regarding this behaviour; the relationship between users' preferences regarding instructors' behaviour and the observational data related to this behaviour; and the relationship between users' perceptions and preferences.

The mixed methods approach used was a multilevel triangulation design (see Chapter 1, Figure 1.5) based on the combination of four sources of data. Three of these corresponded to quantitative (QUAN) data derived from an observation instrument (SOCIF), a questionnaire (QUECIF), both of which referred to the pedagogical behaviour of fitness instructors, and a satisfaction survey administered to users. The fourth corresponded to qualitative (Qual) data obtained via open-ended questions to users about their preferences regarding instructors' behaviour.

Participants

The instructor sample comprised 62 qualified fitness instructors from Portuguese gyms. They were aged between 21 and 34 years (mean: 25.39 ± 2.85) and 51.6 per cent of them were male. A complete group, resistance-training class was videotaped for each instructor (mean duration: 45 minutes). The sample of users comprised all those participants in the observed classes who agreed to answer the questionnaire (447 participants). Users ranged in age from 18 to 66 years (mean: 34.71 ± 10.54) and the majority were female (93.04 per cent).

Instruments

There were four evaluation instruments. The first two were an observation system (Observation System of Fitness Instructors' Pedagogical Behaviour – Group Classes (SOCIF – Group Classes)) and a questionnaire (Questionnaire Regarding Fitness Instructors' Pedagogical Behaviour – Group Classes (QUECIF – Group Classes), both developed and validated by Franco (2009). The categories of the observation system were matched to the questionnaire items. The third instrument was a specific question built into the QUECIF concerning users' preference regarding instructors' behaviour. This was treated as a measure of overall user satisfaction. Finally, the fourth instrument was a series of open-ended questions to users about their preferences in relation to instructors' behaviour.

Instrument 1: SOCIF – Group Classes

The Observation System of Fitness Instructors' Pedagogical Behaviour – Group Classes (SOCIF – Group Classes) gathers information about fitness instructors' pedagogical behaviour in group activities (aerobics, step, slide, hip hop, water fitness, resistance training, combat, indoor cycling, stretching). The system covers 33 behaviours organized into six criteria: Instruction, Interaction, Activity, Monitoring, Organizing and Other Behaviours.

A team of four observers were first trained (Mars 1989) in how to code the videos with SOCIF, using the software Match Vision Studio 3.0 (Castellano *et al.* 2008). After the training phase they then worked individually to code the recordings. Inter-observer reliability was tested using Cohen's kappa and yielded values greater than or equal to 75 per cent (kappa ≥ 0.75), which can be considered excellent (Pestana and Gageiro 2005). Each observer then re-coded the same video at least one week later, as suggested by Mars (1989), in order to test intra-observer reliability. The values of Cohen's kappa were again greater than or equal to 75 per cent (kappa ≥ 0.75).

Instrument 2: QUECIF – Group Classes

The Questionnaire of Fitness Instructors' Pedagogical Behaviour – Group Classes (QUECIF – Group Classes) consists of 33 questions, each corresponding to one of the pedagogical behaviour categories from the observation system. It was used here to gather information about users' perceptions and preferences, and items were scored on a six-point Likert scale: 0 – none; 1 – very little; 2 – a little; 3 – average; 4 – a lot; 5 – very much.

Instrument 3: Question about overall satisfaction

The QUECIF included a question about users' satisfaction with their instructor's pedagogical behaviour, and this was scored on a seven-point Likert scale: 1 – overall dissatisfied; 2 – very dissatisfied; 3 – dissatisfied; 4 – neither satisfied nor dissatisfied; 5 – satisfied; 6 – very satisfied; 7 – overall satisfied.

Instrument 4: Questions about users' preferences

Users were asked several open-ended questions to determine their preferences and specific satisfaction in relation to instructors' behaviour, and the material obtained was subjected to a content analysis. In the context of the triangulation design this qualitative data helps to provide more specific explanations of the quantitative data.

Procedure

User satisfaction can be regarded as a positive affective state resulting from the discrepancy between preferences and perceptions (Chelladurai and Riemer 1997, 1998). Thus, for each instructor behaviour we determined the specific satisfaction of users, given by the difference between preference and perception (specific satisfaction = preference − perception).

Prior to data collection, informed consent was obtained from the gyms' directors, the instructors and users. A team of six research assistants were trained in the data collection procedures, and the relevant material was set out before the start of each class so as to avoid interfering with its normal duration. As group-based resistance training is accompanied by music the microphone receiver was connected directly to the digital video camera in order to obtain a better definition recording of the instructor's voice. The instructor's microphone (transmitter) was cordless and did not increase the volume of his/her voice, thereby avoiding any interference with the intervention. Also with the aim of avoiding interference, the research assistants (two per class) remained at the end of the fitness studio and did not look directly at either the instructor or the users. At the end of each class a brief explanation about the questionnaire was given, and users then completed it individually in a quiet place so as to ensure confidentiality.

For each of the instructor behaviours the percentage duration was calculated by dividing the duration of the observed behaviour by the class duration. A descriptive analysis was then performed of instructors' observed behaviour, user preferences, users' specific satisfaction and overall user satisfaction. Correlation coefficients, either Pearson's R or Kendall's tau-b, were used to test the associations set out in the study objectives.

Results

Table 6.4 presents the descriptive statistics for the observed behaviour of instructors, users' preferences and perceptions about instructors' behaviour, and users' specific satisfaction for the various pedagogical behaviours. Table 6.5 shows the descriptive statistics for overall user satisfaction.

Table 6.6 shows the associations between the observed behaviour of instructors and users' preferences and perceptions about instructors' behaviour with respect to the various pedagogical behaviours.

The results of the association between overall satisfaction and specific satisfaction (specific satisfaction = preference − perception) should be interpreted as follows (Chelladurai 1984): negative value: when participants perceive that the behaviour approximates or exceed what they prefer, they have a greater overall satisfaction with the instructor; positive value: when participants perceive that the behaviour exceed what they prefer, they have a lower overall satisfaction with the instructor.

Table 6.4 Means (M) and standard deviations (SD) corresponding to the observed behaviour of instructors (OB), users' preferences (UPr), users' perceptions (UP) and users' specific satisfaction (SS) for each instructor behaviour

Criteria	Behaviour	OB (%) M±SD	UPr M±SD	UP M±SD	SS M±SD
Instruction	Information WE	32.98±11.82	4.12±0.99	4.12±0.92	0.01±0.98
	Information WtE	13.15±6.19	3.92±1.30	3.81±1.36	0.11±1.34
	Demonstration With Information	3.65±2.68	4.22±0.92	4.18±0.93	0.04±0.93
	Demonstration Without Information	0.45±0.83	1.05±1.59	1.48±1.81	−0.41±1.91
	Correction WE	1.01±0.87	4.09±0.98	3.93±1.06	0.16±1.25
	Correction WtE	3.33±2.32	4.07±1.17	3.75±1.32	0.30±1.25
	Positive Evaluation WE	1.16±1.06	3.96±1.05	3.58±1.20	0.40±1.25
	Positive Evaluation WtE	0.91±0.77	3.76±1.32	3.32±1.46	0.44±1.50
	Negative Evaluation WE	0.09±0.17	3.74±1.33	3.20±1.42	0.62±1.36
	Negative Evaluation WtE	0.13±0.20	3.56±1.49	2.81±1.70	0.78±1.56
	Questioning WE	0.58±0.52	3.80±1.13	3.41±1.33	0.40±1.28
	Questioning WtE	0.91±0.72	3.74±1.33	3.26±1.55	0.53±1.47
Interaction	Positive Affectivity WE	1.81±1.96	3.11±1.59	3.38±1.53	−0.26±1.57
	Positive Affectivity WtE	1.45±1.27	3.01±1.68	2.76±1.79	0.25±1.11
	Negative Affectivity WE	0.02±0.08	0.59±1.21	0.44±1.12	0.17±1.18
	Negative Affectivity WtE	0.04±0.13	0.55±1.17	0.31±0.95	0.26±1.11
	Encouragement WE	0.80±0.94	4.32±0.76	4.17±1.01	0.14±1.09
	Encouragement WtE	0.38±0.55	4.08±1.12	3.74±1.39	0.33±1.27
	Conversation With Users WE	0.28±0.56	1.45±1.54	0.74±1.30	0.72±1.41
	Conversation With Users WtE	0.70±0.89	1.57±1.54	0.69±1.24	0.89±1.44
	Conversation With Others WE	0.01±0.02	0.39±0.86	0.21±0.74	0.16±0.93
	Conversation With Others WtE	0.01±0.04	0.48±0.96	0.26±0.81	0.22±0.91
Activity	Participatory Exercise	0.04±0.34	4.10±1.02	4.24±1.08	−0.12±1.10
	Independent Exercise	4.67±4.26	0.92±1.43	0.84±1.51	0.08±1.35
Monitoring	Observation WE	19.72±7.09	3.20±1.50	3.14±1.63	0.04±1.52
	Observation WtE	8.54±5.84	3.21±1.59	3.08±1.68	0.16±1.44
	Attention to Users' Int WE	0.24±0.61	3.55±1.17	3.36±1.48	0.21±1.45
	Attention to Users' Int WtE	0.50±0.63	3.48±1.38	3.08±1.61	0.42±1.48
	Attention to Others' Int WE	0.00±0.02	0.41±0.95	0.30±0.91	0.14±1.01
	Attention to Others' Int WtE	0.01±0.00	0.60±1.11	0.36±1.00	0.26±1.01
Organizing	Managing WE	0.16±0.25	2.53±1.67	2.34±1.89	0.19±1.66
	Managing WtE	7.49±2.56	2.65±1.62	2.23±1.85	0.47±1.51
Other Behav.	Other Behaviours	0.37±0.52	0.58±1.13	0.30±0.97	0.30±1.06

Note: WE: With Exercise; WtE: Without Exercise; Int: Interventions.

Table 6.5 Mean (M), standard deviation (SD) and frequency (%) for each level of overall user satisfaction

M±SD	1 Overall dissatisfied (%)	2 Very dissatisfied (%)	3 Dissatisfied (%)	4 Neither satisfied nor dissatisfied (%)	5 Satisfied (%)	6 Very satisfied (%)	7 Overall satisfied (%)
6.45±0.70	0	0.5	0	0	7.2	38.4	54.0

Discussion

Observed behaviour of instructors

The behaviour of instructors is mainly focused on the pedagogical functions of instruction and monitoring. Behaviours 'with exercise' predominate over those 'without exercise', which would seem appropriate in terms of making the class more dynamic, an important goal for fitness instructors (Brehm 2004; Franco *et al.* 2004). It also seems advantageous that the mean duration of 'positive evaluation' is higher than that of 'negative evaluation', given the contribution that positive feedback has on users' motivation (Massey *et al.* 2002), satisfaction (Allen and Howe 1998) and exercise adherence (Carron *et al.* 1999; Nicaise *et al.* 2006). Positive affectivity was also more common than negative affectivity, which again seems propitious given the importance that behaviours associated with positive affectivity, such as smiling, may have in relation to enthusiasm and, consequently, exercise adherence (Loughead *et al.* 2001).

If one considers the effect which encouragement may have on users' motivation to perform strength exercises (Massey *et al.* 2002), such as in resistance-training classes, as well as on user satisfaction (Allen and Howe 1998; Loughead and Carron 2004) and adherence (Carron *et al.* 1999), the duration values obtained for this behavioural category seem rather low. It may be that in order to show their appreciation of users' efforts, instructors are more likely to combine encouragement with exercise. The results also show that independent exercise was one of the categories with the highest mean duration. The fact that instructors are simply exercising, without even observing users, would not seem to be the most appropriate behaviour, although it may at least serve as a model for users.

Users' preferences regarding instructors' behaviour

Information, particularly with exercise, is one of the most preferred behaviours:

> I prefer an instructor who explains how to perform the exercises . . . speaking and making gestures.

The category 'Demonstration without Information' had a lower mean preference score than did 'Demonstration with Information'. The qualitative results suggest

Table 6.6 Association between the observed behaviour of instructors (OB), users' preferences (UPr), users' perceptions (UP), users' specific satisfaction (SS) and overall
user satisfaction (OS) for each instructor behaviour

Criteria	Behaviour	OB/UP	OB/UPr	UP/UPr	OB/OS	SS/OS
Instruction	Information WE	0.071	0.097*	0.410***	0.022	−0.123**
	Information WtE	0.107**	−0.049	0.411***	0.027	−0.121**
	Demonstration With Information	−0.028	0.030	0.437***	−0.013	−0.032
	Demonstration Without Information	−0.014	−0.024	0.345***	0.079*	−0.001
	Correction WE	0.098**	−0.031	0.281***	−0.028	−0.085
	Correction WtE	0.058	−0.021	0.399***	−0.031	−0.178***
	Positive Evaluation WE	0.030	−0.015	0.333***	−0.028	−0.157***
	Positive Evaluation WtE	−0.026	-0.088*	0.355***	−0.051	−0.194***
	Negative Evaluation WE	0.026	−0.036	0.400***	−0.048	−0.094*
	Negative Evaluation WtE	0.056	0.007	0.439***	0.005	−0.091*
	Questioning WE	0.212***	0.113**	0.381***	0.052	−0.133**
	Questioning WtE	0.143***	0.049	0.420***	0.076*	−0.159***
Interaction	Positive Affectivity WE	0.179***	0.140***	0.411***	0.067	−0.036
	Positive Affectivity WtE	0.126***	0.111**	0.378***	0.046	−0.043
	Negative Affectivity WE	0.120**	0.081	0.428***	0.103*	0.061
	Negative Affectivity WtE	0.247***	0.105*	0.424***	0.073	−0.071
	Encouragement WE	0.107**	0.038	0.366***	0.087*	−0.221***
	Encouragement WtE	0.119**	0.036	0.443***	0.065	-0.192***
	Conversation With Users WE	0.082*	0.086*	0.465***	−0.028	−0.025
	Conversation With Users WtE	0.137***	0.072	0.423***	−0.023	0.012
	Conversation With Others WE	0.139**	0.128**	0.333***	0.070	0.068
	Conversation With Others WtE	0.015	−0.039	0.432***	−0.027	−0.045
Activity	Participatory Exercise	0.062	0.019	0.447***	0.060	0.033
	Independent Exercise	0.058	0.044	0.502***	−0.059	0.112*
Monitoring	Observation WE	0.035	0.042	0.435***	−0.031	−0.111*
	Observation WtE	0.060	−0.016	0.535***	0.006	−0.063
	Attention to Users' Int WE	0.068	0.057	0.364***	0.058	−0.139**
	Attention to Users' Int WtE	0.083*	0.053	0.446***	0.061	−0.112*
	Attention to Others' Int WE	0.171***	0.028	0.343***	−0.140**	0.033
	Attention to Others' Int WtE	0.046	0.002	0.430***	−0.054	0.006
Organizing	Managing WE	−0.084*	0.007	0.481***	0.013	−0.045
	Managing WtE	0.057	0.024	0.530***	0.050	0.017
Other Behav.	Other Behaviours	0.028	0.028	0.390***	0.059	−0.124**

Notes: WE: With Exercise; WtE: Without Exercise; Int: Interventions.

* $p \leq 0.05$; ** $p \leq 0.01$; *** $p \leq 0.001$.

that users regard demonstration/modelling as being important in terms of understanding the exercise, especially when accompanied by additional information:

> I prefer an instructor who demonstrates how to do the next exercise and explains it at the same time.

The highest mean preference score corresponded to the category 'Encouragement with Exercise', i.e. users prefer such encouragement to be accompanied by exercise:

> I prefer an instructor who encourages you to maintain or increase your effort and commitment to exercise, and who does the exercise with you.

Behaviours in which the instructor shows no direct in the users, such as 'Independent Exercise', 'Conversations with Others', 'Attention to Others' Intervention', and 'Other Behaviours', present lower user preference scores.

Relationship between users' perceptions and preferences and the observed behaviour of instructors

According to the Multidimensional Model of Leadership (Chelladurai 1990) users should only feel satisfied if there is congruence between the instructor's actual behaviour and the behaviour which users would prefer. Although, for most of the behaviours studied, the observed behaviour of instructors was not congruent with users' preferences, there was always congruence between users' perceptions and preferences, which may explain why they report being satisfied with their instructor (Riemer and Chelladurai 1995).

Relationship between overall satisfaction and the observed behaviour of instructors

Only a few significant associations were found between overall satisfaction and the observed behaviour of instructors. In this regard, it should be remembered that preferences and satisfaction are subjective opinions of users, while their perceptions reflect a point of view about a certain reality. Given that a significant positive association between perceived and observed behaviour was only found for about half the categories, and considering that users' perceptions were always congruent with their preferences, it may make more sense to relate user satisfaction to their opinions about what happened in behavioural terms, rather than what was actually observed, as the latter may not correspond to what users perceived.

Relationship between overall satisfaction and users' specific satisfaction

When users perceive that the behaviours related to either exercise instruction (Information, Correction, Positive Evaluation, Negative Evaluation and

Questioning) or encouragement are close to or exceed what they would prefer, then they report higher levels of overall satisfaction. These behaviours were those with the highest mean scores in terms of users' preferences. These results are consistent with previous findings regarding the relationship between satisfaction and pedagogical behaviours such as information, correction, positive evaluation and encouragement (Allen and Howe 1998; Black and Weiss 1992; Chelladurai 1990; Loughead and Carron 2004; Massey *et al.* 2002; Papadimitriou and Karteroliotis 2000; Theodorakis *et al.* 2004; Wininger 2002).

'Independent exercise' was the only behaviour that showed a significant relationship with a positive sign, which means that if the instructor does more independent exercise than users prefer, they will report lower levels of overall satisfaction with the instructor's behaviour. The category 'independent exercise' was assigned one of the lowest mean scores in terms of users' preferences.

By contrast, there was a significant relationship, with a negative sign, between overall satisfaction and monitoring behaviours in which the instructor shows interest and pays attention to users (Observation, Attention to Users' Intervention), which means that when users perceive that some of these behaviours are close to or exceed what they prefer, they will report higher levels of overall satisfaction with the instructor's pedagogical behaviour.

Conclusions

This case study has described the observed behaviour of instructors in group resistance-training classes, as well as the preferences of users regarding the instructors' pedagogical behaviours. Most of the behaviours which users prefer correspond to actual instruction and encouragement to exercise. The least preferred behaviours correspond to those situations in which users feel that the instructor is not paying them enough attention. Accordingly, users are also more satisfied with instructors' pedagogical behaviour when it is related to instruction or encouragement, or when it takes the form of monitoring behaviour that reflects an interest in users to a degree that matches or exceeds their preferences.

Only about half the categories showed a significant positive association between observed behaviour and users' perceptions, suggesting that users' perceptions may not reflect the reality of certain behaviours. However, despite the lack of congruence between the observed behaviour of instructors and users' preferences in several behavioural categories, users' perceptions were always congruent with their preferences.

In terms of practical applications the result suggest that instructors should focus on encouraging the efforts of users and on giving actual instruction, using information, demonstration with information, correction, positive and negative evaluation (although not to the extent of denigrating users' performance) and questioning. Instructors should also pay attention to users through behaviours such as observation and attention to users' interventions, and avoid situations that might suggest a lack of interest, such as independent exercise, conversation and attention to individuals who are not participating in the class. In sum, the training syllabus for fitness instructors should seek to develop their knowledge and skills in relation to those behaviours and strategies that promote users' learning, motivation and satisfaction.

Acknowledgements

We gratefully acknowledge the support of the Spanish government project *Avances tecnológicos y metodológicos en la automatización de estudios observacionales en deporte* (Dirección General de Investigación, Ministerio de Ciencia e Innovación) [Grant number PSI2008-01179]. We also gratefully acknowledge the support of the Generalitat de Catalunya government project GRUP DE RECERCA E INNO-VACIÓ EN DISSENYS (GRID). Tecnología i aplicació multimedia i digital als dissenys observacionals, Departament d'Innovació, Universitats i Empresa, Generalitat de Catalunya [Grant number 2009 SGR 829]. We also gratefully acknowledge ESDRM-IPS; CIDESD; gyms, instructors and participants

Note

So as to protect the identity of participants the photo images used to illustrate the T-patterns do not correspond to real images. Each still photo illustrates each one of the events occurring within the pattern, listed in the order in which they occur within the pattern.

References

Allen, J. B., and Howe, B. L. (1998). Player ability, coach feedback, and female adolescent athletes' perceived competence and satisfaction. *Journal of Sport and Exercise Psychology, 20*, 280–299.

Anguera, M. T. (2003). Observational methods. In R. Fernández-Ballesteros (ed.), *Encyclopedia of Psychological Assessment, Vol. 2* (pp. 632–637). London: Sage.

Anguera, M.T. (2005). Microanalysis of T-patterns: analysis of symmetry/asymmetry in social interaction. In L. Anolli, S. Duncan, M. Magnusson and G. Riva (eds), *The hidden structure of social interaction: From genomics to culture patterns* (pp. 51–70). Amsterdam: IOS Press.

Baringer, D.K. and McCroskey, J.C. (2000). Immediacy in the classroom. *Communication Education, 49*, 178–186.

Berends, I.E., and Van Lieshout, E.C.D.M. (2009). The effect of illustrations in arithmetic problem-solving: Effects of increased cognitive load. *Learning and Instruction 19* (4), 345–353.

Bericat, E. (1998). *La integración de los métodos cuantitativos y cualitativos en la investigación social*. Barcelona: Ariel.

Black, S.J., and Weiss, M.R. (1992). The relationship among perceived coaching behaviors, perceptions of ability, and motivation in competitive age-group swimmers. *Journal of Sport and Exercise Psychology, 14*, 309–325.

Brehm, B.A. (2004). *Successful fitness motivation strategies*. Champaign, IL: Human Kinetics.

Buck, R., and VanLear, C.A. (2002). Verbal and nonverbal communication: distinguishing symbolic, spontaneous, and pseudo-spontaneous nonverbal behavior. *Journal of Communication, 52* (3), 522–541.

Camerino, O., Chaverri, J., Anguera, M.T., and Jonsson, G.K. (2012). Dynamics of the game in soccer: Detection of T-patterns. *European Journal of Sport Science 12* (3), 216–224.

Carron, A.V., Hausenblas, H.A., and Estabrooks, P.A. (1999). Social influence and exercise involvement. In S.J. Bull (ed.), *Adherence issues in sport and exercise* (pp. 1–17). Chichester, West Sussex: John Wiley & Sons Ltd.

Castañer, M. (2009). SOCOP: Sistema d'observació de la comunicació paraverbal del docent. *Temps d'Educació 36*, 231–246.

Castañer, M. and Camerino, O. (2006). *Manifestaciones Básicas de la Motricidad*. INEFC. Publicacions de la Universitat de Lleida.

Castañer, M., Camerino, O., Anguera, M.T., and Jonsson, G.K. (2010). Observing the paraverbal communicative style of expert and novice PE teachers by means of SOCOP: A sequential analysis. *Procedia Social and Behavioral Sciences, 2* (2), 5162–5167.

Castañer, M., Camerino, O., Anguera, M.T and Jonsson, G.K. (in press). Kinesics and proxemics communication of expert and novice PE teachers. *Quality and Quantity*. DOI: 10.1007/s11135-011-9628-5.

Castañer, M., Miguel, C., and Anguera, M.T. (2009). SOCOP-Coach: An instrument to observe coaches' paraverbal communication in match competition situations. *Redaf Revista Electrónica de Desporto e Actividade Física, 2* (2), 2–10.

Castañer, M., Miguel, C., Anguera, M.T., and Jonsson, G.K. (2011). Observing the paraverbal communication of coaches in competitive match situations. Proceedings of the 7th International Conference on Methods and Techniques in Behavioral Research Proceeding, 10 edn (pp. 243–246). New York: ACM. .

Castellano, J., Perea, A., Alday, L., and Hernández-Mendo, A. (2008). The measuring and observation tool in sports. *Behavior Research Methods, 40* (3), 898–905

Chelladurai, P. (1984). Discrepancy between preferences and perceptions of leadership behavior and satisfaction of athletes in varying sports. *Journal of Sport Psychology, 6*, 27–41.

Chelladurai, P. (1990). Leadership in sport: A review. *International Journal of Sport Psychology, 21*, 328–354.

Chelladurai, P., and Riemer, H.A. (1997). A classification of facets of athletes' satisfaction. *Journal of Sport Management, 11*, 133–159.

Chelladurai, P., and Riemer, H.A. (1998). Measurement of leadership in sport. In J.L. Duda (ed.), *Advances in sport and exercise psychology* (pp. 227–253). Morgantown, WV: Fitness Information Technology.

Cook, M. (2001). *Dirección y entrenamiento de equipos de fútbol*. Barcelona: Paidotribo.

Creswell, J.W., and Plano Clark, V.L. (2007). *Designing and conducting mixed methods research*. Thousand Oaks, CA: Sage.

Cristophel, D. (1990). The relationships among teacher immediacy behaviors, student motivation and learning. *Communication Education, 39*, 323–340.

Crowder, E.M., and Newman, D. (1993). Telling what they know: The role of gestures and language in children's science explanations. *Pragmatics and Cognition, 1*, 341–376.

De Vries, R.E., Bakker-Pieper, A., Siberg, R.A., Van Gameren, K., and Vlug, M. (2009). The content and dimensionality of communication styles *Communication Research, 36* (2), 178–206.

Ekman, P. (1985). *Methods for measuring facial action*. In K. Scherer and P. Ekman (eds), *Handbook methods in nonverbal behavior research* (pp. 45–83). Cambridge: Cambridge University Press.

Ekman, P., and Friesen, W.V. (1969). The repertoire of nonverbal behavior categories:

Origins, usage, and coding. *Semiotica, 1*, 49–98. In A. Kendon (ed.), *Nonverbal communication, interaction and gesture.* The Hague: Mouton.

Franco, S. (2009). Comportamento pedagógico dos instrutores de fitness em aulas de grupo de localizada: Comportamento observado, percepção, preferência e satisfação dos praticantes. Unpublished Doctoral Thesis, INEFC-Lleida, Lleida.

Franco, S., Cordeiro, V., and Cabeceiras, M. (2004). Perception and preferences of participants about fitness instructors' profiles:- Comparison between age groups and different activities. Paper presented at the 9th Annual Congress of the European College of Sport Science, Clermont-Ferrand, France.

Hackfort, D., and Birkner, H.A. (2003). Triangulation as a basis for diagnostic judgments. *International Journal of Sport and Exercise Psychology, 1*, 82–94.

Gallaher, P.E. (1992). Individual differences in non-verbal behavior dimensions of style. *Journal of Personality and Social Psychology, 63* (1), 133–145.

Hall, E.T. (1968). Proxemics. *Current Anthropology, 9* (2–3), 83.

Jones, S.E., and LeBaron, C.D. (2002). Research on the relationship between verbal and nonverbal communication: Emerging integrations. *Journal of Communication, 52* (3), 499–521.

Jonsson, G.K., Anguera, M.T., Blanco-Villaseñor, A., Losada, J.L., Hernández-Mendo, A., Ardá, T., Camerino, O., and Castellano, J. (2006). Hidden patterns of play interaction in soccer using SOF-CODER. *Behavior Research Methods, Instruments and Computers, 38* (3), 372–381.

Lacy, A.C., and Goldston, P.D. (1990). Behavior analysis of male and female coaches in high school girls' basketball. *Journal of Sport Behavior, 13* (1), 29–39.

Lemke, J.L. (1999). Typological and topological meaning in diagnostic discourse. *Discourse Processes, 27,* 173–185.

Lippke, S., Knäuper, B., and Fuchs, R. (2003). Subjective theories of exercise course instructors: Causal attributions for dropout in health and leisure exercise programmes. *Psychology of Sport and Exercise, 4* (2), 155–173.

Loughead, T.M., and Carron, A.V. (2004). The mediating role of cohesion in the leader behavior: Satisfaction relationship. *Psychology of Sport and Exercise, 5,* 355–371.

Loughead, T.M., Colman, M.M., and Carron, A.V. (2001). Investigating the mediational relationship of leadership class cohesion, and adherence in an exercise setting. *Small Group Research, 32* (5), 558–575.

Magnusson, M.S. (2005). Understanding social interaction: Discovering hidden structure with model and algorithms. In *The hidden structure of interaction: From neurons to culture patterns* (pp. 3–22). Amsterdam: IOS Press.

Mars, H. (1989). Observer reliability: Issues and procedures. In P.W. Darst, D.B. Zakrajsek and V.H. Mancini (eds), *Analysing physical education and sport instruction* (pp. 53–80). Champaign, IL: Human Kinetics.

Massey, C.D., Maneval, M.W., Phillips, J., Vincent, J., White, G., and Zoeller, B. (2002). An analysis of teaching and coaching behaviors of elite strength and conditioning coaches. *Journal of Strength and Conditioning Research, 16* (3), 456–460.

McCroskey, J.C., Fayer, J.M., Richmond, V.P., Sallinen, A., and Barraclough, R.A. (1996). A multi-cultural examination of the relationship between nonverbal immediacy and affective learning. *Communication Quarterly, 44*, 297–307.

Mehrabian, A. (1969). Methods and designs: Some referents and measures of nonverbal behaviour. *Behavioral Research Methods and Instrumentation, 1,* 203–207.

Nicaise, V., Cogérino, G., Bois, J., and Amorose, A.J. (2006). Students' perceptions of teacher feedback and physical competence in physical education classes: Gender effects. *Journal of Teaching in Physical Education, 25* (1), 36–57.

Papadimitriou, D.A., and Karteroliotis, K. (2000). The service quality expectations in private sport and fitness centers: A re-examination of the factor structure. *Sport Marketing Quarterly, 9* (3), 157–164.

Pestana, M.H., and Gageiro, J.N. (2005). *Análise de dados para ciências sociais. A complementaridade do SPSS.* Lisboa: Edições Sílabo.

Potrac, P., Brewer, C.J., Jones, R., Armour, K., and Hoff, J. (2000). Toward an holistic understanding of the coaching process. *Quest, 52* (2), 186–199.

Poyatos, F. (1983). Language and nonverbal systems in the structure of face-to-face interaction. *Language Communication, 3* (2), 129–140.

Riemer, H.A., and Chelladurai, P. (1995). Leadership and satisfaction in athletics. *Journal of Sport and Exercise Psychology, 17*, 276–293.

Rodríguez, J.I., Plax, T.G., and Kearney, P. (1996). Clarifying the relationship between teacher nonverbal immediacy and student cognitive learning: Affective learning as the central casual mediator. *Communication Education, 45*, 293–305.

Roth, W.M. (2001). Gestures: Their role in teaching and learning. *Review of Educational Research, 71* (3), 365–392.

Roth, W.M. (2002). Scientific investigations, metaphorical gestures, and the emergence of abstract scientific concepts. *Learning and Instruction, 12*, 285–304.

Simões, V., and Franco, S. (2006). Body Pump® instructor's pedagogical feedback: Comparison between different experienced levels and different academic degrees. Paper presented at the 11th Annual Congress of the European College of Sport Science, Lausanne, Switzerland.

Simões, V., Franco, S., and Rodrigues, J. (2009). Estudo do feedback pedagógico em instrutores de ginástica localizada com diferentes níveis de experiência profissional. *Fitness and Performance Journal, 8* (3), 174–182.

Theodorakis, N., Alexandris, K., Rodriguez, P., and Sarmento, P.J. (2004). Measuring customer satisfaction in the context of health clubs in Portugal. *International Sports Journal, 8* (1), 44–53.

Weinmann, J.M., and Backlund, P.M. (1980). Current theory and research in communicative competence. *Review of Educational Research, 50*, 185–199.

Wininger, S.R. (2002). Instructors' and classroom characteristics associated with exercise enjoyment by females. *Perceptual and Motor Skills, 94*, 395–398.

Summary

This book has aimed to show that research methods can be integrated in line with the growing trend towards a more balanced approach that merges quantitative and qualitative designs and methods of data treatment. Chapter 1 described the wide range of mixed method approaches and designs that are available, while the case studies that make up the core of the book have illustrated how mixed methods offer a new way of understanding and approaching the study of sport, physical education and dance.

Substantive research in different fields

This book is based on various substantive studies that were conducted in relation to three contexts: sport, motor behaviour and physical education.

Chapters 2 and 3 focused on the field of sport and the research they describe covered the following areas: (a) analysis of the dynamics of play in team sports, specifically, rugby, basketball and handball; (b) the influence of environmental factors and the detection of technical errors in combat sports, in this case, judo and fencing; and (c) the relationship between technical efficacy and physiological performance in freestyle swimming and in rugby.

Chapters 4 and 5 went beyond the domain of sport and considered motor behaviour and the specific context of dance. The research here involved: (a) an analysis of motor patterns in children's play and a comparison with the patterns observed in parkour; (b) a study of professional choreographies and the spontaneous generation of movement when dancing contact improvisation; (c) ways of improving motor behaviour and performance and motor laterality; and (d) an illustration of how a kinematic analysis based on aesthetic appraisals can complement the use of motion capture technology in the context of dance.

Finally, Chapter 6 focused on the field of physical education, and specifically on what we consider to be a key aspect of the teaching process, namely the communication of coaches, instructors and teachers. The quality of communicative interaction has a direct influence on the effectiveness of motor behaviour, and this can be seen not only in the performance of sports coaches but also in the transmission skills of physical education teachers. In this regard, the research described in Chapter 6 concerns: (a) the optimization of nonverbal communication in secondary school physical education teachers; (b) the communication of coaches in competitive situations; and (c) the behaviour of fitness instructors.

The mixed methods designs used

What the above substantive studies have in common is that they all draw upon the emerging research trend of mixed methods. Based on the theoretical framework that was set out in Chapter 1, the various case studies show how it is possible to combine and implement a range of instruments in relation to different mixed methods designs, thereby enabling a complementary analysis of the quantitative and qualitative data that can be obtained through the study of motor behaviour and sport.

Chapter 1 described four mixed methods designs, the use of which was then illustrated throughout the book. The four designs are: *triangulation designs, dominant embedded designs, exploratory sequential designs* and *explanatory sequential designs*. Triangulation designs were applied in most of the case studies involving sport (performance in rugby, freestyle swimming and fencing), as well as in relation to contact improvisation (dance) and the communicative skills of coaches in competitive situations. Some of the case studies used a variation of this design. For example, *convergent triangulation* was applied in order to analyse interaction contexts in basketball and technical errors in judo, while *multilevel triangulation* was used to study the performance of dance choreographies, satisfaction levels among users of fitness instructors and to study coaches' communication in competitive match situations.

Embedded designs were applied to assess the laterality of motor behaviour, while the variant known as an *embedded correlational design* was used to study the aesthetics of dance in relation to kinematic parameters.

Exploratory sequential designs were applied in the studies of tactical defence in handball and the optimization of nonverbal communication in physical education teachers.

Finally, an explanatory sequential design was used to study and compare the spontaneous motor skills associated with children's behaviours in playgrounds and young adults' behaviour in parkour.

Instruments and techniques for gathering data

Various instruments and data gathering techniques are used in the mixed methods designs illustrated in this book. One instrument that was used in all the case studies, except for the aesthetic appraisal of dance, involved the construction of a specific category system for the systematic observation of behaviour. However, several other instruments are described at one point or another in the book. For example, *semantic differentials* were used in the case studies that analysed contemporary dance productions and the aesthetics of motor behaviour in the same field. *Recall interviews* were the preferred method in the case studies about the dynamics of play in handball and dancers' performance in contact improvisation, whereas *semi-structured interviews* were used in the analysis of motor skills in children's playgrounds and in parkour, as well as in the study of dance choreographies. The studies of motor laterality and the optimization of nonverbal communication in physical education teachers made use of *focus groups*, while a *structured questionnaire* was the tool used to assess satisfaction among users of fitness instructors. The aesthetic appraisals of dance in relation to kinematic parameters were made using not only a *motion capture system* but also an *open-ended questionnaire*, which was also the method used to evaluate coaches' communication in competitive situations. Motor laterality was assessed by means of a *standardized test*, while in the case study of rugby a wireless GPS unit was used to obtain *standardized temporal parameters*. Finally, the studies of performance in both rugby and freestyle swimming measured *physiological parameters*.

Conclusion

In terms of both their substantive contribution and the methodologies they apply, the fourteen case studies in this book provide researchers with an opportunity to open their minds to a range of ideas and concepts. If nothing else, they should serve to raise awareness of the kind of research that is now being conducted in the fields of sport, physical education and dance.

Taking as an analogy the Saussurian dichotomy between language and speech, one might say that our task here has been to discover and define the elements that make up the 'language' and 'speech' of scientific methodology. Although the 'language' of research may be clearly quantitative or qualitative in nature, its richness, its originality and its variety depend on how each ad hoc design, how each study 'speaks' to the scientific community. In this regard, the time has come for research in all fields to move beyond the traditional separation of quantitative and qualitative approaches. The extent to which this will occur depends on whether, scientifically speaking, we continue to rely on this dualism or, alternatively, seek to reconcile what is in fact a false dichotomy. Achieving the latter would, with respect to the fields addressed by this book, imply abandoning a standardizing, linear mentality and moving towards a more ramified and multi-faceted approach, one that is truly capable of revealing the richness and diversity of behaviour to be found in motor activity and sport.

Index

An environmentally friendly book printed and bound in England by www.printondemand-worldwide.com

#0216 - 140915 - C0 - 234/156/13 - PB - 9780415532273